The Bedside
Guardian 2014

The Bedside Guardian 2014

EDITED BY BECKY GARDINER

guardianbooks

Published by Guardian Books 2014

2 4 6 8 10 9 7 5 3

Copyright © Guardian News and Media Ltd 2014

Becky Gardiner has asserted her right under the Copyright, Designs
and Patents Act 1988 to be identified as the editor of this work

First published in Great Britain in 2014 by
Guardian Books
Kings Place, 90 York Way
London N1 9GU

www.guardianbooks.co.uk

A CIP catalogue record for this book is available from the British Library

ISBN 978-0852-65563-4

Cover design by Two Associates
Typeset by seagulls.net

Printed and bound in Great Britain by CPI Group (UK) Ltd,
Croydon CR0 4YY

Contents

SUMMER

Foreword

JEANETTE WINTERSON

Since 1951 the *Guardian* has published an annual of its journalism. These are zeitgeist pieces that contain and critique the happenings of the year, the national mood, international politics; stories of the moment and stories like lighthouses, flashing across the wrecks, rocks, and near-misses of the way we live now.

What we value as a society is often not reflected by the governments we elect – even majority governments. Blair's determination to go into Iraq, the lies and cover-ups made necessary by that act of arrogance and its terrible consequences, has made it difficult to trust anything politicians tell us about war or terrorism, because they will turn round later and say it was all in the national interest, even when the nation – us – wants nothing to do with it.

In the coalition government's response to the Snowden files, we see official hypocrisy bulging out as aggressive self-righteousness. There is no question that Snowden's courage and the *Guardian*'s fearlessness is in the public interest. Yet exposing the secret dealings of intelligence agencies and the military is always depicted as a crime of some kind – hopefully with a prison sentence attached. The *Guardian* had to destroy its own computers, overseen by MI5, and Alan Rusbridger appeared before the home affairs committee over issues of national security. That the newspaper won a Pulitzer Prize for the Snowden reporting is some vindication of its public bravery.

It has been interesting watching the *Guardian* battle for public awareness of mass surveillance by the intelligence services here and around the world, while a different kind of surveillance – phone hacking – was put under scrutiny. The Leveson Inquiry (cost to the taxpayer: £5.5m) and the trial of News International employees and their associates (cost to the taxpayer: approximately £100m) were showy displays of democracy and accountability that changed ... what?

Whatever phone hacking exposed, we have discovered that ruining people's lives to sell newspapers is not a crime.

The *Guardian* has been a campaigning newspaper from its beginnings in Manchester – edited there for 50 years by CP Scott. The Scott Trust was founded to keep the *Guardian* free of unwanted financial pressures that might compromise its ethics. No oligarch or family dynasty is hiding behind the *Guardian*, pulling the strings. It is a newspaper for everyone, anyone, who is interested in a better understanding of Britain and the world.

Whether or not you broadly agree with the *Guardian*'s politics, whether or not you argue with its journalism, it would be hard to claim that its reporting is not honest and honourable. Its comment pages and longer articles are often heroic attempts to stop the ideological right in Britain making things up – and I do mean making things up – about welfare, immigration, the economy.

Amelia Gentleman, George Monbiot and Tanya Gold are not mad pamphleteers spouting agitprop – you need the tabloids for that – they are class-A journalists who force the facts in our faces and ask about the consequences – whether it's subsidy farming for the rich, Iain Duncan Smith's benefits 'reforms' that have thrown so many people into breadline despair and borderline mental health, or the rewriting of the past to pretend a time that never was.

There's an excellent Martin Kettle piece in this volume about bendy history – or what might have happened if two world wars had come out differently. This isn't 'unhistorical shit', as EP Thompson put it, nor is it rewriting the past. Rather, it's looking at outcomes as possibilities, not as Greek chorus Fates. The left believes that life is propositional. Human beings can and do change. Society changes. We do not have to accept doomster versions of high unemployment as inevitable. Of greed as natural. Of social justice as softy politics.

The great thing about this yearbook is the sense that the left really is about alternatives of every kind. That there must be a challenge to nonsense masquerading as wisdom in a suit, whether it's business that doesn't want to pay a living wage, corporations that don't like paying tax, or Ukippers who blame migrants for our economic collapse. Those ideologies need stories that make their world-view look true.

But what kind of a world are we living in – and what kind of a world do we want to live in? That's the challenge I get from the *Guardian*.

It's great to see fourth-wave feminism riding proud in these pages. Zoe Williams on the childcare scandal (no, we're not Tory wives and we're not staying at home), Kira Cochrane warning 'Misogynists watch out', and Polly Toynbee's guide to sexual harassment for the Lib Dems. If you think there's too much feminism in here, recall that Britain ranks 65th (below Rwanda) for representation of women in parliament.

There's room for jokes, too (a blowfly goes into a bar and asks, 'Is this stool taken?'). There's SamCam sketchery and the irreplaceable Simon Hoggart. Mostly, though, this is serious stuff about serious stuff, and we need it as an antidote to the increasing inanity of soundbite life where catchy headlines and half-baked outrage is the fodder of the nation. Britain feels like a lottery world – where nothing matters because nothing will change except by chance. Trials and inquiries come and go, banks rig the Libor rate and it's business as usual. G4S is investigated by the Serious Fraud Office, has to repay more than £100m of taxpayers' money – but still gets to bid for contracts funded by more taxpayers' money. What is the point of protest? What is the point of voting?

The *Guardian* makes the point every day.

I shall be buying several copies of this book – but not from Amazon. Order from your brave little bookshop that pays taxes and business rates, and employs someone who likes reading. If the piece included here on Amazon doesn't make you boycott them for life, nothing will. With workers tagged like prisoners in a *Blade Runner* warehouse of timed packings and clock-outs to go to the loo, employed on low wages with little or no job security, a job with Amazon is part of the new slavery modern capitalism calls opportunity.

In 2012, on £4.2bn of UK earnings, Amazon's main British subsidiary paid just £3.2m in corporation tax. Go figure.

September 2014

Introduction

BECKY GARDINER

Keith Vaz MP: 'Do you love this country?'
Alan Rusbridger: 'I'm slightly surprised to be asked the question but, yes ...'

It was December 2013, and the *Guardian*'s editor-in-chief, Alan Rusbridger, had been called to give evidence to a parliamentary committee about the paper's handling of National Security Agency leaks from the whistleblower Edward Snowden. Barack Obama had already welcomed the debate provoked by the stories; so had various US security chiefs. But in Britain, most politicians and intelligence officials – even some journalists – were still doing their best to shoot the messenger. The *Guardian* had been under attack for several months, and the *Daily Mail* had not long published an editorial headlined: 'The Paper that Helps Britain's Enemies'.

But even so, the question the committee chairman, Keith Vaz, asked Rusbridger was a curious one: 'Do you love this country?'

'Yes,' Rusbridger replied, he loved this country: '[and] one of the things I love about this country is that we have [the] freedom to write, and report, and to think.'

An anthology of this kind can't hope to do justice to the Snowden leaks – the news stories kept on coming, and the international debate about privacy and security they have provoked

5

will continue for many years yet. I have included only one inter-view with Snowden, who at the time of writing is still living in exile in Russia. His bravery is remarkable.

But in this year's *Bedside*, as always, you will find journalists on the *Guardian* and its sister paper, the *Observer*, taking full advan-tage of their freedom to write, and report and to think, whether it's Russell Brand railing against celebrity culture; Harry Leslie Smith wearing his Remembrance Day poppy for the last time; Peter Beaumont witnessing the shelling of children in Gaza; or Carole Cadwalldr experiencing first-hand the exploitation behind Amazon's success. The *Guardian* is genuinely pluralistic, giving space to many different views. But its centre of gravity is centre-left, and certain values permeate the journalism: a public-service ethos, courage, a belief in social justice. You will see all this in evidence in this collection. And some humour, too.

As well as capturing a *Guardian* sensibility, *The Bedside Guardian* serves as a snapshot of the year – the 12 months from the autumn of 2013. In Britain, it was a year bookended by two historic votes: the first by MPs who, responding to public pressure, defied the government and voted against intervention in Syria; the second by the people of Scotland, who after a year of intense debate even-tually voted No to independence. It was also the year in which, for the first time in modern history, neither Labour nor the Conser-vatives won a British national election. Nigel Farage's victory at the European elections was, as he said himself, 'an earthquake' – but the tremors have been felt for years, as Suzanne Moore says on page 186.

Meanwhile, at the Old Bailey, journalists were in the dock. The phone-hacking trial was the culmination of five years' tireless reporting by Nick Davies. His devastating piece on the ultimate failure of that trial to tackle the real issues behind hacking is on page 231. And on page 149, you'll find a previously unpublished Steve Bell cartoon (it couldn't be printed on the day for legal reasons).

Hacking was not the only trial to dominate the news. I could have filled these pages with distressing accounts of historic sex abuse. Instead, I have included just one piece: Simon Hattenstone on the rise and fall of Max Clifford (page 189).

If these trials were the death rattle of an era – and I hope they were – a chorus of women were gathered around the deathbed, calling sexism out in politics, in the street, even in *The Great British Bake Off*. Some readers may feel I have included too much feminism, but I make no apology for that – I wanted to celebrate what Kira Cochrane calls the new wave of 'rebel women' (page 77).

Internationally, 2013–14 saw more than its share of violence and terror. From Ukraine to Syria, our reporters on the ground showed great courage in covering these events, while our columnists and specialists helped readers make sense of them. Again, I could have filled these pages with their work, but a book designed for bedtime can only take so much horror.

If it was difficult for the first *Bedside* editor to choose the best pieces we have run, it is impossible now. When the first anthology was published, in 1951, there were 12–18 daily pages to choose from. Now we publish an astonishing 3,000 pieces a week, 24 hours a day, across three continents. I read everything that appeared in print, together with those online articles that were most widely shared on social media, but it is inevitable that many great pieces of journalism passed me by.

Making the final cut was painful. Two thirds of the articles I had picked out were eventually culled, after much dithering. So my apologies to those colleagues who feel they have done great work that should have been included here, but wasn't – you are almost certainly right. The best journalism does not necessarily make the best *Bedside* piece: news reporting can lose impact over time; only a handful of long pieces can be squeezed in; investigations tend to be too involved for a book, and blogs too conversational. As a result, some of the paper's most valued reporters, some of its most powerful investigations (gambling, food adulteration, slavery, slave wages in Qatar) and some of its liveliest online writers have not made it into this edition. And, of course, the cutting-edge work of our digital developers, data bloggers and our multimedia and interactive teams is beyond the scope of this or any printed book.

Having apologised to some colleagues, I must thank others: Alan Rusbridger, for asking me to edit this book; Hugh Muir and Martin Wainwright, former *Bedside* editors, for showing me where to start; Lindsay Davies from Guardian Books, for being so wise and encouraging throughout. The *Guardian*'s picture editor, Roger Tooth, helped choose the powerful photographs. Jack Podmore, from the analytics team, identified the online-only articles readers shared the most (allowing readers to guide me to pieces I may otherwise have missed). Jeremy Alexander from the sports desk did his best to help me overcome my sport blindspot. Clare Brown – as always – gave me endless support, administrative and otherwise. I would also like to thank all those friends and colleagues who made my 16 years at the Guardian such a great pleasure.

At the beginning of this *Bedside* year, the *Guardian* was under attack for its reporting of the Snowden leaks. By the end, that hostility was, by and large, history: in 2014 the *Guardian* won the Newspaper of the Year award, the European Press Prize for journalism, and the Pulitzer Prize. It has been a very good year, and I hope I have done it justice.

September 2014

Autumn

Live blog: MPs vote down military intervention in Syria

Andrew Sparrow

8.46 A.M. BST
After last night's U-turn by David Cameron – he announced that tonight's vote will specifically not authorise military action – it looked as though this afternoon might be an anticlimax. But this morning it became clear that we've still got a day of drama ahead. Labour are not ruling out voting against the government.

9.02 A.M. BST
Nick Clegg's LBC phone-in
Q: What is the government's position on Syria?
Clegg says MPs will be voting on what Britain should do 'in principle' about the use of chemical weapons in Syria. Many people will be thinking 'why now?' The answer is that the gassing of men, women and children is a heinous crime ... If the world does not act, it may rue the day in the future.

9.06 A.M. BST
Q: You are wholly convinced Assad used the weapons.
Yes, says Clegg. All the evidence points to that.
Q: What evidence?
Clegg says there is evidence from doctors.
Q: But you would not get a conviction in court.
Clegg says it is hard to see how anyone else could have done it.

10.06 A.M. BST

Nick Clegg's interviews – summary

Repeatedly, he tried to stress the differences between the way the coalition is handling Syria and the way Labour handled Iraq. I'm not Blair, he seemed to be saying. Yet, when it came to justifying intervention, he was channelling the spirit of St Tony.

10.48 A.M. BST

Ed Miliband has also been talking to broadcasters this morning. 'We've got to learn the lessons of Iraq, because people remember the mistakes, and I'm not willing to have those mistakes made again. And one of the most important lessons from Iraq is about giving the United Nations the proper chance to do its work.'

12.24 P.M. BST

Here are some YouGov figures, showing only 25 per cent of the public in favour of Britain taking part in missile attacks against Syria.

1.37 P.M. BST

Lunchtime summary

- Downing Street has published a letter from a three-page note from the joint intelligence committee saying the Syrian government was to blame for the chemical weapons attack. The JIC concluded that it was 'highly likely' that Bashar al-Assad's regime was to blame, and that there are 'no plausible alternatives'. But at least one Conservative MP has already branded the evidence 'inconclusive'.
- Labour sources have said within the last few minutes that Labour MPs will definitely vote against the government's motion.

2.13 P.M. BST

> **John Mann MP**
> @ John Mann MP
>
> Current Bassetlaw polling on Syria
> For bombing 1 (the 1 young Conservative)
> Against bombing everyone else
> (and lots of people were asked)
>
> 10:17 AM – 29 Aug 2013

2.32 P.M. BST

Jenny Willott, a Lib Dem MP, says she is 'undecided' about the Syria issue (she's a government whip!).

4.56 P.M. BST

Lord Goldsmith, the attorney general who approved the Iraq war, says he has some 'concerns' about the government's legal case.

6.37 P.M. BST

- Justin Welby, the Archbishop of Canterbury, has said that military intervention would be 'deeply unjust' if it diminished the prospects of peace and reconciliation (he implied strongly that it would).
- David Davis, the Tory backbencher, has warned that Britain could be 'conned' into military intervention in Syria by the rebels. He said the chemical weapons could have been used by Assad's troops, by a rogue regime military unit, or by rebels 'with the direct aim of dragging the West into the war'.

7.12 P.M. BST

Here are some extracts from George Galloway's speech:

Only 11 per cent of the public, according to the *Daily Telegraph*, support Britain becoming involved in a war in Syria. Can ever a British government have imagined sending its men and women to war with the support of just 11 per cent in public opinion?

First, that there is no compelling evidence that the Assad regime is responsible for this crime yet. Not that they are not bad enough to do it. Everybody knows they are bad enough to do it. The question is, are they mad enough to do it?

To launch a chemical weapons attack in Damascus on the very day that a UN chemical weapons inspection team arrives in Damascus must be a new definition of madness. And of course if he is that mad, how mad is he going to be once we've launched a blizzard of Tomahawk cruise missiles upon his country?

7.48 P.M. BST

Lord Dannatt, the former head of the army, has said that servicemen and women should not be forced to fight a campaign without public support.

'It's been very interesting this week what has been happening in our country. The drums of war were banging very loudly two or three days ago. The people didn't like it. The ... debate has changed.'

10.23 P.M. BST

Jon Trickett
@ jon_trickett

🔵 Follow

A number of Tories in the no lobby with Labour

10.20 PM – 29 Aug 2013

10.31 P.M. BST

The government has lost by 285 votes to 272 – a majority of 13.

10.33 P.M. BST

Cameron says he believes in respecting the will of the House.

He says he 'gets' the message.

10.51 P.M. BST

James Forsyth
@ JGForsyth

Result today a huge embarrassment to Cameron.
Up until this vote, he'd had a very good summer.
Politics is now turned upside down

10.37 PM – 29 Aug 2013

Owen Jones
@OwenJones84

Worth pointing out how historic this is. British has been
subservient to US foreign policy since Suez in 1956.
A big moment.

10:38 PM – 29 Aug 2013

10.55 P.M. BST

Douglas Carswell MP
@DouglasCarswell

Democracy works. Mucky, messy, infuriating. But the best
way of running our country

10.50 PM – 29 Aug 2013

13 SEPTEMBER

The GQ awards: 'It's amazing how absurd it seems'

RUSSELL BRAND

Russell Brand was in hot water after cracking a Nazi joke at the expense of GQ awards sponsors, Hugo Boss. Here, he gives his side of the story:

I have had the privilege of scuba diving. I did it once on holiday, and I'm aware that it's one of those subjects that people can get pretty boring and sincere about, and sincerity, for we British, is no state in which to dwell, so I'll be brief. The scuba dive itself was nuministic enough, a drenched heaven; coastal shelves and their staggering, sub-aquatic architecture, like spilt cathedrals, gormless, ghostly fish gliding by like Jackson Pollock's pets. Silent miracles. What got me, though, was when I came up for air, at the end. As my head came above water after even a paltry 15 minutes in Davy Jones's Locker, there was something absurd about the surface. How we, the creatures of the land, live our lives, obliviously trundling, flat feet slapping against the dust.

It must have been a while since I've attended a fancy, glitzy event, because as soon as I got to the GQ awards I felt like something was up. The usual visual grammar was in place – a carpet in the street, people in paddocks awaiting a brush with something glamorous, blokes with earpieces, birds in frocks of colliding colours that, if sighted in nature, would indicate the presence of poison. I'm not trying to pass myself off as some kind of Francis of Assisi, Yusuf Islam, man of the people, but I just wasn't feeling it. I ambled into the Opera House across yet more outdoor carpets, boards bearing branding, in this case Hugo Boss, past paparazzi, and began to queue up at the line of journalists and presenters, in a slightly nicer paddock, who offer up mics and say stuff like:

'Who are you wearing?'

'I'm not wearing anyone. I went with clobber; I'm not Buffalo Bill.'

Noel Gallagher was immediately ahead of me in the press line and he's actually a mate. I mean, I love him: sometimes I forget he wrote 'Supersonic' and played to 400,000 people at Knebworth because he's such a laugh. He laid right into me, the usual gear: 'What the fook you wearing? Does Rod Stewart know you're going through his jumble?' I try to remain composed and give as good as I get, even though the paddock-side banter is accompanied by looming foam-tipped eavesdroppers, hanging like insidious mistletoe.

In case you don't know, these parties aren't like real parties. It's fabricated fun, imposed from the outside. A vision of what squares imagine cool people might do set on a spaceship. Or in Moloko. As we come out of the lift there's a bloody great long corridor flanked by gorgeous birds in black dresses, paid to be there, motionless, left hand on hip, teeth tacked to lips with scarlet glue. The intention, I suppose, is to contrive some Ian Fleming super-uterus of well fit mannequins to midwife you into the shindig, but me and my mate Matt just felt self-conscious, jigging through Robert Palmer's oestrogen passage like aspirational Morris dancers. Matt stared at their necks and I made small talk as I hot-stepped towards the pre-show drinks. Now, I'm not typically immune to the allure of objectified women, but I am presently beleaguered by a nerdish, whirling dervish, and am eschewing all others. Perhaps the clarity of this elation has awakened me. A friend of mine said: 'Being in love is like discovering a concealed ballroom in a house you've long inhabited.' I also don't drink, so these affairs where most people rinse away their Britishness and twittishness with booze are for me a face-first log flume of backslaps, chitchat, eyewash and gak.

After a load of photos and what-not, we descend the world's longest escalator, which are called that even as they de-escalate, and in we go to the main forum, a high-ceilinged hall, full of circular, cloth-draped, numbered tables, a stage at the front, the letters 'GQ', 12-foot high in neon at the back; this aside, though – neon for ever the moniker of trash – this is a posh do, in an opera house full of folk in tuxes.

Everywhere you look there's someone off the telly: Stephen Fry, Pharrell, Sir Bobby Charlton, Samuel L Jackson, Rio Ferdinand, Justin Timberlake, foreign secretary William Hague and mayor of London Boris Johnson. My table is a sanctuary of sorts; Noel and his missus Sara, John Bishop and his wife Mel, my mates Matt Morgan, Mick and Gee. Noel and I are both there to get awards and decide to use our speeches to dig each other out. This makes me feel a little grounded in the unreal glare, normal.

Noel's award is for being an 'icon' and mine for being an 'oracle'. My knowledge of the classics is limited, but includes awareness that an oracle is a spiritual medium through whom prophecies from the gods were sought in ancient Greece. Thankfully, I have a sense of humour that prevents me from taking accolades of that nature on face value, or I'd've been in the tricky position of receiving the GQ award for being 'best portal to a mystical dimension', which is a lot of pressure. Me, Matt and Noel conclude it's probably best to treat the whole event as a bit of a laugh and, as if to confirm this as the correct attitude, Boris Johnson – a man perpetually in pyjamas regardless of what he's wearing – bounds to the stage to accept the award for 'best politician'. Yes, we agree: this is definitely a joke.

Boris, it seems, is taking it in this spirit, joshing beneath his ever-redeeming barnet that Labour's opposition to military action in Syria is a fey stance that he, as *GQ* politician of the year, would never be guilty of.

Matt is momentarily focused. 'He's making light of gassed Syrian children,' he says. We watch, slightly aghast, then return to goading Noel.

Before long, John Bishop is on stage giving me a lovely introduction, so I get up as Noel hurls down a few gauntlets, daring me to 'do my worst'.

I thanked John, said the 'oracle award' sounds like a made-up prize you'd give a fat kid on sports day – I should know, I used to get them – then that it's barmy that Hugo Boss can trade under the same name they flogged uniforms to the Nazis under and finally flagged the ludicrous necessity for an event such as this one to banish such a lurid piece of information from our collective consciousness.

I could see the room dividing as I spoke. I could hear the laughter of some and louder still the silence of others. I realised that for some people this was regarded as an event with import. The magazine, the sponsors and some of those in attendance saw it as a kind of ceremony that warranted respect. In effect, it is a corporate ritual, an alliance between a media organisation, *GQ*, and a commercial entity, Hugo Boss. What dawned on me as the night went on is that even in apparently frivolous conditions the establishment asserts control, and won't tolerate having that assertion challenged, even flippantly, by that most beautifully adept tool: comedy.

The jokes about Hugo Boss were not intended to herald a campaign to destroy them. They're not Monsanto or Halliburton, the contemporary corporate allies of modern-day fascism; they are, I thought, an irrelevant menswear supplier with a double-dodgy history. The evening, though, provided an interesting opportunity to see how power structures preserve their agenda, even in a chintzy microcosm.

Subsequent to my jokes, the evening took a peculiar turn. Like the illusion of sophistication had been inadvertently disrupted by the exposure. It had the vibe of a wedding dinner where the best man's speech had revealed the groom's infidelity. With Hitler.

Foreign secretary William Hague gave an award to former *Telegraph* editor Charles Moore, for writing a hagiography of Margaret Thatcher, and he used his acceptance speech to build a precarious connection between my comments about the sponsors, my foolish answerphone scandal at the BBC and the Sachs family's flight, 70 years earlier, from Nazi-occupied Europe. It was a confusing tapestry that Moore spun but he seemed to be saying that a) the calls were as bad as the Holocaust and b) the Sachs family may not've sought refuge in Britain had they known what awaited them. Even for a man whose former job was editing the *Telegraph*, this is an extraordinary way to manipulate information.

Noel, who is not one to sit quietly on his feelings, literally booed while Charles Moore was talking, and others joined in. Booing! When do you hear booing in this day and age other than at pantomimes and in parliament? Hague and Johnson are equally at home in either (Widow Twanky and Buttons, obviously) so were not unduly ruffled, but I thought it was nuts. The room by now had a distinct feel of 'us and them' and if there is a line drawn in the sand I don't ever want to find myself on the same side as Hague and Johnson. Up went Noel to garner his gong and he did not disappoint: 'Always nice to be invited to the Tory party conference,' he began. 'Good to see the foreign secretary present when there's shit kicking off in Syria.'

Noel once expressed his disgust at seeing a politician at Glastonbury. 'What are you doing here? This ain't for you,' he'd said. He explained to me: 'You used to know where you were with politicians in the 70s and 80s cos they all looked like nutters: Thatcher, Heseltine, Cyril Smith. Now they look normal, they're more dangerous.' Then, with dreadful foreboding: 'They move among us.' I agree with Noel. What are politicians doing at Glastonbury and the *GQ* awards? I feel guilty going, and I'm a comedian. Why are public officials, paid by us, turning up at events for fashion magazines? Well, the reason I was there was because I have a tour on and I was advised it would be good publicity. What are the politicians selling? How are they managing our perception of them with their attendance at these sequin-encrusted corporate balls?

We witness that there is a relationship between government, media and industry that is evident even at this most spurious and superficial level. These three institutions support one another. We know that however cool a media outlet may purport to be, their primary loyalty is to their corporate backers. We know also that you cannot criticise the corporate backers openly without censorship and subsequent manipulation of this information.

Now I'm aware that this was really no big deal; I'm not saying I'm an estuary Che Guevara. It was a daft joke by a daft comic at a daft event. It makes me wonder, though, how the relationships and power dynamics I witnessed in this relatively inconsequential context are replicated on a more significant scale

For example, if you can't criticise Hugo Boss at the *GQ* awards because they own the event, do you think it is significant that energy companies donate to the Tory party? Will that affect government policy? Will the relationships that 'politician of the year' Boris Johnson has with City bankers – he took many more meetings with them than public servants in his first term as mayor – influence the way he runs our capital?

Is it any wonder that Amazon, Vodafone and Starbucks avoid paying tax when they enjoy such cosy relationships with members of our government?

Ought we to be concerned that our rights to protest are being continually eroded under the guise of enhancing our safety? Is there a relationship between proposed fracking in the UK, new laws that prohibit protest and the relationships between energy companies and our government?

I don't know. I do have some good principles picked up that night that are generally applicable: the glamour and the glitz aren't real, the party isn't real, you have a much better time mucking around trying to make your mates laugh. I suppose that's obvious. We all know it, we already know all the important stuff, like: don't trust politicians, don't trust big business and don't trust the media. Trust your own heart and each other. When you take a breath and look away from the spectacle, it's amazing how absurd it seems when you look back.

30 SEPTEMBER

Review: Sarah Lucas at the Whitechapel: more than the sum of her parts

ADRIAN SEARLE

Not long ago I received a postcard from a reader, complaining about my use of the word 'penises' as a plural. The correct word, he opined, was penes. He also complained about the *Guardian*'s ban on the word 'comedienne'. Once again, I shall annoy him.

There are a lot of penises in Sarah Lucas's Whitechapel exhibition. Big dicks, little fag-end dicks and absolutely humongous members. Lucas is also something of a comedian, but that is to belittle a talent that is uncomfortable, uncompromising, and much broader and richer than that of a potty-mouthed stand-up. Cocks, tits, fags, bums, blokes and their blokeish parts and their blokey ways are all here, along with a giant hunk of Spam and a mobile of concrete pies. Then there are the readers' wives and human toilets. The show, visitors are advised, might not be suitable for children. The real problem is for adults, who might have to answer all the little blighters' questions.

Back to the penes. Droopy ones, vast Henry Mooreish ones: there's no escaping them. Why go to the trouble to depict the whole man when just the dong will do? Lucas objectifies women, too, as an agglomeration of body parts: melon breasts, fried egg breasts, kippers, kebabs and raw chickens, thighs seen in a pair of Spanish hams conjoined with underpants and supine on a grease-stained mattress.

This is more than a mournful and depressing – not to say distressing – view of the human animal and its use-value. Looking at Lucas's partial figures, none of whom have heads, the ways in which they are gendered gets blurred. Are her sausagey, bulging Nuds male or female? They are simply, inescapably human.

Her recent cast bronze figures, which looked so beautiful in a courtyard at the Venice Biennale, and which are now upstairs at this London gallery, seem to morph between male and female, just as your eyes slither and slide over their highly polished surfaces. The contours reflect and dissolve, as you begin to meld with what you are looking at. This is a sexy feeling. I am wary of artists who go in for bronze. It can be like anointing and authorising what they make as 'high art', through the associations and imprimatur of their classy material. But Lucas's really have a point, and need to glow as they do, just as her bunnies – those etiolated figures made from stuffed tights – need their vulnerable and slightly squalid dun-coloured surfaces and visual texture, as they writhe and flop about on their chairs. One wears tiny ballerina shoes, which is somehow very touching.

Lucas's range really comes to the fore and, if there is laughter here, it is hollow and bleak. Of course, when she used Jimmy Savile as the model for her Toby-mug figure of Richard the Lionheart, before the extent of Savile's appalling behaviour became known, Lucas was aware that using the entertainer's face was bound to feel uneasy. Richard stands in the corner near the show's entrance. Nearby, an old red metal bucket lies on a crushed car, like a horrible, yawning invitation. It is all in the placement and relationships she sets up between sculptures. Artists can never know what meanings their work will accrue. Once out in the world, art is a hostage to fortune.

Lucas's work is as much a play of forms as it is of masculine and feminine. Just like the American artist Roni Horn, Lucas works with her own androgyny, and on a kind of mental gendering. In English, objects are not gendered as they are in Romance languages, where the gender assigned to a noun is often at odds with its physical designation. Lucas exploits similar ambiguities.

Inventive, bawdy and abject, tender, violent, revolting and miserable, Lucas's art is as complicated as we are, with our drives and fantasies, our inexplicable needs. She also knows when to leave off, when to stop once things are just right. She can turn a bricolage into a visual mot, a pun or a conundrum. It was all there, right from the beginning, with her bovver boots, her photographs of herself eating a banana, and the things she got her naked boyfriend of the time, the painter Gary Hume, to do with foaming tins of beer and a crate of fruit and veg.

Lucas's Whitechapel show is both enormously enjoyable and awful: awful because much of what she shows us about our relationship to the human body and our psyches is as grim as it is hilarious – the toilet as an extension of the human digestive tract, as receptacle not just of waste but of parts of ourselves, dark thoughts as well as dark matter. She can bring us up short: a cigar and a couple of walnuts are balanced on the rim of a begrimed loo. I imagine the smell of the cigar and the taste of walnuts. It's stomach-churning.

With all sorts of interesting groupings and juxtapositions, this show is a riot. Lucas's figures often confront one another in front of huge, blown-up photographs. Her self-portrait appears and reappears. At the top of the stairs, a photograph of the pensive artist, with a skull at her feet, is illuminated in the reddish glow of a neon coffin. Downstairs is a sort of orchestrated clutter of soft sculptures and concrete figures, abjection, meat, toilets and bawdiness, while the first upstairs space is a kind of wallpapered salon with a mattress sculpture as a centrepiece. The final, light-filled long space is airy and open: you move more freely, between a giant drawing of Trotsky, rendered in cigarettes, to statuesque figures in kinky boots, and on to bigger sculptures.

Lucas has also manufactured several chairs, benches and walls, using MDF and breezeblocks, some of which we can use, while others are occupied by her sculptures. I'd avoid sitting on her breezeblock plinths, though, unless you wish to be impaled by a rubbery, globular, dick-like object. Seated on the benches, you become part of the same world as her sculptures. You can't help thinking what leaky, bendy, absurd beings we are. I almost wanted to get my kit off.

Lucas is one of those artists who have a great touch and a feel for materials: things that droop, dangle and stretch; things that poke and bulge. Sometimes, her figures are as isolated as bodies at a crime scene. I have written about her a lot and she can still surprise me. Lucas, the androgynous, shy, laddish girl from the Holloway housing estate, is now the respected sculptor living in a

Suffolk village. She still deals in the perverse take on the familiar. She defamiliarises us with things we know, things we regard as beneath our attention. Dealing in the repressed, Lucas is irrepressible. I came out of this show not glad – but definitely alive.

4 OCTOBER

The greatest trick Fifa ever pulled was to issue a Qatar weather warning

MARINA HYDE

The indispensable English footballer whose metatarsal will snap four weeks before the 2022 World Cup is currently 12 years old, but Fifa is already worrying stagily about the temperature in which he will perform disappointingly. As for the 12-year-old Nepalese boy whose family are unwittingly saving for the chance to send him off in a few years to die laying the foundations of a stadio-mall, or the 12-year-old Qatari boy wondering not when his people voted for this, but whether they'll ever vote for anything at all ... well, it would be much easier if people did not concern themselves with them.

The greatest trick Fifa ever pulled – or at the very least, one of their top 10 – is acting as though the big question mark over the Qatar World Cup is the weather. By hook and by crooks, a brilliant piece of misdirection has seen almost the entire discussion centred on a roastingly heated debate about the tournament shifting seasons.

I'm not totally across the rules of apocalypse bingo. But I'm pretty sure that the second that people care more about how a winter World Cup will affect the Champions League schedule than the fact it's being built by slaves in a non-democracy, we all move closer to a full house.

A *Guardian* investigation has uncovered abuse of migrant workers in Qatar, with huge numbers dying, and working practices in various infrastructure projects amounting to modern-day slavery. Like Captain Renault in the *Casablanca* gambling den, Fifa professes itself shocked – shocked! – to find this going on in Qatar; and you, wide-eyed readers, will very likely have spent much of the week on the smelling salts yourself. In fact, I can't decide whether I am more shocked by the discovery that workers are appallingly exploited in these building binges in the Emirates, or the discovery that summer in Qatar is quite warm.

Yet even I can't synthesise surprise at leaks from this week's Fifa meeting in Zurich, which indicate they will stick with Qatar for 2022, and not reopen the dubious vote to allow wishy-washy non-authoritarian states another chance. Apologies for the repetition, but Fifa is much less of an international sporting administrator than it is a supranational privateer. It is a parasite body, which descends on the appropriately named 'host' nation every four years, siphons billions of tax-free profit out of it at the same time as overriding its laws and constitution to suit its needs, before buggering off in search of new blood. What on earth does anyone imagine it wants with democracies?

But please don't take it from me – Fifa itself is increasingly clear on the matter. 'I will say something crazy,' declared its chillingly sane secretary general, Jérôme Valcke, back in April, 'but less democracy is sometimes better for organising a World Cup.' A statement that should for ever lay to rest Fifa's nonsense about the tournament's power to change the world for good.

Far from being the catalyst for progress its corporate folklore always holds it to be, the World Cup is in the gift of those irked by so-called advances for the little people – democracy, say, or the right to protest – and who believe it much better staged where those required to pay for it are voiceless.

Or, as Valcke added: 'When you have a very strong head of state who can decide, as maybe Putin can do in 2018, that is easier for us organisers than a country such as Germany ... where you have to negotiate at different levels.'

How trying it must be. Happily, South Africa – Fifa's most recent ATM – rolled over very easily in 2010, with the scale of their obedience so total that Blatter was sufficiently emboldened to put the recently bereaved Nelson Mandela under 'extreme pressure' to show himself at the final. As I say, I don't play apocalypse bingo. But if you had your dabber in your hand, the moment Sepp Blatter successfully pulled rank on the unofficial elder of the entire global village was probably one to cross off.

As for the demonstrations in Brazil ahead of next year's tournament, Blatter seems nostalgic for simpler South American times.

'I was happy Argentina won,' he declared of the victorious hosts of the 1978 World Cup, held under military government. 'This was a kind of reconciliation with the public, of the people of Argentina, with the system, the political system, the military system at the time.' Mmm. Perhaps when Herr Blatter finally retires, having held power longer than most dictators, he could write a musical entitled *Oh, What a Lovely Dirty War!*

What a historian he is, and we can only imagine the spin he will put on the deaths of those labourers in Qatar in 10 years' time. They were not slaves – they were freedom fighters in the unimpeachable cause of football's mission to build a better tomorrow. Or a better food court, or something.

The one thing we'll never hear, of course, is a decent argument for why on earth non-democracies are even eligible to bid for

Fifa's bauble – yet no attempt to get us to chat about the weather should stop this fundamental question being asked of Fifa at every turn. After all, if hosting an Olympics or a World Cup were even remotely likely to advance the cause of human freedom in their countries, does anyone think the likes of China and Qatar would be as keen to host them as they are?

8 OCTOBER

Mrs Cameron's Diary: toilets, serviettes and stove – a dissection of class in modern Britain

CATHERINE BENNETT

Well, major eek, like when you ask someone if they are pregnant and actually they are just big – sort of THAT? As in, the number of people Dave has offended since Mr Cobber went, listen mate, the polls are saying 10 top chavs in place by Monday or trust Lynton, you are royally fucked? I mean, I get how hurt Victoria Beckham was, but Dave is right, Harlow + hair extensions + a footballer = ticks all the boxes?

So Craig Oliver said, chavwise, a flat cap says everything, but Pippa Middleton just hung up? So Anna Soubry was like, trust me, repulsive obesity never lies, oh, no offence #awkward. So Dave asked Fellowes over, as in GIMLET eye for kulaks, & Julian said just mention golf, e.g. Lady Kitchen of Khartoumland might say, 'we have just come from heavenly St Andrews, do you play at all?', & anyone who does not say 'gorl', rhymes with shawl, is a northerner. I'm like, Julian are you SURE #neverforgetLadyMary'sbrazilian.

Well, Mummy said, just be alert for toilet, I'm like, excuse me Tracey Emin says toilet, well obvs, but Alexa CHUNG says toilet, probably Anna Wintour would say toilet if she thought it was a thing? Mummy's like, fine, serviette, is not serviette how you found dear Pickles – they do 'do' napkins north of Scunthorpe? Dave was like, well, I guess if there was a sure-fire sign of working classness science would have found it by now, I'm like *lightbulb* it HAS, as in, 'does not own a wood-burning stove'? Dave is like genius, Craig, who do we know who does not own a wood-burning stove, Craig's like, Andy Coulson?

So it is actually quite embarrassing because Oik comes up with this entire LIST? Dave is like, God, Matthew Hancock a chav, who knew, Oik goes, exactly, Exeter College, he keeps it very quiet. I'm like, OMG, how did we not know that Amber Rudd keeps pigeons, Oik goes, well please do not mention it, the same with Greg Hands, VERY sensitive about his pig, as you'd imagine. Dave's like, totes understand, Oik old man, you must feel the same way about St Paul's, no don't apologise, if there is one thing Lynton insists on, it is celebrating difference :)

22 OCTOBER

The Great British Bake Off: why did our show attract so much vitriol?

RUBY TANDOH

Ten weeks of frenzied baking culminated in a great pastel-coloured explosion of flour, bunting and puns. Within the confines of our little picket-fenced tent, we threw ourselves into the challenges of picnic pies and pretzels, shaking, terrified, dosed up on adrenaline and Rescue Remedy.

Of course, it is the hyperbolic silliness – the make-or-break trifle sponge, custard thefts, and prolonged ruminations over 'The Crumb' – that makes *The Great British Bake Off* so lovable. It is your nan's biscuit tin, a village fete and picnic in the park. It converts banality – the efforts of a gaggle of amateur bakers in a tent in Somerset – into a national spectacle.

That's why I am surprised at just how much nastiness was generated from the show. Despite the saccharine sweetness of the *Bake Off*, an extraordinary amount of bitterness and bile has spewed forth every week from angry commentators, both on social media and in the press. Many took to Twitter, decrying the demise of the show, voicing their hatred for certain bakers, and asserting (week after week!) that they would 'never watch it again' if X or Y got through that episode. Online hordes massed, brandishing rolling pins and placards, ready to tear down the bunting and upturn the ovens. How did a programme about cake become so divisive?

The criticism ranged from the gently cynical to the downright obnoxious, but as the series went on I noticed an increasing degree of personal vitriol and misogyny. We (female) finalists are supposedly too meek, too confident, too thin, too domestic, too smiley, too taciturn ... If I see one more person use the hackneyed 'dough-eyed' pun I will personally go to their house and force-feed them an entire Charlotte Royale.

I am tired of defending myself against the boring, inevitable accusations of flirting with Paul Hollywood, of emotionally manipulating the judges and of somehow surfing into the final on a tidal wave of tears. I'd rather eat my own foot than attempt to seduce my way to victory, and even if I had any intention of playing that card, it's insulting to both the judges to suggest that they'd ever let their professional integrity be undermined in that way.

Of course, this is TV – it is meticulously manufactured – but the judging was always fair. Much of the groundless criticism and claims of cupcake conspiracy are the inevitable consequences of *Bake Off*'s success with viewers.

But I think there's more to it than just this – so much of the criticism levelled at the bakers is gender-specific. My self-doubt has been simultaneously labelled pathetic, fake, attention-seeking and manipulative.

Raymond Blanc waded in on the commentary so helpfully to deride the 'female tears' on the show. (What are 'female tears', anyway? Are they more fragile and delicate than male tears? Do they wear pink?) Kimberley's self-assurance – a character trait so lauded in men – has been rebranded as smugness, cockiness and even malice.

There have been the sadly predictable comments on the bakers' weights (as though it's unfathomable that anybody could enjoy food and yet be slim), and charming debates on which of the finalists is the most 'shaggable'.

And then there's the broader background of misogyny and gender politics against which this has all played out. It's a culture of frilly baking versus macho Michelin stars, of real chefs versus domestic goddesses. Food has become divided and gendered, torn between the serious sport of haute cuisine and the supposedly antithetical world of women pottering around in home kitchens.

Even within baking there's the view that a spelt sourdough is somehow more sincere than a miniature macaroon. It's all nonsense, of course, but as long as this needlessly gendered rift is maintained, both men and women will suffer for it. Of course *Bake Off* is silly, and of course there's nothing life-or-death about making trifle in a tent. But it is no more frivolous than any other reality-TV cooking show, and its contestants are no less serious about what they do.

Well, I'm done with apologising. I have apologised for my bakes, and I have apologised for apologising. I have shied away from the more decorative side of baking for fear of being dismissed as silly.

I've served every bake with a side of self-deprecation, as anything more than total meekness may be mistaken for the sort of confidence that other bakers have been lambasted for. I have defended myself against accusations of being a 'filthy slag' based solely on me being a woman on a TV screen.

If a show as gentle as *Bake Off* can stir up such a sludge of lazy misogyny in the murky waters of the internet, I hate to imagine the full scale of the problem. But it's not something I'm willing to tolerate. Sod the haters. I'm going to have my cupcake and eat it, too.

8 NOVEMBER

This year, I will wear a poppy for the last time

HARRY LESLIE SMITH

Over the last 10 years the sepia tone of November has become blood-soaked with paper poppies festooning the lapels of our politicians, newsreaders and business leaders. The most fortunate in our society have turned the solemnity of remembrance for fallen soldiers in ancient wars into a justification for our most recent armed conflicts. The American civil war's General Sherman once said that 'war is hell', but unfortunately today's politicians in

Britain use past wars to bolster our flagging belief in national austerity or to compel us to surrender our rights as citizens, in the name of the public good.

Still, this year I shall wear the poppy as I have done for many years. I wear it because I am from that last generation who remember a war that encompassed the entire world. I wear the poppy because I can recall when Britain was actually threatened with a real invasion and how its citizens stood at the ready to defend her shores. But most importantly, I wear the poppy to commemorate those of my childhood friends and comrades who did not survive the second world war and those who came home physically and emotionally wounded from horrific battles that no poet or journalist could describe.

However, I am afraid it will be the last time that I will bear witness to those soldiers, airmen and sailors who are no more, at my local cenotaph. From now on, I will lament their passing in private because my despair is for those who live in this present world. I will no longer allow my obligation as a veteran to remember those who died in the great wars to be co-opted by current or former politicians to justify our folly in Iraq, our morally dubious war on terror and our elimination of one's right to privacy.

Come 2014, when the government marks the beginning of the first world war with quotes from Rupert Brooke, Rudyard Kipling and other great jingoists from our past empire, I will declare myself a conscientious objector. We must remember that the historical past of this country is not like an episode of *Downton Abbey*, where the rich are portrayed as thoughtful, benevolent masters to poor folk who need the guiding hand of the ruling classes to live a proper life.

I can tell you it didn't happen that way because I was born nine years after the first world war began. I can attest that life for most people was spent in abject poverty where one laboured under brutal working conditions for little pay and lived in houses not fit to kennel a dog today. We must remember that the war was fought by the working classes, who comprised 80 per cent of Britain's population in 1913.

This is why I find that the government's intention to spend £50m to dress the slaughter of close to a million British soldiers in the 1914–18 conflict as a fight for freedom and democracy profane. Too many of the dead, from that horrendous war, didn't know real freedom because they were poor and were never truly represented by their members of parliament.

My uncle and many of my relatives died in that war and they weren't officers or NCOs; they were simple Tommies. They were like the hundreds of thousands of other boys who were sent to their slaughter by a government that didn't care to represent their citizens if they were working poor and undereducated. My family members took the king's shilling because they had little choice, whereas many others from similar economic backgrounds were strong-armed into enlisting by war propaganda or press-ganged into military service by their employers.

For many of you, 1914 probably seems like a long time ago, but I'll be 91 next year, so it feels recent. Today, we have allowed monolithic corporate institutions to set our national agenda. We have allowed vitriol to replace earnest debate and we have somehow deluded ourselves into thinking that wealth is wisdom. But by far the worst error we have made as a people is to think of ourselves as taxpayers first and citizens second.

Next year, I won't wear the poppy but I will until my last breath remember the past and the struggles my generation made to build this country into a civilised state for the working and middle classes. If we are to survive as a progressive nation we have to start tending to our living because the wounded – our poor, our underemployed youth, our hard-pressed middle class and our struggling seniors – shouldn't be left to die on the battleground of modern life.

13 NOVEMBER

A fashion show that has nothing to do with fashion

JESS CARTNER-MORLEY

It is the most expensive catwalk show ever staged, but it has almost nothing to do with fashion. They're not really into irony at Victoria's Secret, so the joke gets a little lost in the dazzle of white teeth and diamond-encrusted bras and paparazzi cameras, but it's quite funny, when you think about it.

All the signifiers of a fashion show are in place when Victoria's Secret stages its annual extravaganza. The model line-up always includes high-end Paris fashion week names (Cara Delevingne and Jourdan Dunn have featured in recent years) and the show is styled by Sophia Neophitou who, as stylist and collaborator to Roland Mouret and Antonio Berardi and British Fashion Council ambassador, is an undisputed powerhouse of high-fashion taste. The six-inch high heels are designed for the occasion by Nicholas Kirkwood, the talented young shoe designer who was just snapped up by LVMH.

But there's something missing. Call me old-fashioned, but I sort of think the absence of clothes is a dealbreaker as far as fashion goes. At the Victoria's Secret show, instead of clothes, the models wear underwear and massive fluffy angel wings. I've been a fashion editor for 15 years, I've seen all kinds of crazy accessories anointed a fashion must-have, but massive fluffy angel wings? Nope. Not a catwalk trend. Never.

I know what you're thinking: it's about sex, stupid. Well, here's the thing: I don't see that Victoria's Secret is really about sex, either. The presentation of the Victoria's Secret Angels, to give the catwalk models their faintly creepy official title, is look-but-don't-touch in the extreme. Like a very grand ballgown, or a bridal dress with a train, the wings form a kind of exclusion zone, making it physically difficult to get close. Also, even if you did find a woman dressed in an oversized Angel Gabriel costume sexy, which seems a little dubious, you'd have difficulty getting intimately acquainted. The wings Alessandra Ambrosio wore in the 2011 show were gold-plated antique copper decorated with 105,000 Swarovski crystals. They weighed almost 10kg. There is as much neon, crystal and metallic on the VS runway as there is satin and marabou. The VS catwalk cipher might be look-at-me, but it's hard to argue that it is come-and-get-me. The name Victoria's Secret was chosen, in 1977, to set a mood-music of sobriety and respectability, and that wholesomeness is still there, despite the acres of flesh on show.

When you visit the store, you notice how little of the product is sexy in the sense of being designed for sex. Much of the shop floor is dominated by bras bulked up by gel or foam padding. In these, a woman may send a sexual signal when dressed, but she will need to undress alone. The vast 'Pink' sub-brand of pyjamas, sweatshirts and logoed vests sells an aesthetic of the tween sleepover, not booty call. But there is no doubt it works: last year, sales at Victoria's Secret totalled almost £4bn.

The VS brand has very little to do with actual sex, and everything to do with sexiness as a status symbol. The brand has as much to do with women looking at other women, as it does with men looking at women: for every 17-year-old boy ogling the models' arses, there is a 16-year-old girl staring at their abs. VS deliberately emphasises the intense competition among models to appear on the catwalk; among the most 'liked' posts of the endless Instagram photos of Angels-in-training are those that feature the models in boxing gloves, punching their way to a catwalk turn that could earn them a seven-figure pay cheque.

The Victoria's Secret show takes the cheerleader tradition, and removes the boring old football game. Sportsmanship is old hat; the 21st century is all about being hot. This is the Superbowl, for those gifted with lovely hair, beautiful bottoms and superhuman endurance for juice fasting. These days you can be a champion – an Angel, a higher being – just by being sexy. That's a trend, for sure. But it's got nothing to do with fashion, so don't blame us.

15 NOVEMBER

Why even atheists should be praying for Pope Francis

JONATHAN FREEDLAND

That Obama poster on the wall, promising hope and change, is looking a little faded now. The disappointments, whether over drone warfare or a botched roll-out of health care reform, have left the world's liberals and progressives searching for a new pin-up to take the US president's place. As it happens, there's an obvious candidate: the head of an organisation those same liberals and progressives have long regarded as sexist, homophobic and, thanks to a series of child abuse scandals, chillingly cruel. The obvious new hero of the left is the pope.

Only installed in March, Pope Francis has already become a phenomenon. His is the most talked-about name on the internet in 2013, ranking ahead of 'Obamacare' and 'NSA'. In fourth place comes Francis's Twitter handle, @Pontifex. In Italy, Francesco has fast become the most popular name for new baby boys. Rome reports a surge in tourist numbers, while church attendance is said to be up – both trends attributed to 'the Francis effect'.

His popularity is not hard to fathom. The stories of his personal modesty have become the stuff of instant legend. He carries his own suitcase. He refused the grandeur of the papal palace, preferring to live in a simple hostel. When presented with the traditional red shoes of the pontiff, he declined; instead, he telephoned his 81-year-old cobbler in Buenos Aires and asked him to repair his old ones. On Thursday, Francis visited the Italian president – arriving in a blue Ford Focus, with not a blaring siren to be heard.

Some will dismiss these acts as mere gestures, even publicity stunts. But they convey a powerful message, one of almost elemental egalitarianism. He is in the business of scraping away the trappings, the edifice of Vatican wealth accreted over centuries, and returning the church to its core purpose, one Jesus himself might have recognised. He says he wants to preside over 'a poor church, for the poor'. It's not the institution that counts, it's the mission.

All this would warm the heart of even the most fervent atheist, except Francis has gone much further. It seems he wants to do more than simply stroke the brow of the weak. He is taking on the system that has made them weak and keeps them that way.

'My thoughts turn to all who are unemployed, often as a result of a self-centred mindset bent on profit at any cost,' he tweeted in May. A day earlier he denounced as 'slave labour' the conditions endured by Bangladeshi workers killed in a building collapse. In

September he said that God wanted men and women to be at the heart of the world and yet we live in a global economic order that worships 'an idol called money'.

There is no denying the radicalism of this message, a frontal and sustained attack on what he calls 'unbridled capitalism', with its 'throwaway' attitude to everything from unwanted food to unwanted old people. His enemies have certainly not missed it. If a man is to be judged by his opponents, note that this week Sarah Palin denounced him as 'kind of liberal' while the free-market Institute of Economic Affairs has lamented that this pope lacks the 'sophisticated' approach to such matters of his predecessors. Meanwhile, an Italian prosecutor has warned that Francis's campaign against corruption could put him in the crosshairs of that country's second most powerful institution: the mafia.

As if this weren't enough to have Francis's 76-year-old face on the walls of the world's student bedrooms, he also seems set to lead a church campaign on the environment. He was photographed this week with anti-fracking activists, while his biographer, Paul Vallely, has revealed that the pope has made contact with Leonardo Boff, an eco-theologian previously shunned by Rome and sentenced to 'obsequious silence' by the office formerly known as the 'Inquisition'. An encyclical on care for the planet is said to be on the way.

Many on the left will say that's all very welcome, but meaningless until the pope puts his own house in order. But here, too, the signs are encouraging. Or, more accurately, stunning. Recently, Francis told an interviewer the church had become 'obsessed' with abortion, gay marriage and contraception. He no longer wanted the Catholic hierarchy to be preoccupied with 'small-minded rules'. Talking to reporters on a flight – an occurrence remarkable in itself – he said: 'If a person is gay and seeks God and has good will, who am I to judge?' His latest move is to send the world's Catholics a questionnaire, seeking their attitude to those vexed questions of modern life. It's bound to reveal a flock whose practices are, shall we say, at variance with Catholic teaching. In politics, you'd say Francis was preparing the ground for reform.

Witness his reaction to a letter – sent to 'His Holiness Francis, Vatican City' – from a single woman, pregnant by a married man who had since abandoned her. To her astonishment, the pope telephoned her directly and told her that if, as she feared, priests refused to baptise her baby, he would perform the ceremony himself. (Telephoning individuals who write to him is a Francis habit.) Now contrast that with the past Catholic approach to such 'fallen women', dramatised so powerfully in the current film *Philomena*. He is replacing brutality with empathy.

Of course, he is not perfect. His record in Argentina during the era of dictatorship and 'dirty war' is far from clean. 'He started off as a strict authoritarian, reactionary figure,' says Vallely. But, aged 50, Francis underwent a spiritual crisis from which, says his biographer, he emerged utterly transformed. He ditched the trappings of high church office, went into the slums and got his hands dirty.

Now inside the Vatican, he faces a different challenge – to face down the conservatives of the curia and lock in his reforms, so that they cannot be undone once he's gone. Given the guile of those courtiers, that's quite a task: he'll need all the support he can get.

Some will say the world's leftists and liberals shouldn't hanker for a pin-up, that the urge is infantile and bound to end in disappointment. But the need is human and hardly confined to the left: think of the Reagan and Thatcher posters that still adorn the metaphorical walls of conservatives, three decades on. The pope may have no army, no battalions or divisions, but he has a pulpit – and right now he is using it to be the world's loudest and clearest voice against the status quo. You don't have to be a believer to believe in that.

18 November

'Syria is not a revolution any more – this is civil war' (extract)

GHAITH ABDUL-AHAD

For three men in northern Syria, the second civil war started shortly after the first staggered into a quagmire of sectarian violence. The goals of the first war – freedom, Islam, social equality – were replaced by betrayal, defeat and anger towards rival militias, jihadis and foreign powers fighting in Syria.

Like many others, the three men are bewildered at what has become of their war. Their alliances – and their goals – are shifting. The regime is far away, the jihadis are near – and seem unstoppable. Their resources are dwindling; their families are shattered. Their villages and farm lands are lost to regime militias. Their allies are at best unreliable, and at worst actively conspiring against them.

They are a businessman, a smuggler and an army defector who became respectively the political officer, treasurer and military commander of a once-formidable battalion in northern Syria.

The businessman is the shrewdest: a tall, wide-shouldered man with a square head and thinning hair. A devout Salafi, he was once a rich man in Homs, but after two and a half years of war, most of his fortune has been spent on arms and ammunition. What remains of his wealth is being slowly drained by the families of his dead, injured and missing relatives, many of them languishing in refugee camps.

On a cold autumn evening he sat in the courtyard of a newly built house on the Turkish side of the Syrian border.

'I need Bashar [al-Assad] to last for two more years,' said the businessman. 'It would be a disaster if the regime fell now: we would split into mini-states. We'll be massacring each other – tribes, Islamists and battalions.

'Maybe if the regime lasts for a few more years we can agree on the shape of the new Syria. At least then we might end up with three states rather than 10,' he said. Meanwhile, the killings and massacres will continue, until sectarian cleansing has been carried out in all of Syria's cities and regions, he added. 'There will be either Alawites or Sunnis. Either them or us. Maybe in 10 years we will all be bored with fighting and learn how to coexist.' He paused, then added: 'In 10 years maybe, not now.'

The battalion that the three men were part of was once the darling of the rebels' foreign backers: Qatari royalty, Saudi preachers and Kuwaiti MPs all donated money and funnelled weapons to them. The businessman regularly met Turkish military intelligence officers on the border who safeguarded his arms shipments from Mediterranean ports.

But as jihadi influence grew among the opposition forces, the battalion's position came under threat. A clash was inevitable. A jihadi leader was assassinated and the battalion was forced from its footholds in the oil-rich east. Some of its men left to join other factions or set up their own.

Gulf dignitaries accused the three men of sowing dissent in the Muslim community and financial backers switched their support to other battalions with a stricter Islamic outlook.

The businessman stared up at the night sky, and smoked his last cigarette of the day. 'This is not a revolution against a regime any more, this is a civil war,' he said.

The next day, in a sparsely furnished living room with thinly whitewashed walls, the smuggler and the businessman argued about a missing shipment of rockets. The smuggler had worked the secret routes across Lebanon's border from the age of 11; he was shot at for the first time aged 12 and ran his own network when he was barely 17. He is proud never to have owned an ID card or a passport in his life. He fidgeted and moved constantly, tapping on his smartphone, buying arms, selling rockets, importing cars and arranging schooling for his many nephews and nieces.

He opened Google Earth on his phone, zooming in closer and closer until the screen showed a small grey square: the house where his family used to live. 'Before, all my family was in Syria, and I worried about them. Now, they've got out but I have lost my land. I have reached a point of despair,' he said.

'I feel I can't breathe. I have 20 people to look after – to feed them and school them. I was in the revolution at the beginning, and I used to think that was going to be progress – but now we have lost everything. We don't talk about military plans and hitting the regime – now the plotting is against each other.'

The third man worked as a shepherd as a child, spending long weeks trekking alone with his sheep in the arid hills of southern Syria. School was a two-mile (3km) hike; like many young Bedouins, he joined the military as soon as he graduated from high school. He eventually became a lieutenant.

Soon after the revolution began in early 2011, he defected, joining other rebel officers in the north. He made his reputation when his unit attacked an army base and captured several tanks. He became the commander of one of the rebel forces' first armoured battalions.

In those days, he was lean and tense, with a wispy Che Guevara beard; his looks and his heroism inspired devotion in his men. He read history books, and drew lessons from the Russian partisans' tactics in the second world war.

Like most Bedouins, he spoke rarely, and when he did, he was frank to the point of rudeness. But amid the chaos of civil war, he was keen to impose discipline: every morning he would drive around his base, inspecting his men's uniforms and weapons. 'How do you impose discipline?' he would muse. 'I don't pay them money and I can't put them in jail. The bond between you and your men comes from battle: if they respect you as a fighter, they will follow you.'

After travelling into Syria, the businessman and the smuggler arrived where the lieutenant was staying with some of his men. Dressed in a dirty white vest and combat trousers, he seemed much older. The lieutenant ate lunch in silence before finally addressing his two friends. 'I am now in an impossible situation. The army is ahead of me and they are surrounding from behind.'

'They' were the al-Qaida-linked group Islamic State of Iraq and al-Sham (Isis), which is directly linked to the main al-Qaida group in Iraq.

Recognised as a ferocious fighting force, it has also won a reputation for efficiency and governance in the areas it runs – a fact reflected in a name locals use for the faction: *Dawla* – the Arabic word for 'the state'.

'I can't defeat them and the army. I am about to collapse. I can hold out for a month or two at most. Isis are expanding in a fearful way.

'I tell other commanders: "Let's make a deal, let's unite against the jihadis. If we take over the northern border strip we can strangle them."' He flashed a bitter smile before continuing: 'But we can't even decide to unite against Bashar – how can we unite against Islamists?'

The three men drove down to the battalion base. The lieutenant pointed at a town of low-rise buildings. This was al-Dana, the jihadi capital of the region.

'They control cities: once you control a town you control the surrounding villages,' the lieutenant said.

When they reached the base, the lieutenant sank down in a corner. He seemed weary. 'I have been fighting for two years and a half. Tell me: what have I achieved? All I think about is attacking this checkpoint, getting that tank.

'In all this time did I ever think of establishing governance? Did I consider working with the civilians in the areas under my control to get electricity or provide anything? The jihadis are better: they provide governance. In two and a half years, I have built nothing. Kill me, and my battalion collapses. Kill the jihadis, and the institutions they have founded will survive.'

The lieutenant's men had been attacking a government outpost in a farmhouse on Hama's eastern plains. After three days, the house was reduced to rubble but the troops inside were still holding out.

Ancient Russian tanks – rebel and loyalist – were lobbing shells at each other across a pistachio grove like street children throwing stones in an alleyway. The explosions sent orange columns of dust into the haze of the setting sun. Near the outpost, a government tank was smouldering, and a young girl lay dead, hit by shrapnel. A group of rebels crawled through the fields for a mile until they reached the edge of the outpost.

But before they managed to scale the fortifications they were spotted – a shell landed nearby, and machine gun fire broke out, pinning them down. Two fighters kicked the dirt with their heels, trying to make a shallow trench. Bullets whistled through the trees, shredding leaves and tree trunks. On the other side of the dyke, government troops fired at the rebels from hatches in the ruined outpost.

'If they all fight like this, this army won't give up until Bashar is dead,' said the commander of the rebel attackers.

But by early evening the regime troops abandoned their position, falling back under cover of heavy shelling. The rebels packed the ruined outpost with explosives and blew it up. The attack had killed one rebel and wounded 11. The unit had used ammunition worth £43,000, and the only salvageable government weapon was a machine gun.

'For three days I've been attacking this checkpoint,' said the lieutenant. 'I ask myself why, but I don't know. Maybe because I can. Maybe because I need to keep my men busy. But honestly, I don't know the purpose of all this. In Syria, everyone has lost. No one is winning.'

A few days later, the smuggler, the lieutenant and another rebel officer were walking in an Istanbul shopping centre packed with Arab tourists. After two and a half years, the smuggler and the lieutenant said they had finally decided to leave Syria and the war for good.

They stopped at a Starbucks, where they sat laughing at each other's jokes. They had Nike shopping bags and new jeans, and the smuggler was – as usual – fidgeting with his phone. 'I don't know what we are doing here,' he laughed. 'Back home, the world is collapsing.'

Later, in the food court upstairs, the smuggler and the lieutenant ate lunch with another man, a people-smuggler, who told them how they could be spirited across the border into Greece and from there into Italy, where they could start a new life with their families.

By the end of the meal, they had agreed on a plan. The man told them to be ready to leave the next day – $2,000 (£1,250) would be deposited with a colleague, to be handed over when they reached Italy.

The businessman came to Istanbul the next day and drove to a large hotel for a conference of centre-right Islamists. The lobby was filled with preachers and dignitaries from around the Arab world, Syrian rebel commanders, and a group of Kuwaiti politicians. On one side, a Sudanese man in extravagant head-gear held court. Further on, an Emirati sheikh chatted amiably with an Iraqi MP wanted on charges of terrorism. The mix felt like the crowd in the *Star Wars* bar.

In the midst of this, in walked the businessman. He struggled to keep a straight face as he walked between the small circles of men speaking in grandiose terms about the glory of Islam, western conspiracies and the Syrian tragedy.

'We kept telling them: if you keep supporting the jihadis you will destroy the revolution. That Kuwaiti MP who now talks of moderation was the same one who sent the money to the jihadis.'

One afternoon a few days later, the lieutenant, the smuggler and the other commander went out for a walk in the warm sunshine. Children chased pigeons; tourists posed for pictures. Overhead, a plane was coming into land. The commander pulled the collar of his shirt, speaking into an imaginary microphone: 'Air defence! Air defence!'

'Airplane approaching! You could bring it down with a heavy machine gun,' retorted the lieutenant. The commander made a finger pistol and took aim – but the two men stopped their macabre game when they realised they were enjoying it too much.

By now, the excitement of being in Istanbul had waned: the three men walked the streets aimlessly. The lieutenant was adamant that he wanted to leave the war but every time the people-smuggler called, he postponed the trip a few more days. One evening, he admitted that he had tried to leave once before: he had stayed away for 25 days, but found he could not live in the world of peace: he missed the excitement, the combat, the camaraderie.

'While I'm here, I'm laughing and smiling, but I choke with tears every time I remember the men I have left behind – men who fought with me, men who were injured for me.'

He was sitting in a cafe perched on a hill, with the lights of oil tankers and ferries blinking from the Bosphorus below.

'If I go, they will accuse me of treason – but I am fed up with this life. I cannot attack the regime while I'm being attacked by jihadis from behind.'

The lieutenant left the cafe, and there was no news of him for weeks. Nobody knew if he was still in Turkey, or if he had gone with the people-smuggler and made his way to Italy.

When he finally called, he sounded relieved and almost cheerful. 'I just couldn't do it,' he said. 'I couldn't leave. I went back to Syria, to fight.'

19 November

Childcare – don't reduce us to a sheaf of payslips

ZOE WILLIAMS

Solve childcare and you win the election. This is the calculation politicians make – whether they set about it like Nick Clegg, rolling out childcare for the poorest under-twos, or like Ed Miliband, promising 8 a.m. to 6 p.m. care for school kids, or you take David Cameron's rather perverse course of making childcare slightly cheaper for rich people. Nobody can afford to walk away from the territory. There are votes in them there kindergartens.

A practical family mind, planning what to do with its young rather than how to cast its vote, might ask some questions that aren't about the bottom line. Would you necessarily want to leave your two-year-old in the care of a state whose Department of Education under-secretary, Liz Truss, famously worries about them 'running around with no sense of purpose'? How does one measure purpose, exactly? Is it with a test? Do you want your toddler tested, or even your four-year-old?

And that's a pretty long day that Miliband's offering, isn't it, 8 a.m. to 6 p.m.? It's longer than my day, and I've had all social anxiety bleached out of me by the slightly-too-hot wash of life. Sorry, of course this is all off-topic: this discussion is about childcare; those questions were about education. And by the terms of today's politics, those are two totally different things, albeit performed by the same people, upon the same people, in the same place.

More to the point, I was being off-message – you're not allowed to ask whether a solution for the mother also works for the child, since that's de facto unfeminist. Women, by modern logic, win by having economic agency and lose by being economically excluded. Children, having no productive contribution to make, are either a neutral value in the equation, an appendage of the mother, or a negative value, a drain on the mother. What if the mother wants to hang out with the child, not because she has been subjugated by the patriarchy but because she thinks the child is awesome? What if the father does too? Well, that point of view makes no financial sense, so unfortunately cannot be included in our discussion.

All we hear is a series of conversations about the 'economic case' for childcare. It's often billed as the 'softer yet stronger' economic policy, just as women are (egregiously, in my view) presented as the 'softer yet stronger' sex. The shadow minister for children, Lucy Powell, contrasted, on *Comment Is Free*, 'business case after business case for boys' toys like planes and trains' against 'the case for childcare as a key economic driver to get women – and it is still mainly women – back into work'. Leaving aside the wisdom of trying to turn rail infrastructure into a gendered issue (in this day and age!), this remark distils the approach of the mainstream, which holds economic productivity as the highest goal of the human being.

Yet if you raise those 'stay-at-homes', the vexatious mothers who are in no rush to get back to work, who want to savour what is, set against 40 or, in the future, more like 50 years of a career, the unbearably short and precious time span of a childhood – well, then you have allied yourself to a different sort of Tory. The breadwinner Tory, the marriage tax-break Tory, the Tory for whom getting women back into the kitchen is the first stage of getting the world back to rights. This entire conversation is caught between the Ukip frying pan and the Treasury fire: re-domestication on one side; a monetising, price-tag-on-everything agenda on the other.

Received wisdom has moved so far from lived experience that it's almost comical. Nobody apart from Godfrey Bloom still thinks women should be full-time mothers as a function of their sex. Nobody apart from the Career Bitch of the *Daily Mail*'s imagination wants full-time, free nurseries running from birth straight into wraparound, free schooling. It's not like parking a car. Wherever you leave your children – and that's great, if it's convenient and free – you're still left with the problem of not being around them.

What almost everybody wants is this: the option of working full-time if they want or need to, without spending every penny they make on childcare, but the ability to work part-time if they'd rather divide their lives more equitably between home and work; an abundance of interesting and flexible jobs, so they can get away from their children for the sake of their sanity, but not so much work that they cease to be the main influence in their children's lives.

People want the freedom to react to things – an illness, an irrational hatred of nursery – without that signifying a lack of professional commitment. Never mind women, this is what all parents want: some recognition, from the workplace and beyond, that there is more to life than making money, and yet that making money is a blessed diversion from full-time making a mess.

These are very simple ideas, but to execute, or even show oneself able to understand them, would take a significant shift in political stance. Not only would politicians need to stop talking about workforce participation as the only meaningful yardstick of successful social policy, they'd also have to stop talking about employers as these godlike creators of wealth and talk of them instead as people with as much responsibility to act like human beings as the rest of us.

We will all have periods in our lives when we are producing sod all that anybody could buy, when we are economically stagnant; some of those will be our happiest moments. We can't allow this debate to reduce us all to a sheaf of payslips.

27 NOVEMBER

'Whooah ... Livin' in Mayfair!' Prince William's Bon Jovi moment reimagined

STUART HERITAGE

After Prince William joined Jon Bon Jovi to sing 'Livin' on a Prayer' – a song about a poverty-stricken couple struggling to make ends meet – Stuart Heritage imagined lyrics he might feel more comfortable with.

Thomas used to work with the stocks
Then the markets collapsed
Now he's down to his last pair
Of Crocs, which sucks

Henrietta's down in the dumps
Her butler's on strike
She has to make her own lunch
Boiled dove, boiled dove

They say we've got to hold on to what we've got
Doesn't really matter
If we need it or not
We've got big houses, and rifles we bought
For fun – let's give them a shot

Whooah, we're halfway there
Livin' in Mayfair
All my neighbours are Russians I swear
Livin' in Mayfair

Henrietta's awfully miffed
Her pony has got gout
And it was a gift
from Mum, her mum

Thomas dreams of running away
When he cries in the night
His hedge fund reminds him
It's OK, someday

We've got to hold on to what we've got
'Cause it doesn't really matter
If we earned it or not
We went to good schools and that's a lot
For cash, we'll just sell our yachts

Whooah, we're halfway there
Livin' in Mayfair
My gap year was wicked I swear
Livin' in Mayfair

We've got to hold on, ready or not
You'll wear your red trousers when they're all you've got

Whooah, we're halfway there
Livin' in Mayfair
Eat this swan, it's delicious I swear
Livin' in Mayfair

1 DECEMBER

My week as an Amazon insider (extract)

CAROLE CADWALLADR

The first item I see in Amazon's Swansea warehouse is a package of dog nappies. The second is a massive pink plastic dildo. The warehouse is 800,000 square feet, or, in what is Amazon's standard unit of measurement, the size of 11 football pitches. It is a quarter of a mile from end to end. There is space, it turns out, for an awful lot of crap.

But then there are more than 100m items on its UK website: if you can possibly imagine it, Amazon sells it. And if you can't possibly imagine it, well, Amazon sells it too. To spend 10 and a half hours a day picking items off the shelves is to contemplate the darkest recesses of our consumerist desires, the wilder reaches of stuff, the things that money can buy: a One Direction charm bracelet, a dog onesie, a banana slicer, a fake twig. I work mostly in the outsize 'non-conveyable' section, the home of diabetic dog food, and bio-organic vegetarian dog food, and obese dog food; of 52-inch TVs, and six-packs of water shipped in from Fiji, and over-sized sex toys – the 18-inch double dong (regular-sized sex toys are shelved in the sortables section).

On my second day, the manager tells us that we alone have picked and packed 155,000 items in the past 24 hours. Tomorrow, 2 December – the busiest online shopping day of the year – that figure will be closer to 450,000. And this is just one of eight warehouses across the country. Amazon took 3.5m orders on a single day last year. Christmas is its Vietnam – a test of its corporate mettle and the kind of challenge that would make even the most experienced distribution supply manager break down and weep. In the past two weeks, it has taken on an extra 15,000 agency staff in Britain. And it expects to double the number of warehouses in Britain in the next three years. It expects to continue the growth that has made it one of the most powerful multinationals on the planet.

Right now, in Swansea, four shifts will be working at least a 50-hour week, hand-picking and packing each item, or, as the *Daily Mail* put it in an article a few weeks ago, being 'Amazon's elves' in the '21st-century Santa's grotto'.

If Santa had a track record in paying his temporary elves the minimum wage while pushing them to the limits of the EU working time directive, and sacking them if they take three sick breaks in any three-month period, this would be an apt comparison. It is probably reasonable to assume that tax avoidance is not 'constitutionally' a part of the Santa business model as Brad Stone, the author of a new book on Amazon, *The Everything Store: Jeff Bezos and the Age of Amazon*, tells me it is in Amazon's case. Neither does Santa attempt to bully his competitors, as Mark Constantine, the founder of Lush cosmetics, who last week took Amazon to the high court, accuses it of doing. Santa was not called before the Commons public accounts committee and called 'immoral' by MPs.

For a week, I was an Amazon elf: a temporary worker who got a job through a Swansea employment agency. Amazon is the future of shopping; being an Amazon 'associate' in an Amazon 'fulfilment centre' – take that for doublespeak, Mr Orwell – is the future of work; and Amazon's payment of minimal tax in any jurisdiction is the future of global business. A future in which multinational corporations wield more power than governments.

Amazon is successful for a reason. It is brilliant at what it does. 'It solved these huge challenges,' says Brad Stone. 'It mastered the chaos of storing tens of millions of products and figuring out how to get them to people, on time, without fail, and no one else has come even close.' We didn't just pick and pack more than 155,000 items on my first day. We picked and packed the right items and sent them to the right customers. 'We didn't miss a single order,' our section manager tells us with proper pride.

To work in a 'fulfilment centre' is to be a tiny cog in a huge global distribution machine. It's an industrialised process, on a truly massive scale, made possible by new technology. The place might look like it's been stocked at 2 a.m. by a drunk shelf-filler: a typical shelf might have a set of razor blades, a packet of condoms and a *My Little Pony* DVD. And yet everything is systemised, because it has to be. It's what makes it all the more unlikely that at the heart of the operation, shuffling items from stowing to picking to packing to shipping, are those prone-to-malfunctioning things we know as people.

It's here, where actual people rub up against the business demands of one of the most sophisticated technology companies on the planet, that things get messy. It's a system that includes unsystemisable things like hopes and fears and plans for the future and children and lives. And in places of high unemployment and low economic opportunities, places where Amazon deliberately sites its distribution centres – it received £8.8m in grants from the Welsh government for bringing the warehouse here – despair leaks around the edges. At the interview we're shown a video. 'Like you, I started as an agency worker over Christmas,' says one man in it. 'But I quickly got a permanent job and then promoted and now, two years later, I'm an area manager.'

Amazon will be taking people on permanently after Christmas, we're told, and if you work hard, you can be one of them. In the Swansea/Neath/Port Talbot area, an area still suffering the body blows of Britain's post-industrial decline, these are powerful words, though it all starts to unravel pretty quickly. There are four agencies who have supplied staff to the warehouse, and their reps work from desks on the warehouse floor. I ask one of them how many permanent employees work in the warehouse but he mishears me and answers another question entirely: 'Well, obviously not everyone will be taken on. Just look at the numbers. To be honest, the agencies have to say that just to get people through the door.'

It does that. It's what the majority of people in my induction group are after. I train with Pete – not his real name – who has been unemployed for the past three years. Before that, he was a care worker. He lives at the top of the Rhondda valley, and his partner, Susan (not her real name either), an unemployed IT repair technician, has also just started. It took them more than an hour to get to work. 'We had to get the kids up at five,' he says. After a 10-and-a-half-hour shift, and about another hour's drive back, before picking up the children from his parents, they got home at 9 p.m. The next day, they did the same, except Susan twisted her ankle on the first shift. She phones in but she will receive a 'point'. If she receives three points, she will be 'released', which is how you get sacked in modern corporatese.

And then there's 'Les', who is one of our trainers. He has a special, coloured lanyard that shows he's an Amazon 'ambassador', and another that says he's a first aider. He's worked at the warehouse for more than a year and over the course of the week I see him, speeding across the floor, going at least twice the rate I'm managing. He's in his 60s and tells me how he lost two stone in the first two months he worked there from all the walking. We were told when we applied for the jobs that we may walk up to 15 miles a shift. He'd been a senior manager in the same firm for 32 years before he was made redundant and landed up here. How long was it before you got a permanent job, I ask him. 'I haven't,' he says, and he holds up his green ID badge. Permanent employees have blue ones, a better hourly rate, and after two years share options, and there is a subtle apartheid at work.

'They dangle those blue badges in front of you,' says Bill Woolcock, an ex-employee at Amazon's fulfilment centre in Rugeley, Staffordshire. 'If you have a blue badge you have better wages, proper rights. You can be working alongside someone in the same job, but they're stable and you're just cannon fodder. I worked there from September 2011 to February 2012 and on Christmas Eve an agency rep with a clipboard stood by the exit and said: "You're back after Christmas. And you're back. And you're not. You're not." It was just brutal. It reminded me of stories about the great depression, where men would stand at the factory gate in the hope of being selected for a few days' labour. You just feel you have no personal value at all.'

Why haven't they given you a proper job, I ask Les, and he shrugs his shoulders but elsewhere people mutter: it's friends of the managers who get the jobs. It's HR picking names at random. It's some sort of black magic nobody understands. Walking off shift in a great wave of orange high-vis vests, I chat to another man in his 60s. He'd been working in the Unity mine, near Neath, he told me, until a month ago; the second time he'd been laid off in two years. He'd worked at Amazon last Christmas too. 'And they just let me go straight after, no warning or anything. And I couldn't have worked any harder! I worked my socks off!'

When I put the question to Amazon, it responded: 'A small number of seasonal associates have been with us for an extended period of time and we are keen to retain those individuals in order that we can provide them with a permanent role when one becomes available. We were able to create 2,300 full-time permanent positions for seasonal associates in 2013 by taking advantage of Christmas seasonality to find great permanent employees but, unfortunately, we simply cannot retain 15,000 seasonal employees.'

And this is what Amazon says about its policy relating to sickness: 'Amazon is a company in growth and we offer a high level of security for all our associates. Like many companies, we employ a system to record employee attendance. We consider and review all personal circumstances in relation to any attendance issues and we would not dismiss anyone for being ill. The current system used to record employee attendance is fair and predictable and has resulted in dismissals of 11 permanent employees out of a workforce of over 5,000 permanent employees in 2013.'

It's worth noting that agency workers are not Amazon employees.

On my third morning, at my lowest point, when my energy has run out and my spirits are low, it takes me six minutes to walk to the airport-style scanners, where I spend a minute being frisked. I queue a minute for the loos, get a banana out of my locker, sit down for 30 seconds, and then I get up and walk the six minutes back to my station.

To work at Amazon is to spend your days at the coalface of consumerism. The vast majority of people working in the warehouse are white, Welsh, working class, but I train with a man who's not called Sammy, and who isn't an asylum seeker from Sudan, but another country, and I spend an afternoon explaining to him what the scanner means when it tells him to look for a Good Boy Luxury Dog Stocking or a Gastric Mind Band hypnosis CD.

We want cheap stuff. And we want to order it from our armchairs. And we want it to be delivered to our doors. And it's Amazon that has worked out how to do this. Over time, like a hardened drug user, my Amazon habit has increased. In 2002, I ordered my first non-book item, a *This Life* series one video; in 2005, my first non-Amazon product, a second-hand copy of a biography of Patricia Highsmith; and in 2008, I started doing the online equivalent of injecting intravenously, when I bought a TV on the site. 'We are the most customer-centric company on earth,' we're told in our induction briefing, shortly before it's explained that if we're late we'll get half a point, and after three of them we're out. What constitutes late, I ask. 'A minute,' I'm told.

At the Neath working men's club down the road, one of the staff tells me that Amazon is 'the employer of last resort'. It's where you get a job if you can't get a job anywhere else. And it's this that's so heartbreaking. What did you do before, I ask people. And they say they're builders, hospitality managers, marketing graduates, IT technicians, carpenters, electricians. They owned their own businesses, and they were made redundant. Or the business went bust. Or they had a stroke. They are people who had skilled jobs, or just better-paying jobs. And now they work for Amazon, earning the minimum wage, and most of them are grateful to have that.

Amazon isn't responsible for the wider economy, but it's the wider economy that makes the Amazon model so chilling. It's not just the nicey-nice jobs that are becoming endangered, such as working in a bookshop, as Hugh Grant did in *Notting Hill*, or the jobs that have gone at Borders and Woolworths and Jessops and HMV, it's pretty much everything else too: working in the shoe department at John Lewis, or behind the tills at Tesco. Swansea's shopping centre down the road is already a planning disaster; a wasteland of charity shops and what Sarah Rees of Cover to Cover bookshop calls 'a second-rate Debenhams and a third-rate Marks and Spencer'.

'People know about their employment practices, and all the delivery men hate them, but do people remember that when they click? Probably not,' she says. It's cheaper, often, for her to order books on Amazon than through her distributor. 'There is just no way to compete with them on price.'

There is no end to Amazon's appetite. 'It's expanding in every conceivable direction,' Brad Stone tells me. 'Their ambition is to sell everything. They already have their digital services and their enterprise services. They've just started selling art. Groceries are the next big thing. They're going very strongly after that because it will cut down costs elsewhere. If they can start running their own trucks in major metro areas, they can cut down the costs of third-party shippers.'

And everywhere it kills jobs. Shops employ 47 people for every $10m in sales, according to research done by a company called ILSR. Amazon employs only 14 people per $10m of revenue. In

Britain, it turned over £4.2bn last year, which is a net loss of 23,000 jobs. And even the remaining jobs, the hard, badly paid jobs in Amazon's warehouses, are hardly future-proof. Amazon has just bought an automated sorting system called Kiva for $775m. How many retail jobs, of any description, will be left in 10 years' time?

Our lust for cheap, discounted goods delivered to our doors promptly and efficiently has a price. We just haven't worked out what it is yet.

It's taxes, of course, that pay for the roads on which Amazon's delivery trucks drive, and the schools in which its employees are educated, and the hospitals in which their babies are born and their arteries are patched up. Taxes that all its workers pay, and that, it emerged in 2012, it tends not to pay. On UK sales of £4.2bn in 2012, it paid £3.2m in corporation tax. In 2006, it transferred its UK business to Luxembourg and reclassified its UK operation as simply 'order fulfilment' business. The Luxembourg office employs 380 people. The UK operation employs 21,000. You do the math.

Brad Stone tells me that tax avoidance is built into the company's DNA. From the very beginning it has been 'constitutionally oriented to securing every possible advantage for its customers, setting the lowest possible prices, taking advantage of every known tax loophole or creating new ones'. It's something that Mark Constantine, the co-founder of Lush cosmetics, has spent time thinking about. He refuses to sell through Amazon, but it didn't stop Amazon using the Lush name to direct buyers to its site, where it suggested alternative products they might like.

'It's a way of bullying businesses to use their services. And we refused. We've been in the high court this week to sue them for breach of trademark. It's cost us half a million pounds so far to defend our business. Most companies just can't afford that. But we've done it because it's a matter of principle. They keep on forcing your hand and yet they don't have a viable business model. The only way they can afford to run it is by not paying tax. If they had to behave in a more conventional way, they would struggle.

'It's a form of piracy capitalism. They rush into people's countries, they take the money out, and they dump it in some port of convenience. That's not a business in any traditional sense. It's an ugly return to a form of exploitative capitalism that we had a century ago and we decided as a society to move on from.'

It's an unignorable fact of modern life that, as Stuart Roper of Manchester Business School tells me, 'some of these big brands are more powerful than governments. They're wealthier. If they were countries, they would be pretty large economies. They're multinational and the global financial situation allows them to ship money all over the world. And the government is so desperate for jobs that it has given away large elements of control.'

It's a mirror image of what is happening on the shop floor. Just as Amazon has eroded 200 years' worth of workers' rights through its use of agencies, so it has pulled off the same trick with corporate responsibility. MPs like to slag off Amazon and Starbucks and Google for not paying their taxes but they've yet to create the legislation that would compel them to do so.

'They are taking these massive subsidies from the state and they are not paying back,' says Martin Smith of the GMB union. 'Their argument is that they are creating jobs but what they are doing is displacing and replacing other jobs. Better jobs. And high-street shops tend to pay their taxes. There is a £120bn tax gap that is only possible because the government pays tax benefits to enable people to survive. When companies pay the minimum wage they are in effect being subsidised by the taxpayer.'

Back in Swansea, on the last break of my last day, I sit and chat with Pete and Susan from the Rhondda and Sammy, the asylum seeker from Sudan. Susan still wants a permanent job but is looking more doubtful about it happening. Her ankle is still swollen. Her pick rate has been low. We've been told that, next week, the hours will increase by an hour a day and there will be an extra day of compulsory overtime. It will mean getting their children up by 4.30 a.m. and Pete is worried about finding a babysitter at three days' notice. When I ask Sammy how the job compares with the one he had in Sudan, where he was a foreman in a factory, he thinks for a minute then shrugs: 'It's the same.'

There have always been rubbish jobs. Ian Brinkley, the director of the Work Foundation, calls Amazon's employment practices 'old wine in new bottles'. Restaurants and kebab shops have done the same sort of thing for years. But Amazon is not a kebab shop. It's the future. Which may or may not be something to think about as you click 'add to basket'.

4 DECEMBER

Where is the redemption for Christine Keeler?

TANYA GOLD

A campaign is launched for the posthumous rehabilitation of Stephen Ward, whom we can only call the celebrity osteopath at the centre of the Profumo affair. He introduced the 19-year-old Christine Keeler to both John Profumo, the secretary of state for war in Harold Macmillan's government, and the Russian naval attaché, Yevgeny Ivanov, in 1961. When it emerged that Keeler had slept with both men, Ward was charged with living off the immoral earnings of prostitutes. He took an overdose and was found guilty while still in a coma. He died three days later. Profumo, who had lied to parliament about his involvement with Keeler, resigned. In 1964 the government fell.

Geoffrey Robertson QC has written a book, published this week, called *Stephen Ward Was Innocent, OK*. It charges the rattled establishment with the vindictive framing of Ward, and this is surely true: the police were instructed to 'get' Ward. Andrew Lloyd Webber joins the absolution choir with his musical *Stephen Ward*, which opens this week. It does not surprise that Lloyd Webber would choose Ward as his hero: in *Phantom of the Opera*, he made a murderer a romantic hero, gave him a ruffled shirt.

But the principal victim of the affair was neither Ward nor Profumo, who performed an ostentatious penance, cleaning toilets at Toynbee Hall in London's East End, emerging occasionally, to attend Margaret Thatcher's 70th birthday party or to collect a CBE from the Queen. It was Christine Keeler.

Keeler was an abused child. In her memoir, *Secrets and Lies*, she tells, with no awareness of how her childhood was linked to what came after, how her stepfather touched her and asked her to run away with him, because he didn't love her mother (she was 12); how he beat her mother and drowned the puppies; how the fathers of the children she babysat touched her; how she got pregnant at 17 and aborted the child herself, with a knitting needle.

This was the child-woman Ward picked up in 1959, after seeing her dance in a Soho nightclub: she was 17, he 46. This was the woman Harold Macmillan called a tart.

Is it true? She lived with Ward, platonically; he was not interested in her sexually, but he liked her to sleep with other men. He used her to gain the favour of the powerful; he took her to orgies; he sent her to find him prostitutes; he called her his 'little baby'.

The memoir is a sequence of unfunny *Carry On* clips – Keeler being chased round desks, her arse red with pinching, invariably being asked: 'How could you not want to go out with such an important man?' The central image of the Profumo affair – Keeler swimming naked in the pool at Cliveden, while Ward and Profumo watch – seethes with what would normally be eroticism, but here is something more helpless. 'I enjoyed it,' she said of sex with Profumo, 'for he was kind and loving afterwards.' She says he got her pregnant – and why should we disbelieve her? (She had another life-threatening abortion.) Another lover, Lucky Gordon, abducted and raped her; she was so inured to sexual violence and coercion, she consented to see him again.

Keeler believes that Ward spied for the Russians and this is plausible: she also names Roger Hollis, who was head of MI5, as a spy, as Peter Wright did in *Spycatcher*. But whether Ward was using Keeler to get information, or simply as a breathing toy, he used her. When, during Gordon's trial, she claimed she did not know two men who prevented him assaulting her, she went to jail for perjury.

In the way of things, the men of the Profumo affair have redemption, and why not? It was long ago, this abuse of a teenage girl – now that is a familiar tune. Jimmy Savile's victims, diminished and disbelieved, will hear bitter echoes in Keeler's tale. But, to the predator, everything. When he died in 2006, the *Telegraph* called Profumo 'a man who made one terrible mistake but sought his own redemption in a way which has no precedent in public life either before or since'. Stephen Ward might win a musical theatre award, albeit through someone else, and his case may be reopened, the miscarriage of justice righted. Where is the redemption of a woman who calls herself 'a dirty joke'. Where is that?

5 December

George Osborne blown off course

SIMON HOGGART

Simon Hoggart, who joined the Guardian *in 1968 and was the paper's parliamentary sketchwriter for more than 20 years, died on 5 January 2014, aged 67. This is his last sketch.*

Poor George Osborne. After three and a half years he finally has some good news to bring us – and he's upstaged by the weather. In the Commons he was talking about growth being way up, employment up, wages up and borrowing down. On the TV, all anyone could see was smashed cars, cancelled trains and worse storms on the way. Last year he could have used a tornado or two to cover up the pasty tax and similar disasters; now a delay in fuel duty rise could not compete with nature's fury.

The autumn statement is actually a recent, fairly meaningless, wheeze, now largely governed by convention. The convention is, the chancellor gloats.

Gordon Brown's speeches used to be bloated with gloating. He'd paint a vague picture of lesser nations, unblessed by his guid-ance, seeing their citizens reduced to living in cardboard boxes and eating what the supermarkets threw out at closing time.

Osborne did much the same. We were improving faster than any other advanced industrial nation, he told us. Eat your hearts out, Germany and France! In America the president's aides are scratching their heads and wondering how they can create their own British miracle. And, in a few short years, we will be a creditor nation, with our very own surplus! Forget Mr Micawber – we can expect no more misery but unbounded joy.

Behind the chancellor, Tories kept up a wall of noise, laughing and jeering at the misery guts on the benches opposite. Do the coalition's MPs really believe this stuff? Probably half of them do, and the other half find it expedient to pretend to. Even Andrew Tyrie, who chairs the Treasury committee, a man who smiles as often as an undertaker whose budgie has just died, managed to beam happily, at least some of the time.

And David Cameron, who must have heard all this stuff often, sitting next to Osborne, managed to look impressed, as if he could not quite believe this cornucopia of good news. His mouth would open in delighted astonishment, his whole face wrinkled with excitement, he smiled like the Cheshire cat after a large sherry, and he did something I can only call pursing his nose. At one point I think I caught him whistling with delight.

The chancellor even had the nerve to tell us that we were all in this together – with the very rich paying the most. Depends how you define 'the most', I suppose; in cash or just proportionately? He didn't say.

He did try to warn us that all was not yet well. Austerity would have to continue. But he knew who the real villains were. He opened solemnly. 'Mr Speaker, Britain's economic plan is working. But the job is not yet done. The biggest risk comes from those who would abandon the plan.'

By which he meant Ed Balls, who had the difficult task of responding to this cascade of new jobs, falling deficits, postponed taxes, increased pensions, investment grants and purses full of gold for hard-working families.

The shadow chancellor, as is his style, began at maximum volume and turned up the controls. By the end his voice was shredded. If he had pretended to be any angrier, he would have been coughing up his own intestines.

He did what he could. All of this would have happened sooner if it weren't for three flatlining years; living standards were continuing to fall. Like Owen Paterson's badgers, the government was moving the goalposts. They were shooting Labour's foxes. The chancellor himself had called Cameron's plans for a married couples' tax allowance a 'turkey'.

There was more wildlife in his reply than in that John Lewis ad. Except that by now he sounded more like King Lear, raging against the storm that was blowing even harder outside.

6 DECEMBER

The Mandela I knew

When Nelson Mandela died on 5 December 2013, tributes poured in. Here are just two of the many the Guardian *published.*

Mandela used the time in prison for rigorous self-examination, not just in a personal sense but examination of the political goals and vision that were driving him and the ANC. One of his strengths was his ability to look at himself; this was something he deepened and broadened during 27 years in prison. He had a willingness in our discussions in jail to say 'maybe we were wrong', which didn't play well in many quarters.

When you are in prison, your first instinct is to say: 'Shut up, don't question yourself ... if you question yourself, you weaken yourself in the eyes of the enemy.' And yet he would ask: 'Were we right, when we resisted removal from Sophiatown' – a multi-racial township cleared in 1954 – 'with the slogans "We shall not move" and "Over our dead bodies"?' We were not ready to defend our people when push came to shove, yet we created a slogan that created an expectation. He would ask: 'What is it about a slogan? What's its role? What's its foundation?'

Our years in prison were also vital in that they gave us a chance to interact with our white jailers – we were cheek by jowl with them on Robben Island; they were almost imprisoned with us – to try to begin to understand what was driving them.

When we went to prison most of us were not speaking Afrikaans. I argued with Mandela about whether we should study the language. He'd say: 'Let's do it together.' I'd say I'm not interested in this language; first of all, it's not even an international language, and second it's the language of the oppressor. He'd reply: 'Look, man, we're in for a long struggle, a protracted struggle. It's going to be a war of attrition.' He'd say: 'How are we going to lead the enemy forces into an ambush? To do that we look at the enemy's commander and try to understand him. To do that, we've got to read his literature, read his poetry. So shall we study Afrikaans?'

MAC MAHARAJ, *politician, friend and fellow prisoner*

On the evening of 6 August 1990, I sat around a small radio with a group of young activists and wept. Nelson Mandela had just announced that the African National Congress's armed struggle had been suspended. For the angry youths we were then, it meant capitulation. In our view, Mandela had offered everything, even though the apartheid regime had offered nothing in return. We cursed him.

That evening hundreds of ANC leaders swarmed into black townships across the country, addressing – cajoling – young men and women at rallies and meetings. They begged for calm. They said this was a strategic retreat, not surrender. But the anger would not go away. Mandela, we muttered, had gone soft.

In the Pretoria Minute, the document in which both parties agreed to end the armed struggle, we saw nothing of Mandela's vision for a new South Africa. In the townships, thousands of black people were dying as a result of action by the armed forces and government-sponsored 'black-on-black violence'.

This would not be the last time that we, the young ones, would be angry with Mandela. In 1996, when the Truth and Reconciliation Commission got into its stride, we wondered again: why is he bending over backwards to accommodate white people?

Numerous black people took to the TRC stage and told of the torture and hunger they had suffered at the hands of the apartheid government. Mothers appeared and wept for lost sons and daughters. Young women told of rape and violation by white policemen. And from South Africa's white people there was a white silence. None of them, it seemed, had supported apartheid.

Whose Truth Commission was it? We wanted to look into the eyes of the killers and torturers and get at least an admission of guilt.

None came. Instead, they hired batteries of lawyers and spokespersons to defend themselves. Even while the commission sat, many guilty people were destroying intelligence files containing incriminating evidence.

And Mandela? Well, Mandela, now president of our country, kept saying that the commission would, in time, be of benefit to all South Africans. And he was right, of course, just as he had been when he signed the Pretoria Minute six years earlier. Many of us now recognise the beauty of the TRC: it was for us – to bring about our own confrontation with what happened, and to enable our own healing.

Mandela was not always the one. I grew up in the 1970s when it was all about the Black Consciousness Movement, and he didn't really count. Nelson Mandela was an old guy, talked of reverentially by my father, but to us he seemed distant, a shadow.

However, the activists of the 1970s were driven into exile by the apartheid regime, and in exile they began to be absorbed into the ANC. Early in the 80s they began to return to the country with the cry that the struggle must be intensified from within. They exhorted the youth to call for Mandela's release. Having been a shadowy figure, he now became immediate and urgent to us. The apartheid regime vilified him as a communist and agitator. The more they did, the more we loved him.

By 1986 Mandela's name was so powerful that for many black South Africans the immediate focus of the struggle wasn't freedom from apartheid – we simply wanted Mandela out of jail. Few of us knew what he looked like; few of us had ever seen pictures of him (they were banned). In the late 1980s student activists began putting sketches of him on T-shirts. It was an invitation for immediate beating and detention.

Mandela hauled the young ones into a new South Africa. Along the way, particularly in the 1990s, he was called everything from soft to a stooge of the regime. But today we know the necessity of his actions.

How do I remember Nelson Mandela? In George Orwell's famous story a young British policeman stationed in Burma walks towards an elephant that has just killed a villager. There are 2,000 Burmese following him. He is the only one with a gun. They all want him to kill the elephant. He knows that it would be wrong to do so because the elephant no longer poses a threat to anyone. But he is scared of looking a fool – and regarded as weak – by the villagers. So he shoots the elephant. When Mandela came out of prison there were millions of us behind him. We all urged him at the top of our voices to act radical, to shoot the apartheid elephant and cause a conflagration. He did not.

He is the greatest, most courageous and honest leader we ever had. He gave us – the so-called 'lost generation' of South Africa – a future. He saved us.

JUSTICE MALALA, *journalist*

6 DECEMBER

How far can privatisation go?

IAN JACK

The phrase 'selling the family silver' became the most celebrated if not the deepest criticism of Mrs Thatcher's privatisation programme, though Harold Macmillan never used those exact words. At a dinner of the Tory Reform Group – wets, moderates, Europhiles, none of them 'one of us' – the former prime minister devised a more extended metaphor that drew on an aristocratic lifestyle that had been failing since its heyday in his Edwardian childhood. When individuals or estates ran into financial trouble, he said, they would commonly sell a few of their assets. 'First the Georgian silver goes [laughter, applause]. Then all that nice furniture that used to be in the saloon. Then the Canalettos go [laughter, applause].'

He began to wander a bit. 'And then the most tasty morsel, the most productive of all, they got rid of Cable and Wireless, and having got rid of the only part of the railways that paid, and a part of the steel industry that paid, and having sold this and that, the great thing of the monopoly telephone system came on the market. They [sic] were like the two Rembrandts that were still left [laughter] and they went, and now we're promised in the king's speech a further sale of anything that can be scraped up. You can't sell the coal mines, I'm afraid, because nobody will buy them [laughter, prolonged applause].'

When Macmillan made the speech, on 8 November 1985, he was 91 and had just over a year left to live. He still cut an attractive figure – the inverted V of his bow tie matched the weary droop of his moustache and eyebrows – though his reference to the king's speech suggested that a few marbles were coming unstuck in what was once one of the sharpest minds in British politics. The audience loved him. He was the last British prime minister to have served in the first world war, where he was badly wounded, and the last born during Victoria's reign; a 'born actor', people said, because he was always so effortlessly droll. His references to oil paintings and precious tableware, his correct but vintage use of the word 'saloon': this kind of thing endeared him to the public for much the same reasons as *Downton Abbey* did 25 years later – as an amusing and slightly camp version of a previous age.

He disavowed the speech only a few days afterwards, telling the House of Lords that he'd been misunderstood. All he was questioning was the government's wisdom in treating the capital raised by privatisation as income; as a Conservative he was 'natu-rally in favour of returning into private ownership ... all those means of production and distribution which are now controlled by state capitalism'. But the metaphor had made its mark, and the fact is that Macmillan's 'family silver' and British Gas's 'Tell Sid' slogan are probably the best-remembered phrases from the early years of the war against public ownership. Oddly, given that privatisation was to have such profound effects on British life, both in their different ways raised a smile; did we know what was coming?

At the time of Macmillan's speech, privatisation had hardly begun. British Rail's ferries and hotels were the first to go (how strange it now seems that the best hotels in almost every city outside London were owned and run – usually well – by public servants in the most literal sense). But British Telecom, British Steel, British Airways, British Shipbuilders and Rolls-Royce – all of them listed as targets in the Tories' 1983 manifesto – had still to complete their journey from the public sector, and the big privatisations that would affect every household had yet to come. Gas, water, electricity: people puzzled as to how the same stuff flowing through the same pipes and wires could be owned by different companies, and yet somehow it became so in the name of competition. Then came the British Airports Authority and British Rail and large chunks of the Ministry of Defence, while many public institutions such as local authorities and the NHS outsourced much of their activity and shrank sometimes to the role of regulator. Nigel Lawson triumphantly announced 'the birth of people's capitalism', but many private companies sold out to foreign ownership; others were taken over by private equiteers; others again subsumed into octopus-like businesses such as Serco and G4S, which picked up the contracts for outsourced work ranging from Royal Navy tugboats to nursing assistants.

This landscape is familiar to us, but what would Macmillan have made of it? What kind of country-house metaphor would be equal to the modern situation where the electricity is owned in France, the football clubs by emirs and the publishing houses (including Macmillan's own) in Germany and the US? Or a state that has recently sold off the Royal Mail too cheaply (a habit that began with British Rail's hotels 30 years ago), that has privatised its blood plasma service and is about to sell its profitable stake in cross-Channel trains, and which has its eye on all kinds of small treasures (air traffic control, Ordnance Survey, the Royal Mint) that in future may raise a few bob and enable a tax cut? Comparisons with the sale of silver sugar tongs and Canalettos hardly seem adequate. Surely the crumbling house itself has a For Sale sign nailed to it at a crazy angle, with stickers attached to the inhabitants – the dowager, the servants, even the dogs – for they too have a value as the consumers of the stuff their new owner will sell them.

The words of the novelist and reporter James Meek ring ever truer. 'The commodity that makes water and roads and airports valuable to an investor, foreign or otherwise, is the people who have no choice but to use them,' Meek wrote last year in the *London Review of Books*. 'We have no choice but to pay the price the toll keepers charge. We are a human revenue stream; we are being made tenants in our own land, defined by the string of private fees we pay to exist here.'

But why not take it further and outsource the air force, the army and the navy? Mercenaries from poorer countries would be cheaper, accepting even worse rates of pay than the average British infantryman. Why not outsource the police, given that prison warders are already privatised? Why not outsource the government? It has cut so many parts from itself that it does no more than bleed on its stumps. Finally, why not outsource the political class that without interruption since 1979 has promoted the denigration of public service while upholding the idea of private profit, or at best done nothing to stop it. How interesting it would be to oversee the tendering process for the last – to weigh up the rival claims of political teams from, say, Finland, Germany and Iceland to transform the House of Commons into a more intelligent and courteous debating chamber that had outgrown the Oxford Union. How good it would be if the shouters and petty point-scorers could be replaced, on the male side at least, with grave pipe-smokers who spoke in charming English and wanted only the best for the country they had come to supervise – a colony almost, deserving enlightened rule.

10 December

Meet the rebel women

KIRA COCHRANE

The campaign for women's liberation never went away, but this year a new swell built up and broke through. Since the early summer, I've been talking to feminist activists and, as I tried to keep up with the protests, marches and talks, my diary became a mess of clashing dates. The rush was such that in a single weekend in October, you could have attended a feminist freshers' fair in London, the North East Feminist Gathering in Newcastle, a Reclaim the Night march in Edinburgh, or a discussion between different generations of feminist activists at the British Library (this sold out in 48 hours, was moved to a room four times bigger, and sold out again).

You could have joined one of the country's 149 local grassroots groups, or shared your experience of misogyny on the site Laura Bates, 27, started in April 2012. Her Everyday Sexism Project has proved so successful that it was rolled out to 17 countries on its first anniversary this year, tens of thousands of women world-wide writing about the street harassment, sexual harassment, workplace discrimination and body-shaming they encounter. The project embodies that feminist phrase 'the personal is polit-ical', a consciousness-raising exercise that encourages women to see how inequality affects them, proves these problems aren't individual but collective, and might therefore have political solu-tions. This year, 6,000 stories that have been sent to the project about harassment or assault on public transport – the majority never reported to authorities – were used to train 2,000 police officers in London, and create a public awareness campaign. In its first few weeks, says Bates, the reporting of harassment on public transport soared. Everyday Sexism currently has more than 108,000 followers on Twitter. Of course, following a social media account isn't the same as joining a political party, but to put this engagement in perspective, Tory membership is now at 134,000.

Welcome to the fourth wave of feminism. This movement follows the first-wave campaign for votes for women, which reached its height 100 years ago, the second-wave women's liberation movement that blazed through the 1970s and 80s, and the third wave declared by Rebecca Walker, Alice Walker's daughter, and others, in the early 1990s. That shift from second to third wave took many important forms, but often felt broadly generational, with women defining their work as distinct from their mothers'. What's happening now feels like something new again. It's defined by technology: tools that are allowing women to build a strong, popular, reactive movement online.

Just how popular is sometimes slightly startling. Girlguiding UK introduced a campaigning and activism badge this year and a summer survey of Mumsnet users found 59 per cent consider themselves feminists, double those who don't. Bates says that, for her, modern feminism is defined by pragmatism, inclusion and humour. 'I feel like it is really down-to-earth, really open,' she says, 'and it's very much about people saying: "Here is something that doesn't make sense to me, I thought women were equal, I'm going to do something about it."'

As 2013 unfolded, it became impossible to ignore the rumble of feminist campaigners, up and down the country. They gathered outside the Bank of England in early July, the first burst of a heatwave, dressed as aviators, suffragettes and warrior queens, organised by Caroline Criado-Perez, 29, shouting for women's representation on bank notes and beyond.

They demonstrated outside the *Sun* headquarters, organised by Yas Necati, 17, in a protest against Page 3, the biggest image of a woman that appears each day in the country's biggest-selling newspaper – a teenager or twentysomething smiling sunnily in her pants. Necati, a student at sixth-form college, laughed shyly as she told me about the mocked-up pages she has sent *Sun* editor David Dinsmore, suggesting feminist comedians, artists and writers to appear on the page instead. One of her favourites showed a woman flashing bright blue armpit hair. The No More Page 3 petition started by Lucy-Anne Holmes, 37, in August 2012, has been signed by 128,000 people.

Ikamara Larasi, 24, started heading a campaign to address racist and sexist stereotypes in music videos, just as students began banning summer hit 'Blurred Lines' on many UK campuses, in response to its sexist lyrics. Jinan Younis, 18, co-founded a feminist society at school, experienced online abuse from some boys in her peer group – 'feminism and rape are both ridiculously tiring,' they wrote – and wasn't deterred. Instead, she wrote an article about it that went viral. When I spoke to her in September, she was juggling shifts in a call centre, babysitting for neighbours and preparing for university, while helping out with a campaign to encourage feminist societies in schools countrywide. UK Feminista, an organisation set up in 2010 to support feminist activists, has had 100 people contact them this year, wanting to start their own school group. In late August, their national day of action against lads' mags included 19 protests across the UK.

Thousands more feminists raised their voices online. Bates and Soraya Chemaly, 47, were among those who set up a campaign against misogynist pages on Facebook, including groups with names such as 'raping a pregnant bitch and telling your friends you had a threesome'. Supporters sent more than 60,000 tweets in the course of a swift, week-long push, convincing the social-media behemoth to change its moderation policies.

Southall Black Sisters protested outside the offices of the UK Border Agency against racist immigration laws and propaganda – including the notorious 'Go Home' vans. They also marched in solidarity with protesters in Delhi, who began a wave of demonstrations following the death of a woman who was gang-raped in the city last December; protests against rape culture that soon spread to Nepal, Bangladesh, Pakistan and Sri Lanka. The African LGBTI Out & Proud Diamond Group demonstrated opposite Downing Street after allegations emerged of the sexual abuse of women held at Yarl's Wood immigration removal centre.

The Fawcett Society continued to show how cuts to benefits, services and public-sector jobs pose 'triple jeopardy' to women (in 2013 women's unemployment reached a 26-year high). Rape Crisis South London spearheaded a successful campaign to criminalise the possession of pornography that depicts rape. And 40 Days of Choice challenged the anti-abortion campaigners who have become worryingly prominent in the UK recently.

The Edinburgh fringe hosted a surprising run of feminist comedians, including Mary Bourke, with her show *Muffragette*. Bourke memorably noted in a BBC interview this summer that the open-mic circuit has become a 'rape circle' in recent years. Feminist stand-ups were ready to respond. Nadia Kamil, 29, performed a set including a feminist burlesque, peeling off eight layers of clothing to reveal messages such as 'pubes are normal' and 'equal pay' picked out in sequins. She also explained the theory of intersectionality through a vocoder, and gave out badges with the slogan 'Smash the Kyriarchy'. (She hoped audience members would look up any words they were unfamiliar with later, such as 'kyriarchy' and 'cis'.)

Bridget Christie, 42, won the Foster's Edinburgh comedy award with *A Bic for Her*, in which she railed against sexist comments by racing driver Stirling Moss, and talked about 'ethical filing' – taking sexist magazines off shop shelves and dumping them straight in the bin. She wasn't encouraging other people to do this, she emphasised. She just wanted to point out that she had been doing it for months – months – with no problem at all.

Women marched through London for Million Women Rise and Reclaim the Night, and organised events in 207 countries for One Billion Rising, a day of demonstrations to highlight the UN statistic that one in three women will be raped or beaten in her lifetime. As part of this event, the UK parliament debated whether sex and relationship education should be on the national curriculum, and six months later, in her summer holidays, Lili Evans, 16, started the Campaign4Consent with Necati, calling for consent education in schools.

A chorus rose against online misogyny. Criado-Perez highlighted the string of rape threats sent to her on Twitter, writer Lindy West published the comments she received ('There is a group of rapists with over 9,000 penises coming for this fat bitch,' read one), and the academic and broadcaster Mary Beard, Lauren Mayberry from the band Chvrches, and Ruby Tandoh from *The Great British Bake Off* all spoke out on this issue. If you want to know how deeply some people resent the idea of women's advancement, the stream of online misogyny has been perhaps the most obvious, ugly backlash yet.

But bald attempts to silence women only made the movement larger and louder. They convinced those who had never thought about misogyny before that it was clearly still alive, and convinced those who were well aware of it to keep going.

When Nimko Ali, 29, spoke out against female genital mutilation, with her group, Daughters of Eve, she received death threats. She kept speaking strongly, wittily, discussing both her own experience of FGM and her 'fanny forward' list of supporters, putting an issue long marginalised firmly on the political agenda. In November, Alison Saunders, the new director of public prosecutions, suggested she expected the first prosecution for FGM to happen in the UK fairly soon.

Some of those leading the biggest campaigns, including Bates, only started calling themselves feminists in the last few years, which shows how nascent this wave is. Larasi bursts out laughing when I ask if she has always considered herself a feminist. 'Definitely not,' she says. She has been working at the black women's organisation Imkaan for three or four years, and was raised by a feminist mother, but it was only last year that she started using the term to describe herself. She began identifying specifically as a black feminist in February 2013. This means she doesn't feel she has to 'pick a side', she says, between the movements for women's rights and for racial equality, and she is now a member of the thriving Black Feminists group in London – there is also one in Manchester.

The majority of activists I speak to define themselves as intersectional feminists – or say they try to live up to this description – and when I mention this to Kimberlé Crenshaw, the US law professor who coined the term intersectionality in 1989, she's genuinely surprised. The theory concerns the way multiple oppressions intersect, and although, as Crenshaw says, it can be interpreted in a wide variety of ways, today's feminists generally seem to see it as an attempt to elevate and make space for the voices and issues of those who are marginalised, and a framework for recognising how class, race, age, ability, sexuality, gender and other issues combine to affect women's experience of discrimination. Younis considers intersectionality the overriding principle for today's feminists, and Ali says she constantly tries to check her privilege, to recognise how hierarchies of power are constructed.

There are women and men of all ages involved in this movement – at a Lose the Lads' Mags protest in York, for instance, I met an activist who had been at the women's liberation conference in 1978. But many of those at the forefront are in their teens and 20s, and had their outlook formed during decades in which attitudes to women were particularly confusing.

They grew up being told the world was post-feminist, that sexism and misogyny were over, and feminists should pack up their placards. At the same time, women in the public eye were often either sidelined or sexualised, represented in exactly the same way as they had been in the 70s, albeit beneath a thin veil of irony. Finn Mackay says when she started the London Feminist Network in 2004, the two main issues motivating those who joined were the massive growth of the beauty industry, and 'pornification' – the infiltration of pornographic imagery into the mainstream via *Playboy*-branded pencil cases, for instance, and the trend for pubic waxes. Those concerns have continued, and help explain the focus of many current feminist campaigns, which address the wallpaper of women's lives, the everyday sexism – lads' mags, Page 3, rape pages on Facebook, cosmetic surgery advertising – and calls for positive representation on bank notes and in broadcasting.

But the feminist consciousness of the fourth wave has also been forged through the years of the financial crash and the coalition government, and many activists have been politicised and influenced by other movements, particularly the student campaign against fees, but also the wider campaign against cuts and the Occupy movement. The quick, reactive nature of many of the feminist campaigns cropping up today reflects the work of activists more generally in a biting world of unemployment and underemployment, workfare, zero-hours contracts, bedroom taxes, damaging rhetoric against immigrants, the disabled and those who need support from the state.

With so many pressing issues, feminists are fighting on several fronts, and the campaigns of the past few years have often been started by individuals or small groups, who have responded to issues they feel strongly about, and can usefully address. Holmes and Necati both grew up with the *Sun* at home, which has shaped their opposition to Page 3. Criado-Perez was outraged by all-male discussions of teenage pregnancy and breast-cancer treatment on the *Today* programme, so set up a database of female experts, The Women's Room, with Catherine Smith in 2012. In the first three days of that year, seven women were killed by men, and Karen Ingala Smith, chief executive of the charity Nia, started counting the toll of misogynist murders. Her Counting Dead Women project puts names and stories to the statistics we often hear, and is asking the government to take an integrated approach to understanding violence against women.

There are, of course, differences of opinion when it comes to which subjects feminism should be addressing. How could there not be, in a movement that represents half the population, and aims for liberation for all? But what's exciting about these individual campaigns is the way they're building a movement capable of taking on structural, systemic problems. As the philosopher Nina Power notes, there are teenage girls today, growing up with Twitter and Tumblr, who have a perfect grasp of feminist language and concepts, who are active on a huge range of issues – some of those I talk to are starting to work on economic analyses of women's predicament, the ways in which neoliberal policies, such as the rolling back of the state and low taxes for the rich, have shaped modern inequalities.

The movement's concerns are for ever shifting, and will likely do so powerfully when some of today's young activists encounter the pay gap, childcare costs and pregnancy discrimination in their own lives. 'What is it going to be like,' says Power, 'to have this generation of people who are totally attuned to all these terms and categories and thinking through all these issues from a very young age?' Brought up to know they are equal to men, fourth-wave feminists are pissed off when they're not treated as such, but have more than enough confidence to shout back.

Misogynists, watch out.

26 DECEMBER

What if the Germans had won the first world war?

MARTIN KETTLE

People who see a divine hand or the iron laws of dialectical materialism at work in human affairs bridle at the question: 'What if things had turned out differently?' To EH Carr, historian of Soviet Russia, to speak of what might have happened in history, as opposed to what did happen, was just a 'parlour game'. To EP Thompson, author of *The Making of the English Working Class*, such counterfactual speculation was 'unhistorical shit'.

Other historians have confessed to being more intrigued. 'The historian must constantly put himself at a point in the past at which the known factors will seem to permit different outcomes,' wrote Johan Huizinga. It is important to recognise that, at any moment in history, there are real alternatives, argued Hugh Trevor-Roper.

Happily, none of this argument deters the writers of fiction or the public. Germany's possible defeat of Britain in 1940 is by some distance the national treasure trove of might-have-beens. As long ago as 1964, the film *It Happened Here* by Kevin Brownlow and Andrew Mollo raised the then unthinkable thought that collaboration would have thrived in Hitler's Britain. More recently, a succession of novels, including Robert Harris's *Fatherland*, *Resistance* by Owen Sheers and CJ Sansom's *Dominion* – which imagines a Vichy Britain in 1952 ruled by Lord Beaverbrook and Oswald Mosley – have explored the same theme.

By comparison, the first world war has been the subject of far less counterfactual speculation. Niall Ferguson is one of the exceptions, in an essay which considers the possibility that Britain might have stood aside from the European war in August 1914. And although his essay suffers from the fact that the Eurosceptic Ferguson is overeager to portray the kaiser as the godfather of the later European Union, his account of the cabinet debates of 1914 is fascinating because Herbert Asquith's Liberal government could so easily have decided to stay out of the war – and very nearly did.

With the centenary of the first world war almost upon us, 2014 is likely to witness plenty of debate about the right forms of commemoration and about whether the war achieved anything. At present, argument about the war mainly consists of two mutually uncomprehending camps. On the one hand, there are those who, as Margaret MacMillan put it recently, think the war was 'an unmitigated catastrophe in a sea of mud'. On the other, there are those who insist that it was nevertheless 'about something'. At the time, says MacMillan, people on all sides thought they had a just cause. 'It is condescending and wrong to think they were hoodwinked.'

But what was the something that the first world war was about? To answer that it was a war between empires, which it surely was, is fine as long as some effort is made to distinguish between the empires. But this rarely happens in a debate that is polarised between collective myths of national sacrifice on the one hand (certainly in Britain and France) and an indiscriminate muddy catastrophe on the other.

The more one tries to examine and maybe get beyond these dominant narratives, as we should next year and as the centenary rolls on, the more a bit of the counterfactual may help the process.

The first world war came to an end in November 1918, when the German armies surrendered near Compiegne. But it could plausibly have ended in a very different way in spring 1918, if Ludendorff's offensive on Paris and towards the Channel had succeeded. It nearly did so. And what might 20th-century Europe have been like if it had?

Obviously, it would have been dominated and shaped by Germany. But what kind of Germany? The militaristic, conservative, repressive Prussian power created by Bismarck? Or the Germany with the largest labour movement in early-20th century Europe? German history after 1918 would have been a contest between the two – and no one can say which would have won in the end.

But one can say that a victorious Germany, imposing peace on the defeated allies at the treaty of Potsdam, would not have had the reparations and grievances that were actually inflicted upon it by France at Versailles. As a consequence, the rise of Hitler would have been much less likely. In that case, neither the Holocaust nor the second world war would necessarily have followed. If Germany's Jews had survived, Zionism might not have had the international moral force that it rightly claimed after Hitler's defeat. The modern history of the Middle East would therefore be very different – partly also because Turkey would have been among the victors in 1918.

In the kaiser's Europe, defeated France would be the more likely seedbed for fascism, not Germany. But with its steel and coal still in German-controlled Alsace-Lorraine, France's military and naval potential would have been contained. Meanwhile, defeated Britain would have seen its navy sunk in the Heligoland

Bight, have been forced to cede its oil interests in the Middle East and the Gulf to Germany, and have been unable to contain Indian nationalism. In practice, the British empire would have been unsustainable. Today's Britain might have ended up as a modest north European social democratic republic – like Denmark without a prince.

Meanwhile America, whose entry into the war would have been successfully pre-empted by Germany's victory, would have become a firmly isolationist power and not the enforcer of international order. Franklin Roosevelt would solve America's postwar economic problems in the 1930s, but he would never fight a war in Europe – though he might have to fight one against Japan. The Soviet Union, with a wary but powerful neighbour in victorious Germany, would have been the great destabilising factor, but it might not have been invaded as it was in 1941. And with no second world war there might never have been a cold war either.

A parlour game? Obviously. But at least we can see that the outcome mattered. Europe would have been different if Germany had won in 1918. It would have been grim, repressive and unpredictable in many ways. But there is a plausible case for saying many fewer people would have died in 20th-century Europe. If nothing else, that is worth some reflection. The first world war was a catastrophe in the mud. But it was about something more than tragic sacrifice too. The outcome – what happened and what did not – made a difference. In 2014 we need to get beyond the rival national perspectives and learn to see the war more objectively and thoughtfully than has yet happened.

29 December

I worked on the
US drone program

HEATHER LINEBAUGH

Whenever I read comments by politicians defending the Unmanned Aerial Vehicle Predator and Reaper program – a.k.a. drones – I wish I could ask them a few questions. I'd start with: 'How many women and children have you seen incinerated by a Hellfire missile?' And: 'How many men have you seen crawl across a field, trying to make it to the nearest compound for help, while bleeding out from severed legs?' Or even more pointedly: 'How many soldiers have you seen die on the side of a road in Afghanistan because our ever-so-accurate UAVs [unmanned aerial vehicles] were unable to detect an IED [improvised explosive device] that awaited their convoy?'

Few of these politicians who so brazenly proclaim the benefits of drones have a real clue of what actually goes on. I, on the other hand, have seen these awful sights first hand.

I knew the names of some of the young soldiers I saw bleed to death on the side of a road. I watched dozens of military-aged males die in Afghanistan, in empty fields, along riversides, and some right outside the compound where their family was waiting for them to return home from the mosque.

The US and British militaries insist that this is an expert program, but it's curious that they feel the need to deliver faulty information, few or no statistics about civilian deaths and twisted technology reports on the capabilities of our UAVs. These specific incidents are not isolated, and the civilian casualty rate has not changed, despite what our defence representatives might like to tell us.

What the public needs to understand is that the video provided by a drone is not usually clear enough to detect someone carrying a weapon, even on a crystal-clear day with limited cloud and perfect light. This makes it incredibly difficult for the best analysts to identify if someone has weapons for sure. One example comes to mind: 'The feed is so pixelated, what if it's a shovel, and not a weapon?' I felt this confusion constantly, as did my fellow UAV analysts. We always wonder if we killed the right people, if we endangered the wrong people, if we destroyed an innocent civilian's life all because of a bad image or angle.

It's also important for the public to grasp that there are human beings operating and analysing intelligence from these UAVs. I know because I was one of them, and nothing can prepare you for an almost daily routine of flying combat aerial surveillance missions over a war zone. UAV proponents claim that troops who do this kind of work are not affected by observing this combat because they are never directly in danger physically.

But here's the thing: I may not have been on the ground in Afghanistan, but I watched parts of the conflict in great detail on a screen for days on end. I know the feeling you experience when you see someone die. Horrifying barely covers it. And when you are exposed to it over and over again it becomes like a small video, embedded in your head, for ever on repeat, causing psychological pain and suffering that many people will hopefully never experience. UAV troops are victim to not only the haunting memories of this work that they carry with them, but also the guilt of always being a little unsure of how accurate their confirmations of weapons or identifications of hostile individuals were.

Of course, we are trained not to experience these feelings, and we fight it, and become bitter. Some troops seek help in mental health clinics provided by the military, but we are limited on who we can talk to and where, because of the secrecy of our missions. I find it interesting that the suicide statistics in this career field aren't reported, nor are the data on how many troops working in UAV positions are heavily medicated for depression, sleep disorders and anxiety.

Recently, the *Guardian* ran a commentary by Britain's secretary of state for defence, Philip Hammond. I wish I could talk to him about the two friends and colleagues I lost, within a year of leaving the military, to suicide. I am sure he has not been notified of that little bit of the secret UAV program, or he would surely take a closer look at the full scope of the program before defending it again.

The UAVs in the Middle East are used as a weapon, not as protection, and as long as our public remains ignorant of this, this serious threat to the sanctity of human life – at home and abroad – will continue.

29 DECEMBER

Scientists tell us their favourite jokes: 'An electron and a positron walked into a bar ...'

Two theoretical physicists are lost at the top of a mountain. Theoretical physicist No 1 pulls out a map and peruses it for a while. Then he turns to theoretical physicist No 2 and says: 'Hey, I've figured it out. I know where we are.'

'Where are we then?'

'Do you see that mountain over there?'

'Yes.'

'Well ... *That*'s where we are.'

JEFF FORSHAW, *professor of physics and astronomy,*
University of Manchester

An electron and a positron go into a bar.

Positron: 'You're round.'

Electron: 'Are you sure?'

Positron: 'I'm positive.'

JOANNA HAIGH, *professor of atmospheric physics,*
Imperial College London

A group of wealthy investors wanted to be able to predict the outcome of a horse race. So they hired a group of biologists, a group of statisticians, and a group of physicists. Each group was given a year to research the issue.

After one year, the groups all reported to the investors. The biologists said that they could genetically engineer an unbeatable racehorse, but it would take 200 years and $100bn. The statisticians reported next. They said that they could predict the outcome of any race, at a cost of $100m per race, and they would only be right 10 per cent of the time.

Finally, the physicists reported that they could also predict the outcome of any race, and that their process was cheap and simple. The investors listened eagerly to this proposal. The head physicist reported, 'We have made several simplifying assumptions: first, let each horse be a perfect rolling sphere ... '

EWAN BIRNEY, *associate director, European Bioinformatics Institute*

A blowfly goes into a bar and asks: 'Is that stool taken?'

AMORET WHITAKER, *entomologist, Natural History Museum*

What does the B in Benoit B Mandelbrot stand for?

Benoit B Mandelbrot.

(Mathematician Mandelbrot coined the word fractal – a form of geometric repetition.)

ADAM RUTHERFORD, *science writer and broadcaster*

A weed scientist goes into a shop. He asks: 'Hey, you got any of that inhibitor of 3-phosphoshikimate-carboxyvinyl transferase?'

Shopkeeper: 'You mean Roundup?'

Scientist: 'Yeah, that's it. I can never remember that dang name.'

JOHN A PICKETT, *scientific leader of chemical ecology,*
Rothamsted Research

A psychoanalyst shows a patient an inkblot, and asks him what he sees.

The patient says: 'A man and woman making love.'

The psychoanalyst shows him a second inkblot, and the patient says: 'That's also a man and woman making love.'

The psychoanalyst says: 'You are obsessed with sex.'

The patient says: 'What do you mean, *I* am obsessed? You're the one with all the dirty pictures.'

RICHARD WISEMAN, *professor of the public understanding*
of psychology, University of Hertfordshire

Winter

Live blog: Antarctica mission (extract)

ALOK JHA

Alok Jha joined a group of scientists aboard the Akademik Shokalskiy *to follow in the footsteps of Douglas Mawson's 1911 Antarctic expedition. But things did not go according to plan ...*

DAY 9

It only took 10 days to reach the end of the world. Two days of seasickness, five days on a boat that swung like a pendulum, three days of picking and smashing our way through ice-encrusted ocean and, much sooner than anyone had expected, we were cruising along the coastline of Antarctica. Although our clocks showed it was past 5 p.m., the sun was high and warm, the air was still, and the cold, dark water was flat and calm.

We had reached Commonwealth Bay in East Antarctica.

DAY 11

This morning we took a Zodiac boat and went looking for leopard seals. Mid-morning is the best time, when these huge slug-like creatures haul themselves up on to ice floes to sleep, after a hard night of singing.

DAY 16

Every coast or sea we have visited in Antarctica, we have seen penguins. They come to the shoreline to investigate our ship as we sail past, they hop on and off ice floes, flocks of them fly in formation through the water. Night or day, there are always a dozen penguins, at least, within sight of the ship.

Ornithologist Kerry-Jayne Wilson took me to a small rookery [at Cape Denison, where Douglas Mawson built his base camp]. There were about a hundred penguins sitting on or near nests they had made from piles of rocks. Whenever they stood up, we could see large eggs under their guano-stained bellies. A few hundred metres beyond them, we could see the shoreline where the ocean would have been four years ago. All we saw that day was ice, all the way to the horizon. There was no open water anywhere.

A great number of eggs had been abandoned in the rookeries. Instead of sitting on their eggs, some of the penguins would just stand next to them, occasionally rolling the eggs around between their feet. Most worrying, though, was the number of dead chicks that littered the rookeries – penguins that had not survived to their first moult.

We've seen a lot of penguins in the past week and, whether they are alone or in groups, they like to make a noise. But however close we stood next to the nesting penguins at Cape Denison, they stayed silent, not moving, staring directly ahead.

DAY 18

It will come as no surprise to anyone that, this year, Christmas in Antarctica was white. The pack ice around the *Shokalskiy* stretched from the hull and in all directions, a grey-white field of thick floes and tumbled boulders of ice, interspersed with frozen pools and, in the distance, icebergs. Icicles fell from the metal steps on the outside of the ship and the decks were covered in snow. As winter scenes go, you could do worse.

We were meant to be visiting the Mertz glacier this week – but plans change as fast as the winds in Antarctica. On Christmas Eve, a blizzard hit our ship with 50-knot winds – mild for these parts. By Christmas morning, we were beset with ice.

At the time of writing, the *Shokalskiy* is waiting for icebreaker assistance. We are stuck just off the coast of Cape de la Motte and have been here almost two days.

This is a hard environment, antithetical to the very idea of life. But life still clings on here, in spite of everything. Algae stick to the underside of sea ice, lichen grows improbably across the surface of high-altitude rocks, penguins, birds and seals roam the shorelines, living and dying along the slimmest edges of temperature, water and nutrients.

This is no place for people.

Antarctic veterans will tell you that being on this continent is a privilege. Not just because it is so remote, unique or because you hear indescribable silence or see epic empty landscapes. The privilege comes from being in a place that requires you to engage with it, become attuned to it and make a serious attempt to understand it. The environment here deserves respect.

Right now the continent has us in its grasp and, though help is coming, the continent will decide when to let us go.

DAY 19

The *Xue Long* appeared as a dot on the horizon, against a bright blue sky, to the starboard side of our ice-locked ship just after dinnertime. With temperatures at a pleasantly bearable −1°C, some of the crew went on to the ice and killed time by making igloos. The rest remained onboard and watched the Chinese icebreaker through binoculars as it appeared to make steady progress, silently zigzagging through the ice.

But we woke after a brief sleep to an announcement: after spending 12 hours cutting through seven nautical miles of ice, the *Xue Long* had turned around and headed back towards open water.

It would, the expedition leader said, be a couple of weeks before we were reduced to dehydrated food.

POSTSCRIPT: DAY 26

The whirring blades of the helicopter made so much noise that, once inside, it was impossible to hear anything else. Twelve of us had picked our way carefully across a snow-covered ice field and climbed into the windowless compartment at the back of the aircraft. The doors slid shut and the helicopter, fully laden, lifted into the air.

We had been stuck here, off the coast of Antarctica, for more than a week. Several icebreakers had tried and failed to break a path to our ship, but seeing the endless field of compressed ice from above, and the seemingly tiny *Shokalskiy* embedded within it, brought the situation into a whole new focus.

This ship had been our home for almost a month. Now it might become a permanent feature of the landscape.

The Akademik Shokalskiy *did eventually break free of the ice, and returned to port on 14 January.*

4 JANUARY

Restaurant review: Peyote

MARINA O'LOUGHLIN

Mayfair has become so weird and foreign, I've taken to pretty much avoiding it. If I want weird and foreign, I'll go abroad. Apart from anything else, I'm scared of the natives: its restaurant population, with few exceptions, is savage, ready to scalp you at the first sign of weakness. Order a side dish and see.

So what am I doing wandering up and down Cork Street, unable to find my destination because it's too superior for a sign, and marvelling at the galleries where you need a mink onesie just to survive the frost from opening the door? I've been lured by the promise of upscale Mexican food, something hard to get in the UK, whatever the current rash of burrito joints would have you believe. At Peyote, the menu has been created 'in consultation' – how I love that fudgiest of phrases – with Eduardo García of Mexico City's celebrated Maximo Bistrot. Mexican food done well is a riot of taste-bud-frotting flavours, a cuisine to horn up the most jaded palate. So, yes, I'll travel.

Past the thick velvet curtain is the least ergonomic room I've graced in a while. You need to be Mayfair-thin to negotiate the tables without getting your arse in someone's *arroz*. There's a downstairs room complete with taco counter, but we're not offered this option. I appreciate that our fellow diners – lots of American accents, very hedge-fundy – don't give a monkey's about the odd quid here and there (you should see the wine list), but when I'm offered guacamole and chips while waiting for the pal, I don't anticipate £7.50 for the guac – a weaselly, underpowered version dandruffed with bland *queso fresco*, and not a patch on what I knock up for an al-desko lunch. Plus dips at a further four quid: árbol, *salsa verde cruda*, all riffs on different chillies and tomatillos. Only *salsa de molcajete* has any personality.

Our food comes, as is fashionable, at the whim of the kitchen. But these aren't courses, anyway; they're canapés. Tacos the size of communion wafers, topped with teaspoons of this and that: pork pibil, sludgy and slow-cooked with a backnote of orange and chilli; a morsel of soft-shell crab, cleanly fried, with heavenly *cebollas curtidas* – crisp, pink pickled onions – on top. Nice enough, but at £12 for three, I'd prefer wow. Never mind 'better in Mexico'; at defiantly unswanky street-food event Hawker House, I've had tacos from Breddos that made these taste like damp cardboard.

Quesadilla of *hongos* (mushrooms with gooey cheese) are as bland as rusks and as tiny as the tacos. *Laminado* of yellowtail, a.k.a. tarted-up sashimi, Nobu-style, features creamily beauteous fish, slut-shamed by its microherb and truffle oil dressing. Then tostadas of cactus: coppery-tasting, tinned-textured, teeny-weeny. Top marks, though, for *masa* dough that tastes homemade.

Peyote makes a bit of a thing about its cocktails, but they're as underpowered as the guacamole. The gorgeous velvet margarita, laced with avocado and topped with a purple pansy, transports the pal to poolside drinking at cheap hotels. Only two things leave an impression of loveliness: blowsy sugar-and-cinnamon churros with a pungent chocolate sauce, and the honeyed Mexican wine, LA Cetto chenin blanc, recommended as an accompaniment.

For Peyote – how odd to call it after a hallucinogenic drug – Arjun Waney, the restaurateur behind Roka, Zuma and La Petite Maison, has teamed up with brand consultant Tarun Mahrotri. Perhaps, then, this restaurant is less about passion than about brainstorming. What hasn't Mayfair got? A posh Mexican! Maybe that's unfair: perhaps it's because Waney's neighbouring Coya is coining it, so Latin America is where it's at. Whatever, he's clearly smoking hot at giving rich people what they want: hardly any food for huge wads of cash. Love the lampshades made from plastic bottles by war-displaced artisans in Colombia, though. They go really well with the wall of lockers for personal bottles of rare tequila.

Food 4/10 Atmosphere 5/10 Value for money 3/10

13 JANUARY

Dude, where's my North Sea oil money?

ADITYA CHAKRABORTTY

Last Wednesday, every single Norwegian became a millionaire – without having to lift a lillefinger. They owe the windfall to their coastline, and a huge dollop of good sense. Since 1990, Norway has been squirrelling away its cash from North Sea oil and gas into a rainy-day fund. It's now big enough to see Noah through all 40 of those drizzly days and nights. Last week, the balance hit a million krone for everyone in Norway. Norwegians can't take a hammer to the piggy bank, amassed strictly to provide for future generations. And converted into pounds, the 5.11 trillion krone becomes a mere £100,000 for every man, woman and child. Still, the *oljefondet* (the government pension fund of Norway) owns over 1 per cent of the world's stocks, a big chunk of Regent Street and some of the most prime property in Paris: a pretty decent whipround for just five million people.

Wish it could have been you with a hundred-grand bonus? Here's the really nauseating part: it should have been. Britain had its share of North Sea oil, described by one PM as 'God's gift' to the economy. We pumped hundreds of billions out of the water off the coast of Scotland. Only, unlike the Norwegians, we've got almost nothing to show for it. Our oil cash was magicked into tax cuts for the well-off, then micturated against the walls of a thousand pricey car dealerships and estate agents.

All this was kick-started by Margaret Thatcher, the woman who David Cameron claims saved the country. The party she led still touts itself as the bunch you can trust with the nation's money. But that isn't the evidence from the North Sea. That debacle shows the Conservatives as being as profligate as sailors on shore leave.

Britain got nothing from the North Sea until the mid-70s – then the pounds started gushing. At their mid-80s peak, oil and gas revenues were worth more than 3 per cent of national income. According to the chief economist at Pricewaterhouse Coopers, John Hawksworth, had all this money been set aside and invested in ultra-safe assets it would have been worth £450bn by 2008. He admits that is a very conservative estimate: Sukhdev Johal, professor of accounting at Queen Mary University of London, thinks the total might well have been £850bn by now. That doesn't take you up to Norwegian levels of prosperity – they've more oil and far fewer people to divvy it up among – but it's still around £13,000 for everyone in Britain.

Hawksworth titled his 2008 paper on the subject: 'Dude, where's my oil money?' We don't have any new hospitals or roads to show for it: public sector net investment plunged from 2.5 per cent of GDP at the start of the Thatcher era to just 0.4 per cent of GDP by 2000. It is sometimes said that the money was ploughed into benefits for the miners and all the other workers Thatcherism chucked on the scrapheap, but that's not what the figures show. Public sector current spending hovered around 40 per cent of GDP from Thatcher through to the start of the banking crisis.

So where did our billions go? Hawksworth writes: 'The logical answer is that the oil money enabled non-oil taxes to be kept lower.' In other words: tax cuts. When the North Sea was providing maximum income, Thatcher's chancellor, Nigel Lawson, slashed income and other direct taxes, especially for the rich. The top rate of tax came down from 60p in the pound to just 40p by 1988. He also reduced the basic rate of income tax; but the poor wouldn't have seen much of those pounds in their pockets, as, thanks to the Tories, they were paying more VAT.

What did Thatcher's grateful children do with their tax cuts? 'They used the higher disposable income to bid up house prices,' suggests Hawksworth. For a few years, the UK enjoyed a once-in-a-lifetime windfall; and it was pocketed by the rich. The revolution begun by Thatcher and Reagan is often seen as being about competition and extending markets. But that's to focus on the process and overlook the motivation or the result. As the historian of neoliberalism Philip Mirowski argues, what the past 30 years have been about is using the powers of the state to divert more resources to the wealthy. You see that with privatisation: the handing over of our assets at knock-down prices to corporations and supposed 'investors', who then skim off the profits. The transformation of the North Sea billions into tax cuts for the wealthy is the same process but at its most squalid.

Compare and contrast with the Norwegian experience. In 1974, Oslo laid down the principle that oil wealth should be used to develop a 'qualitatively better society', defined by historian Helge Ryggvik as 'greater equality'. Ten oil commandments were set down to ensure the industry was put under democratic control – which it remains to this day, with the public owning nearly 70 per cent of the oil company and the fields. It's a glimpse of what Britain could have had, had it been governed by something more imaginative and less rapacious than Thatcherism.

If Scotland had held on to the revenues from North Sea oil, the question today would not be how it would manage solo, but how London would fare without its bankrollers over Hadrian's Wall.

Oljeeventyr is how Norwegians refer to their recent history: the oil fairy tale. It conveys the magic of how, in just a few decades, they have been transformed from being the poor Nordic neighbour to being the richest. We have no equivalent term for our North Sea experience, but let me suggest one: a scandal.

20 JANUARY

TV review: *Coronation Street* – farewell Hayley Cropper

LUCY MANGAN

He'd buttoned her cardigan wrong, that's the thing. On the day she'd chosen as her last, Roy had buttoned Hayley's cardigan wrong. 'How did that happen?' he asked in anguish, and he begged her to stay just one more day so that they could do everything better tomorrow. But, suffering from terminal cancer and fearful that the effects of the drugs and pain to come would strip her of the selfhood she had fought so hard over the years to piece together, Hayley couldn't.

I suspect Roy knew from the moment he fell in love with Hayley then-Patterson, back in 1998, that she couldn't stay. Not for ever. Life's just not that kind to the Roy and Hayley Croppers of this world. Each a misfit and isolated in their own way – Hayley by her transgendered identity and Roy by his ... Royness – they found each other, braved the bigots and carved out a life together on Coronation Street. And – thanks to years of loving, careful, delicate performances by two of the finest actors ever to grace those fabled cobbles, Julie Hesmondhalgh and David Neilson – every moment, for the viewer, was a pleasure.

On Monday, in two finely scripted episodes by writers Debbie Oates and Chris Fewtrell, Hayley left both Roy and us. One last shirt ironed, one last hug of Fiz and Tyrone's children, one last barm secured for Chesney, and it was time. 'If there is a bloke up there wi' a clipboard,' said Hayley as they sat together on the sofa, trying to find a way to bear the unbearable, 'I reckon I can look him in the eye.' 'I doubt very much,' said Roy bitterly, 'whether he could say the same.' The fathomless injustice that consumes us all in the face of bereavement distilled into a single small exchange.

When Hayley once – just once – breaks down in tears, Roy has a hanky. Roy always has a hanky. They move into the bedroom and she prepares her pills while he puts on the Vaughan Williams they both like. Roy lies down beside her. He takes his shoes off first, of course. So has she. 'I wouldn't be anywhere else,' says Hayley. 'Nor I,' says Roy. She chokes down her pills, forcing away Roy's hand which has flown up instinctively to save her, and him. And she dies.

Goodbye Hayley, and goodbye Julie Hesmondhalgh. And thank you for everything.

21 January

For all Lord Rennard's supporters: a guide to sexual harassment, and why it matters

POLLY TOYNBEE

What are the women whingeing about? If a grown woman can't handle a hand on her knee, she's probably not fit for the rough and tumble of the workplace. Men do try it on, but surely the women could politely tell the portly peer with the wandering hands that they're not interested. Why quite such a fuss when nothing much actually happened? Either these four women are oversensitive or else they must be part of some conspiracy.

That's the gist of one side of the argument among Lib Dem peers who cheered Lord Rennard last week, two to one in his favour. Now the stand-off has been put back on ice: another inquiry and a disciplinary procedure to see if he brought the party into disrepute by refusing to apologise. He says he can't, for fear of being sued. Others say Nick Clegg should have sat him down and cobbled together one of those non-apologies that go 'Sorry if some people have taken offence'. But with blood boiling on both sides, this only freezes the dilemma. The party is in disrepute.

One MEP said Rennard's behaviour was no different to the bottom-pinching Italian men of yore. But most Rennard defenders adopt the kind of 'common-sense' attitude that has dogged every attempt to improve women's position since the suffragettes. Remember David Cameron's patronising 'Calm down, dear' – there it was again in Clegg's complaint today that the argument around Rennard was 'shrill'. Such mild put-downs are harder to confront than full-frontal misogyny.

But these cases are deadly: Rennard's reputation is shot, but his four women accusers stand disbelieved, with their claims not 'beyond reasonable doubt'. With QC Alistair Webster's report being secret, all we are left with is the impression that one man's evidence seems to have carried more weight than four women complainants, sharia style.

For those who had never heard of Lord Rennard, in the teacup of the Lib Dem party he is a storming figure. Magician of Lib Dem by-election victories, many senior figures owe their selection, election or preferment to him. Few forget the whisker-thin Clegg–Huhne leadership contest when the Christmas post delayed the postal ballots. Those votes were heavily pro-Huhne, but the Clegg side demanded they be ignored: Rennard adjudicated in Clegg's favour.

So Rennard had immense power over the four women aspiring to be Lib Dem candidates. If he did what they claim, then surely only that power would have given this physically unprepossessing man the nerve to try his luck with younger, more attractive women. Did an implied 'come up and see my target seat' let a political supremo make passes at women well out of his league – or did they make it up and risk all for mischief?

Sexual harassment is all about power. When that phrase first flew across the Atlantic, we didn't know how to pronounce it: *ha*rassment or har*ass*ment? Nor did we know how bad it had to be before it counted, along the continuum all the way to rape. Back then groping, pinching and outright sexual threats were commonplace. New girls – and 'girls' we were – were warned of the worst leches, that it was not safe to be alone in their offices. But no one complained because no one would listen, and it would mark you down as trouble and no fun. In a 1980s newsroom where I was the only woman editor, other women came to me wondering what to do about an editor who promoted via his bedroom and demoted those who refused. A man with power at work over a woman can never have a fair and equal relationship: how will it end, what happens to her if they break up? Whose job is at risk? Never his.

Costly employment tribunal cases taken by brave women may make men more circumspect. As cases are now unearthed from yesteryear, some complain they're from another age, another culture: if so, any culture change is only because some women dare to call out their abusers. But read the evidence from the Everyday Sexism Project and the change looks cosmetic, with more than 10,000 complaints about workplace harassment received last year – still so insidious, with victims so vulnerable.

How will women in politics feel on hearing these four complainants only suffered 'behaviour that violates their personal space and autonomy'? Westminster remains a man's palace, its 22 per cent women MPs too few to tip the balance. Neither Tories nor Lib Dems learn from Labour that the only way women break past men's barricades is with women-only shortlists and quotas. Douglas Hurd voiced what both parties think when he said last week that things are 'slightly ludicrous' when parties think 'there ought to be more women in this or that sphere of our life'.

Tory politicians' use and abuse of women subordinates is well documented. The Lib Dems were always bad on women: around Jeremy Thorpe was a curious closet-gay coterie unwelcoming to women. Oddly, that unfriendly-to-women aura remained in not-gay David Steel's milieu. Lib Dem women's voices are few, with no uprising over this. Labour may promote more women, but more than one cabinet minister needed his women staff protected from slobbery kisses and aggressive fumblings.

Power may be an aphrodisiac, but it certainly gives otherwise unappealing men the chutzpah to imagine so. Touching up women at work is a way to exert power, often an act of aggression to keep them in their place: underneath it all, women's realm is the bedroom. The politics of sex are too difficult to navigate, men complain. At work, as at home, the only etiquette question is who has the power. And what women hear again from the Lib Dems is, 'Not you.'

27 January

Dark lands: the grim truth behind the 'Scandinavian miracle'

MICHAEL BOOTH

For the past few years the world has been in thrall to all things Nordic (for which purpose we must of course add Iceland and

Finland to the Viking nations of Denmark, Norway and Sweden). 'The Sweet Danish Life: Copenhagen: Cool, Creative, Carefree,' simpered *National Geographic*; 'The Nordic Countries: The Next Supermodel', boomed the *Economist*; 'Copenhagen really is wonderful for so many reasons,' gushed the *Guardian*.

Whether it is Denmark's happiness, its restaurants, or TV dramas; Sweden's gender equality, crime novels and retail giants; Finland's schools; Norway's oil wealth and weird songs about foxes; or Iceland's bounce-back from the financial abyss, we have an insatiable appetite for positive Nordic news stories. After decades dreaming of life among olive trees and vineyards, these days, for some reason, we Brits are now projecting our need for the existence of an earthly paradise northwards.

I have contributed to the relentless Tetris shower of print columns on the wonders of Scandinavia myself over the years but now I say: enough! *Nu er det nok!* Enough with foraging for dinner. Enough with the impractical minimalist interiors. Enough with the envious reports on the abolition of gender-specific pronouns. Enough of the unblinking idolatry of all things knitted, bearded, rye bread-based and liquorice-laced. It is time to redress the imbalance, shed a little light Beyond the Wall.

Take the Danes, for instance. True, they claim to be the happiest people in the world, but why no mention of the fact they are second only to Iceland when it comes to consuming antidepressants? And Sweden? If, as a headline in this paper once claimed, it is 'the most successful society the world has ever seen', why aren't more of you dreaming of 'a little place' in Umeå?

Actually, I have lived in Denmark – on and off – for about a decade, because my wife's work is here (and she's Danish). Life here is pretty comfortable, more so for indigenous families than for immigrants or ambitious go-getters (Google *Jantelov* for more on this), but as with all the Nordic nations, it remains largely free of armed conflict, extreme poverty, natural disasters and Jeremy Kyle.

So let's remove those rose-tinted ski goggles and take a closer look at the objects of our infatuation ...

DENMARK

Why do the Danes score so highly on international happiness surveys? Well, they do have high levels of trust and social cohesion, and do very nicely from industrial pork products, but according to the OECD they also work fewer hours per year than most of the rest of the world. As a result, productivity is worryingly sluggish. How can they afford all those expensively foraged meals and hand-knitted woollens? Simple, the Danes also have the highest level of private debt in the world (four times as much as the Italians, to put it into context; enough to warrant a warning from the IMF), while more than half of them admit to using the black market to obtain goods and services.

Perhaps the Danes' dirtiest secret is that, according to a 2012 report from the Worldwide Fund for Nature, they have the fourth largest per capita ecological footprint in the world. Even ahead of the US. Those offshore windmills may look impressive as you land at Kastrup, but Denmark burns an awful lot of coal. Worth bearing that in mind the next time a Dane wags her finger at your patio heater.

I'm afraid I have to set you straight on Danish television too. Their big new drama series, *Arvingerne* (*The Legacy*, when it comes to BBC4 later this year), is stunning, but the reality of prime-time Danish TV is day-to-day, wall-to-wall reruns of 15-year-old episodes of *Midsomer Murders* and documentaries on pig welfare. The Danes, of course, also have the highest taxes in the world (though only the sixth-highest wages – hence the debt, I guess). As a spokesperson I interviewed at the Danish centre-right think-tank Cepos put it, they effectively work until Thursday lunchtime for the state's coffers, and the other day and a half for themselves.

Presumably the correlative of this is that Denmark has the best public services? According to the OECD's Programme for International Student Assessment rankings (Pisa), Denmark's schools lag behind even the UK's. Its health service is buckling too. (The other day, I turned up at my local A & E to be told that I had to make an appointment, which I can't help feeling rather misunderstands the nature of the service.) According to the World Cancer Research Fund, the Danes have the highest cancer rates on the planet. 'But at least the trains run on time!' I hear you say. No, that was Italy under Mussolini. The Danish national rail company has skirted bankruptcy in recent years, and the trains most assuredly do not run on time. Somehow, though, the government still managed to find £2m to fund a two-year tax-scandal investigation largely concerned, as far as I can make out, with the sexual orientation of the prime minister's husband, Stephen Kinnock.

Most seriously of all, economic equality – which many believe is the foundation of societal success – is decreasing. According to a report in *Politiken* this month, the proportion of people below the poverty line has doubled over the last decade. Denmark is becoming a nation divided, essentially, between the places that have a branch of Sticks'n'Sushi (Copenhagen) and the rest. Denmark's provinces have become a social dumping ground for non-western immigrants, the elderly, the unemployed and the unemployable, who live alongside Denmark's 22 million intensively farmed pigs, raised 10 to a pen and pumped full of antibiotics (the pigs, that is).

Other awkward truths? There is more than a whiff of the police state about the fact that Danish policemen refuse to display ID numbers and can refuse to give their names. The Danes are aggressively jingoistic, waving their red-and-white *dannebrog* at the slightest provocation. Like the Swedes, they embraced privatisation with great enthusiasm (even the ambulance service is privatised); and can seem spectacularly unsophisticated in their race relations (cartoon depictions of black people with big lips and bones through their noses are not uncommon in the national press). And if you think a move across the North Sea would help you escape the paedophiles, racists, crooks and tax-dodging corporations one reads about in the British media on a daily basis, I'm afraid I must disabuse you of that too. Got plenty of them.

Plus side? No one talks about cricket.

NORWAY

The dignity and resolve of the Norwegian people in the wake of the attacks by Anders Behring Breivik in July 2011 were deeply impressive, but in September the right-wing, anti-Islamist Progress party – of which Breivik had been an active member for many years – won 16.3 per cent of the vote in the general election, enough to elevate it into coalition government for the first time in its history. There remains a disturbing Islamophobic sub-subculture in Norway. Ask the Danes, and they will tell you that the Norwegians are the most insular and xenophobic of all the Scandinavians, and it is true that since they came into a bit of money in the 1970s the Norwegians have become increasingly Scrooge-like, hoarding their gold, fearful of outsiders.

Though 2013 saw a record number of asylum applications to Norway, it granted asylum to fewer than half of them (around 5,000 people), a third of the number that less wealthy Sweden admits (Sweden accepted over 9,000 from Syria alone). In his book *Petromania*, journalist Simon Sætre warns that the powerful oil lobby is 'isolating us and making the country asocial'. According to him, his countrymen have been corrupted by their oil money, are working less, retiring earlier, and calling in sick more frequently. And while previous governments have controlled the spending of oil revenues, the new bunch are threatening a splurge which many warn could lead to full-blown Dutch disease.

Like the dealer who never touches his own supply, those dirty frackers the Norwegians boast of using only renewable energy sources, all the while amassing the world's largest sovereign wealth fund selling fossil fuels to the rest of us. As Norwegian anthropologist Thomas Hylland Eriksen put it to me when I visited his office in Oslo University: 'We've always been used to thinking of ourselves as part of the solution, and with the oil we suddenly became part of the problem. Most people are really in denial.'

ICELAND

We need not detain ourselves here too long. Only 320,000 – it would appear rather greedy and irresponsible – people cling to this breathtaking, yet borderline uninhabitable rock in the North Atlantic. Further attention will only encourage them.

FINLAND

I am very fond of the Finns, a most pragmatic, redoubtable people with a Sahara-dry sense of humour. But would I want to live in Finland? In summer, you'll be plagued by mosquitoes; in winter, you'll freeze – that's assuming no one shoots you, or you don't shoot yourself. Finland ranks third in global gun ownership, behind only America and Yemen; has the highest murder rate in western Europe, double that of the UK; and by far the highest suicide rate in the Nordic countries.

The Finns are epic Friday-night bingers and alcohol is now the leading cause of death for Finnish men. 'At some point in the evening, around 11.30 p.m., people start behaving aggressively, throwing punches, wrestling,' Heikki Aittokoski, foreign editor of

Helsingin Sanomat, told me. 'The next day, people laugh about it. In the US, they'd have an intervention.'

With its tarnished crown jewel, Nokia, devoured by Microsoft, Finland's hitherto robust economy is more dependent than ever on selling paper – mostly, I was told, to Russian porn barons. Luckily, judging by a recent journey I took with my eldest son the length of the country by train, the place appears to be 99 per cent trees. The view was a bit samey.

The nation once dubbed 'the West's reigning educational superpower' (the *Atlantic*) has slipped in the latest Pisa rankings. This follows some unfortunate incidents involving Finnish students – the burning of Porvoo cathedral by an 18-year-old in 2006; the Jokela shootings (another disgruntled 18-year-old) in 2007; and the shooting of 10 more students by a peer in 2008 – which led some to speculate whether Finnish schools were quite as wonderful as their reputation would have us believe.

If you do decide to move there, don't expect scintillating conversation. Finland's is a reactive, listening culture, burdened by taboos too many to mention (civil war-, second world war- and cold war-related, mostly). They're not big on chat. Look up the word 'reticent' in the dictionary and you won't find a picture of an awkward Finn standing in a corner looking at his shoelaces, but you should.

'We would always prefer to be alone,' a Finnish woman once admitted to me. She worked for the tourist board.

SWEDEN

Anything I say about the Swedes will pale in comparison with their own excoriating self-image. A few years ago, the Swedish Institute of Public Opinion Research asked young Swedes to describe their compatriots. The top eight adjectives they chose were: envious, stiff, industrious, nature-loving, quiet, honest, dishonest, xenophobic.

I met with Åke Daun, Sweden's most venerable ethnologist. 'Swedes seem not to "feel as strongly" as certain other people,' Daun writes in his excellent book, *Swedish Mentality*. 'Swedish women try to moan as little as possible during childbirth and they often ask, when it is all over, whether they screamed very much. They are very pleased to be told they did not.' Apparently, crying at funerals is frowned upon and 'remembered long afterwards'. The Swedes are, he says, 'highly adept at insulating themselves from each other'. They will do anything to avoid sharing a lift with a stranger, as I found out during a day-long experiment behaving as un-Swedishly as possible in Stockholm.

Effectively a one-party state – albeit supported by a couple of shadowy industrialist families – for much of the 20th century, 'neutral' Sweden (one of the world's largest arms exporters) continues to thrive economically thanks to its distinctive brand of totalitarian modernism, which curbs freedoms, suppresses dissent in the name of consensus, and seems hellbent on severing the bonds between wife and husband, children and parents, and elderly and their children. Think of it as the China of the north.

Youth unemployment is higher than the UK's and higher than the EU average; integration is an ongoing challenge; and as with Norway and Denmark, the Swedish right is on the rise. A spokesman for the Sweden Democrats (currently at an all-time high of close to 10 per cent in the polls) insisted to me that immigrants were 'more prone to violence'. I pointed out that Sweden was one of the most bloodthirsty nations on earth for much of the last millennium. I was told we'd run out of time.

Ask the Finns and they will tell you that Swedish ultra-feminism has emasculated their men, but they will struggle to drown their sorrows. Their state-run alcohol monopoly stores, the dreaded Systembolaget, were described by Susan Sontag as 'part funeral parlour, part back-room abortionist'.

The myriad successes of the Nordic countries are no miracle; they were born of a combination of Lutheran modesty, peasant parsimony, geographical determinism and ruthless pragmatism ('The Russians are attacking? Join the Nazis! The Nazis are losing? Join the Allies!'). These societies function well for those who conform to the collective median, but they aren't much fun for tall poppies. Schools rein in higher achievers for the sake of the less gifted; 'elite' is a dirty word; displays of success, ambition or wealth are frowned upon. If you can cope with this, and the cost, and the cold (both metaphorical and interpersonal), then by all means join me in my adopted *hyggelige* home. I've rustled up a sorrel salad and there's some expensive, weak beer in the fridge. Pull up an Egg. I hear *Taggart*'s on again!

29 JANUARY

Benefits Street: the hard-working history that Channel 4 left out

JON HENLEY

One hundred years before Deirdre Kelly welcomed Channel 4's cameras into her living room and found unexpected fame – if not, yet, fortune – as mouthy, unemployed, single mother-of-two White Dee from *Benefits Street*, her house was home to a family called Ashforth.

The 1911 census records the occupation of Jesse Ashforth, 38, as 'polisher-silversmith'; his son, also Jesse, 20, likewise. Ellen Ashforth, 41, was (one imagines) occupied with William, nine, Charles, seven, Naomi, four, and baby Ellen, '0'.

Thirty-odd years later, baby Ellen became the mother of Ralph Carpenter. 'They had 13 children, my grandparents,' says Carpenter, who was himself brought up 10 doors down the street. 'Six survived. I don't think it was a very easy life.'

Carpenter's memories of James Turner Street in Winson Green, Birmingham – now better known as Channel 4's infamous 'Benefits Street', so named because a majority of its residents (90 per cent, some say) live on welfare – stretch to the mid-1940s. They are mostly, he says, in black and white.

'We lived in a black-and-white world,' he says. 'The cars, not that there were many, were black. There was the soot, from the factories and smokestacks. And I don't recall a single tree on James Turner Street when I was a boy. A few shops, front rooms really, and the fish-and-chips on Eva Road. But no trees.'

What Carpenter does remember clearly, though, is watching all the men – including his father, Fred, a factory worker like practically everyone else – coming home from work each evening. 'They'd walk home up the street, all of them,' he says. 'All smoking: Woodbines, the great Brummie cigarette. They'd all have bags on their shoulders, knapsacks or haversacks, army surplus, or old gas-mask bags, for their lunches. But they were all there, everyone, walking home. Because everyone worked then. Everybody had a job.'

Whatever you think of this TV series – we seem to see it either as a cynical demonisation of the poor, or a laudable exposure of all that is wrong with our benefits system – what it has not done is explain how the James Turner Street of Carpenter's memory came to be the Benefits Street of 2014.

It is an edifying story, and it begins long before Jesse Ashforth. At the beginning of the 19th century, Winson Green was a small hamlet on Birmingham Heath, a vast stretch of largely uncultivated, open land west of town. The canal, cut in 1769, attracted a smattering of early industry to the area; in the 1850s the railway drew more. By then the Heath was also the site for three big new Birmingham institutions: the Borough Gaol, now HM Prison Birmingham; All Saints Asylum, housing 300 'pauper lunatics'; and – completing an unholy trinity – the Union workhouse, home to 1,100 unfortunates. Then came the houses.

For Birmingham, the City of a Thousand Trades, was booming, the small metalworking shops that had fuelled its earlier growth now joined by bigger mills and factories. And many of those were in Smethwick – next door to fast-urbanising Winson Green.

'The manufacturers of Birmingham,' marvelled Willey's *History and Guide to Birmingham* in 1868, 'are almost infinite in their variety. Almost all articles of utility or ornament are manufactured in the town.

'From a pin to a steam engine, from pens to swords and guns, from "cheap and nasty" wares to exquisite and elaborate gold and silver services ... All things are made in this hive of industry and give employment to its thousands of men, women and children.'

Minutes from where James Turner Street would soon be rising from the ground, Matthew Boulton and James Watt's Soho Foundry, which built the world's oldest working steam engine, had put Smethwick on the map as early as 1796. Now there were countless more manufacturers: Muntz Metal Works lined the hulls of all the Royal Navy's ships; rolling stock for the new railways came from the Birmingham Railway Carriage and Wagon Company; Guest, Keen and Nettlefolds made screws; Tangye Bros produced engines; and Evered made tubing. Phillips Cycles was in Bridge Street; British Pens nearby. For the Great Exhibition of 1851 it was two Smethwick firms, Chance Brothers glassworks and Fox, Henderson and Co, that supplied the 25 acres of glazing that went into the Crystal Palace and the iron frame that held it together.

These factories needed workers, and the workers needed homes. Along with most of its neighbours in Winson Green, James Turner Street – originally Osborne Street – was built by speculative private developers during the 1870s and 1880s. Its first official mention occurs in 1877; council records show it was formally renamed in 1882. (A present-day debate about whom the street was named after – a long-serving schoolmaster at King Edward's School, the owner of gun-barrel-maker Cooper & Turner, or a partner in a famous button-making firm, Hammond, Turner & Sons – seems to have been settled by Carl Chinn, chair of community history at the University of Birmingham, who is sure it was the latter.)

The street took some time to complete. Local amateur historian Bill Dargue points out that the 1890 Ordnance Survey map, doubtless surveyed a couple of years before publication, shows it only half-built. The 1891 census, on the other hand, shows a full street of residents.

The houses they moved into were, says Chinn, a big step up from the cramped and squalid early-19th-century working-class homes nearer the city centre. Building of new 'back-to-backs', as they were known, was banned in 1876, and the terraced houses of Winson Green were of another order altogether.

'This was much-improved housing,' says Chinn. 'Two, sometimes three bedrooms upstairs, a front and a back room downstairs, a separate kitchen. And much better built.'

Chris Upton, reader in public history at Birmingham's Newman University, says the new districts tended to attract the more prosperous working class: 'People with steady jobs, good wages, moving out of the city centre, or to Birmingham from elsewhere. This was respectability: bay window, front garden, back yard, your own privy out the back, running water inside.'

At a time when a skilled or semi-skilled working man earned maybe 30 shillings a week, the rent – and until the later 20th century, these houses were all rented – would be around 5s: less, as a proportion of income, than many people pay today.

'Food, though, was much more expensive in those days,' Upton notes. 'Thirteen, 14s a week to feed a family of four or five. Clothes and shoes were dearer. And school was 2d or 3d a week per child; paid upfront, in the box, every Monday morning. There wasn't often much spare.'

So who were those first residents of James Turner Street? They came, according to that 1891 census, from all over the country: a majority from Birmingham and Warwickshire, but also from Cambridgeshire, Cornwall, Devon, Herefordshire, Leicestershire, London, Norfolk, Staffordshire and Worcestershire.

But what stands out are their jobs. There are smiths, pressers, turners and stampers. Chain-makers, moulders, casters and brass workers. Solderers, burnishers, polishers, tank-makers, engine-fitters, nut- and bolt-makers, cycle-makers, core-makers, angle-iron smiths, axle-turners, brass tap-finishers, machine tool-makers, furnacemen, iron and steel wire-drawers, rule-makers. Metal-bashers, almost to a man.

Not that there weren't other jobs: at No 19 was a gardener, Richard Webb, and at No 37 a jeweller, Thomas Sparkes; many others – silversmiths, gold chain-makers, silver swivel-makers – were also in the jewellery trade. The jewellery quarter, which still produces more than 40 per cent of the UK's handmade jewellery, was a short tram ride away.

Prison warders lived at 60, 63 and 119; railway servants at 25 and 49; there were labourers, bricklayers, a carpenter, a clerk or two. It is noticeable, too, how many wives worked: French polishers, lacquerers, brush-makers, steel pen slitters, burnishers, dress- and shirt-makers, stud- and cuff-makers, button- and brooch-makers, ivory-button sorters. 'There were huge numbers of factory jobs for women,' says Chinn. 'This was manufacturing, not heavy industry. They earned real wages – not as well paid as men, but not pin money.'

Past age 12 or 13, most children were working, too: 15-year-old Clara Johnson was a chain-maker; Harry Woolley, aged 14, was a caster; Alice Baker, 13, a dressmaker; Roland Sparkes, 14, a stamper; Timothy Griffiths, 13, a boiler-maker.

Local employment supported local businesses: the Birmingham street directory for 1903 lists four shops, a greengrocer and two 'beer retailers' in James Turner Street alone (in 1932, there were still five shops, plus a 'motor beading-maker'; in 1951, four. Two lasted into the 1970s).

Life was not necessarily easy. Many families had five, six, even seven children; many also took in lodgers, some with children of their own: No 15 housed labourer George Hirom, his wife Kate, their five children aged between nine and two, plus George Straight, lodger, with his two daughters of 12 and seven.

Poverty was never far away: in the harsh winter of 1895, the *Birmingham Daily Post* records the 'heart-rending privations' of some of those helped by relief societies and charitable institutions: a brass caster with wife and two children, 'on short time for a long period, then had his hand injured: £5 behind with rent and debts'; an unemployed harness stitcher's family 'in danger of starvation'.

Others on James Turner Street, records the paper, turned to crime: William Ashmore, 19, 'a cripple', was jailed for a month in 1900 for the theft of half a hundredweight of nickel silver metal; Samuel Marshall, fitter, and his wife Jane, machinist, were charged with stealing 246lb of brass screw blanks; and, most dreadfully, Thomas Moreton, 36, brass caster, was indicted for the drunken murder of his wife, Elizabeth.

But to most, the city, now growing at a barely imaginable pace, was kind. Between 1891 and 1911, when the Ashforths appear in

White Dee's house, Birmingham's population grew from 478,000 to 840,000. The job titles were changing – there was now, for example, an 'electrical wireman' – but there were more and more of them.

The first world war, though it cost 13,000 Birmingham men their lives, only confirmed the city's status as the vital heart of British industrial production; at its close, prime minister David Lloyd George observed that 'the country, the empire and the world owe to the skill, the ingenuity and the resource of Birmingham a deep debt of gratitude'.

On winsongreentobrookfields.co.uk, a community history website run by amateur historian Ted Rudge, people who lived on and around James Turner Street in the 1920s and 30s recall corner shops that sold faggots and peas on Friday nights, as well as cow heels, pig's trotters and tripe.

Others remember playing in Black Patch Park at the end of the road, buying ½d of cake crumbs, and giving vegetable peelings and leftovers to the people who kept the pigs in Vittoria Street, in exchange for a piece of pork at Christmas. Unless the prison siren sounded for an escapee, another recalls, no one locked their front door.

By now more advanced manufacturing, electrical engineering, cars and motorbikes were emerging as major industries. The second world war added jeeps, planes and munitions. And in the 30 postwar years – despite government planning measures actively restraining growth and transferring jobs to less thriving cities in the north – Birmingham's economy far outperformed that of any other British city outside London.

Between 1951 and 1961 only the capital created more jobs. In only one year between 1948 and 1966 did unemployment in Birmingham rise above 2 per cent (most of the time it was below 1 per cent). The city and its region grew wealthy; by 1961, household incomes in the West Midlands were 13 per cent above the national average, higher even than London and the south-east.

John Cahill, now a Black Country bricklayer, grew up on James Turner Street in the 60s, leaving in 1974 at the age of 16 to join the navy. Cahill's father was a lathe turner, highly skilled, making parts for navigation systems, and his mother also worked in a factory. Even as late as the 70s, Cahill says: 'Everyone was in work, women too. It was the same right along the street. Nobody worried about it. People lost a job today, they had a new one tomorrow. Good jobs; skilled jobs. Good incomes.'

The area was, though, beginning to change. 'By the mid-60s,' says Chinn, 'more and more prosperous working-class people, with good jobs, were starting to think they could do better than a terraced house in Winson Green. They began moving out, west-wards, to newer, leafier suburbs.'

Birmingham's housing stock was, indeed, decaying: Chinn cites a survey from 1971 that found 26,000 households in the city had no running hot water, and a further 28,000 no fixed bath. A second report, in 1979, concluded that 40,000 homes needed 'substantial improvement' or demolition, with 26,000 more likely to be substandard within five years.

Many families, plenty in Winson Green, moved on, some into council housing. The most decayed Victorian terraces came down, among them a whole chunk of James Turner Street, oppo-site Foundry Road primary school where Carpenter, Cahill and many of Rudge's contributors were once pupils.

As the more upwardly mobile moved out, immigrant families from the Caribbean and the Indian subcontinent were moving in, finding – mostly without difficulty – relatively low-skilled metal-bashing jobs, just like the street's very first residents. But not for long.

The implosion of Birmingham's industrial economy was as sudden as it was catastrophic. Two authoritative mid-80s studies,

Crisis in the Industrial Heartland and 'The Midland Metropolis', chart the collapse with chilling clarity. In 1976, they record, Birmingham's GDP per capita was still the highest of any British city outside the south-east; five years later, it was the lowest in England. Relative incomes, the highest in the country in 1970, were by 1983 the lowest. Birmingham lost 200,000 jobs, almost all in manufacturing, in the decade from 1971 to 1981; by 1982, its unemployment rate had skyrocketed to nearly 20 per cent.

'It was dramatic,' says Upton. 'Birmingham went from a high-wage, low-unemployment city to a low-wage, high-unemployment city in a decade. UB40 sang about "One in 10"; it was more like one in eight.'

The consequences, in places such as James Turner Street, were soon apparent. 'It's a spiral of decline,' says Chinn. 'External forces, attacking the working class, because of their address. Manufacturing was the fabric of this city and it was ripped up. You can't divorce that fact from the social and economic problems of former manufacturing districts.'

So the gradual transformation of James Turner Street into Benefits Street should properly be seen, Chinn argues, as a story of successive governments, both Labour and Conservative, failing abjectly to value manufacturing, and of a consequent, near-total collapse of economic opportunity. For those on the sharp end of that collapse, Upton concludes, it boils down almost to 'an accident of history. To living in the right or the wrong place, at the right or the wrong time.'

Carpenter, for his part, has been watching *Benefits Street* with slightly shocked fascination. He remembers Black Patch Park, the road to the Soho Foundry, the men coming home from the factory, as if it were yesterday. But like many of his postwar generation, his opportunities lay elsewhere: he went to art college, travelled abroad, got out.

'Your horizons change,' he says. 'My father died young, in his 50s, though my mother stayed on, for a long time. But no friends, none of our family, live on James Turner Street now. Everyone's left. Moved on. That tells you something, I suppose.'

Additional research by Phil Lewis.

31 JANUARY

Clearing out my parents' house

DEBORAH ORR

Last weekend, six months on from the death of our mother, and six years on from the death of my father, my brother and I were as ready as we would ever be to undertake the abject task of dismantling their home. Anyway, because my mother had died without leaving a will, it took that long under Scottish law for the house to be ours. Which was just as well, in a way, because it gave us time to get used to the strange, disorientating fact of our middle-aged orphanage.

For me, this had been the family home since I was 10. For David, since he was six. Our parents had lived there together for 35 years and my mother for a further five, alone and heartsick. By last weekend, it hadn't been lived in for 14 months, apart from eight difficult days when my mum had been briefly discharged from the hospice in which she died.

That was odd, in itself. My parents had been compulsively security-conscious, and had not liked leaving the house empty, even for a couple of days. Even when they'd been persuaded to do so, my mother, particularly, would fret about burglars. 'Look, Mum,' we wanted to say. 'More than a year, and no burglars. Think of all the holidays you missed.'

Plus, my mother had been passionately house-proud. How astonished she'd have been by the dust – such a hesitant, delicate film. She'd lived her whole life as if failure to run the Hoover over the carpet for just one day would bring down a landslide of filth and decay.

As for the pile of post behind the door, such a thing had never happened. Among the circulars were a few letters from companies threatening legal action for non-payment of a couple of overlooked bills. No bill remained unpaid when my mother was alive. Even the arrival of a red bill was not to be countenanced. Their lives, like their cupboards, were ordered and disciplined.

Some of the things in those cupboards had sat in the dark, lurking, for all of their married lives. The incomplete harlequin tea set, which had been my grandmother's. How many times had my mother told me she wanted me to have it when she was gone? It's in my cupboard now, and I don't know if I'll ever use it either. It had been guarded so well that it's achieved a status that's something akin to a holy relic.

I took the little sideboard – always referred to as 'the bureau' – with the glass doors that had always held the dolls. I took the dolls. They were mine – again – at last. Even in the 1960s, my parents had set themselves against holidays. They scorned those who chose to go abroad on packages – the dreadful heat, the awful food, the foreign languages. 'I see the Mackies are back from Spain,' I remember my mother saying. 'They're not very tanned, are they? Probably couldn't take that fierce sun.' But whenever someone was going away, she'd ask them to bring back a doll in national costume, 'for Deborah's collection'. Enquiring as to their ownership, once I had a home of my own, it was made clear that the collection was not mine but ours. I could have them when she was gone. And I do. I loved them as a kid and I love them now. They're kitsch, I can see that. But not to me.

I took the crochet. Well, most of it. If you'd unravelled all the crochet in that house, the yarn would have girded the world. What weird secrets people keep from their families. Mum always had a bit of crochet on the go, especially after her arthritis made knitting difficult.

'What do you do with all that crochet, Mum?' I'd asked her once.

'It's for charity,' she'd said.

I'd nodded approvingly. But we'd found tons of the stuff, nevertheless, in the bottoms of wardrobes, in laundry baskets we'd assumed were for laundry, under the beds in plastic boxes – scarves, shawls, bed jackets, doilies, little women that go over loo rolls, even four substantial blankets. I now must have south London's most impressive hoard of crochet.

There was an unfinished scarf in her crochet bag. It made my brother and me so sad: that sense of a life rudely interrupted, without notice, with things started but not finished. That's what brings the tears back.

David took the chest of drawers – always referred to as 'the tallboy'. It was part of the 'bedroom suite' they'd bought when they married: wardrobe, dressing table, tallboy. I'd had a little one, too, which was also still there. It was striking how the stuff from their early married lives was of better quality. More recent furniture had plastic veneer or synthetic fibre. The wool carpets of my childhood had gradually been replaced with nylon. My parents had fallen for modernity, hook, line and sinker. Nothing they'd bought after 1980 was really made to last.

Except the house – and even that isn't strictly true. Those houses – wooden and always locally called 'the timbers' – had been built as temporary homes after the second world war. Yet they've lasted better – with bigger rooms and more generous gardens – than homes like our previous flat, which was built much later, and is already long gone.

God, the energy my mother put into getting that house. Siblings of different sexes were expected to share a room until one of them was 10, at which point the council would rehouse the family. You were allowed two refusals and had to take the third offer. I remember going to look at prospective new homes – one with a dead mouse in a neat pile of swept-up droppings, another with human excrement smeared on the walls. My fastidious mother was appalled. So, to head off the horror of the offer we couldn't refuse being worse than the previous two, she'd scoured the streets looking for empty houses (the good ones, by amazing coincidence, she said, seemed always to go to people with some kind of local government connection), until she'd found that one, and haunted the housing office until they gave in and let her have it.

I remember the day we moved in. It was magical. The garden – which was huge for a council house, even then – was full of self-seeded lupins in all colours, as high as me. There was a robust strawberry patch – the start of the jam-making years. When the strawberries were ripe, we'd gorge on them for weeks, and still have enough left over to make jam to last until the next summer. My parents had put most of the garden to grass in recent years, and added a plum tree – the plum chutney years. But I took some pots, containing some of the plants, or at least their descendants, that had already been growing in the garden on that glorious day in 1972.

My parents had been appalled when right-to-buy was introduced. They believed, rightly, of course, that it would change the nature of social housing fundamentally, with the better stock moving into private hands, and only the mousy or shitty places left for people who rented. But as the years and the redundancies rolled by, they'd succumbed, and bought the place. They'd started to feel that their own principles were making fools of them. It's hard to swim against the tide.

We took some daft stuff from that house, my brother and I, like ancient school projects that were falling apart. It seemed awful to bin them when they'd been saved so long. My brother took my dad's last set of golf clubs, and the trolley, even though a) the fast pace of golf-club technology means they're probably obsolete already, b) his flat is tiny and he has absolutely no room for them, and c) he never plays golf any more, and isn't likely to, because the whole culture of the game is different down south. But John loved his golf. It drove my mother nuts. We each have a box of his personalised golf balls, and I have the brass tee that he'd turned at work. It only survives because the cup at the top was a bit too narrow and the balls would topple off in a breeze.

And their ashes – the last vestige of my parents' corporeal being, each in a plastic bag inside an ugly brown plastic so-called 'urn' from the Co-op Funeral Service – those had to be attended to as well. We sprinkled a few of my dad's at the 18th hole at Shotts, his golf club, and mingled the rest, scattering them at the falls of Clyde, a beauty spot we all loved and had always continued to visit as a family, right to the end. The Christmas before Dad died, he walked to the top with us, seemingly as vigorous as ever. I took my mother there on the last day out we had before she died.

Later, when something compelled me to check my mother's empty handbag one last time, I found a little pillbox in it, which I couldn't open because the clasp was stuck. David got it open, and inside were some of my father's ashes. My mum must have clung on to that little box after he'd gone, to comfort herself. She must have gripped it so hard that she jammed it. God love her.

And that's that. We'll never enter that house again. A new family will live there, and one day, perhaps, the children of that house will find themselves doing what we just had to do and saying some profoundly final goodbyes. Daunting and terrible a task as it was, my brother and I found an odd satisfaction or serenity in making that final inventory of our family lives. So I find myself hoping that those new children will indeed one day do the same. My parents moved to that house as young people, and lived there happily ever after. They never stopped feeling lucky and blessed to be nesting there, not for a day (until illness and death took them from it). Which, really, is pretty wonderful.

7 FEBRUARY

Audio transcript: Manika's story

INTERVIEW BY ALEXANDRA TOPPING

This heartbreaking interview with 'Manika' helped to launch the Guardian's ongoing campaign to end female genital mutilation (FGM), which has now been backed by the UN.

'When I came to the UK, I was a student, an international student. I met my first boyfriend in 2011. When I slept with him, what happened is, whenever he tries to have intercourse with me, it feels like something is blocking him. He can't find his way in me until one day what was happening was, because we had been trying and trying and trying, one day he has to come in me with force, and I feel down in me that something breaks and I started bleeding, heavy bleeding, and I had to be rushed to the St Thomas' hospital.

'They asked me, "Is this the first time you have had sex?" And I said, "Yes." And they said, "The amount of blood that normally has to come out is just tiny drops, not this huge amount of blood." I know then that back when I was circumcised they've blocked me because that's part of the tradition.

'I was at the age of eight and I was taken to a place like a bush with my late elder sister and we were cut by this old woman. She hold my legs down and my hands. When they were cutting me they don't want my sister to see me because if she saw me she will definitely be panicked.

'It hurts, it really hurt. I mean it's a pain you can't even ... I don't know ... it's like a pain that ... it's too much. It's like taking a knife and cutting someone's flesh. Just like that. It really hurts.

'Since then I feel like I don't want to have sex. I have it in my mind that I'm still going to have that same pain. It is that same incident that led me to break up with my boyfriend, I would say, because what happen is he tries to have sex with me but I'm always ... you know scared, even if we try, even if I give him the chance I can't let my body to move properly so that I can do it.

'It has affected my late sister who passed away in 2008. It was because of this FGM that she couldn't give birth to her first child. She has to die because she couldn't deliver normally. That was back in the Gambia.

'It's something that I will never ever forgive my parents for doing this to me. I wouldn't say it is a culture, it is just a heartless thing to do to someone, especially a human being. You know. You will not call someone your child and then you take even a needle to pinch him or her, not to mention taking a blade, cutting her flesh out.

'Now they want me to marry my late sister's husband. I'm afraid to go back because I have seen what has happened to my sister. Because she died in front of me and I have seen what happened to her and I don't want to go back.'

7–10 FEBRUARY

'Newspapers were never like this. We were mute.' Readers' tributes to Georgina Henry

Georgina Henry, a Guardian *journalist for 25 years and the creator of* Comment Is Free, *died on 7 February, aged 53. As Alan Rusbridger wrote in his obituary of her, 'Newspaper offices can be hard-boiled places where executives typically win respect rather than love. George was both respected and loved. She was an exceptional person.' Many journalists wrote tributes, and hundreds of readers filled our comment threads with their impressions, memories and thanks – this is a small selection of those read out at Georgina's memorial service.*

CIF is the only forum I've ever loved. Thanks Georgina. You created something quite amazing.
Iruka

I'm not usually really saddened by the passing of people I don't know personally, but with Georgina it was different, because people like her are always meant to be there, fighting the good fight for decent ethical values.
MartynInEurope

Until *CIF* came along, I was virtually 'speechless'.
Esy

She was the only person on earth who could have convinced me to cover a hired Mini in EU flags, and then drive around

Birmingham, looking for a fight.
JHarrisSTAFF

Through that photo, she was also the face of *CIF* – kind, encouraging, with an expression that seemed to hope against hope you'd rise above your base instincts and write something erudite and witty. Well, I hereby apologise for years of disappointment.
ragworm

If Carlsberg made newspaper readers' commenting systems, *CIF* is exactly what they'd come up with.
TheDogShouterer

I liked it at the beginning, when it had a more anarchic, amateur, pioneering feel and you could scroll through the entire thread – it felt like a small, intimate place – then it got taken over by slickery and feckin' web-page designers!
LaxativeFunction

God bless Georgina, if He does exist, which I doubt.
shalone

In this age of fake democracy, this comments section seems like the best we have in this country.
There is a feeling of being listened to. Unlike politicians.
ellatynemouth

A tragically early end to a meaningful life with a genuine legacy – not just *CIF* but the lifeblood that it has given the Graun to endure, survive and hopefully thrive in the digital era.
Hedropsforglory

I can't believe you've put up a whole tribute for Georgina Henry, you idiots!
BrasilBranch

What!?
Bobbrian666

It's a joke. No *CIF* thread is complete without someone complaining that the article shouldn't have been published at all.
MontanaWildhack

George had the glamour, fearlessness, beauty and competence of one of those early aviators.
HenryPorter

In spring of 2009 I had the pleasure of meeting Georgina.

I had blagged my way into a conference on digital journalism here in Athens with the intention of picking a fight with her.

After Georgina's talk, questions were invited from the floor, so I stood up and said, 'I'm one of the people on the thread you just talked about. I'm Kizbot.' At this, she loudly blurted out, 'I thought you were a man!', which raised a laugh and threw me off my stride a bit. But I wasn't about to back down, so I put it to her that it was a bit off that the *Guardian* had banned one of the people who had made the comment platform what it was and that JayReilly should be reinstated. 'But he called Tony Blair a cunt!' she cried, in front of an audience of Greece's finest journalists. I really was speechless and could think of no retort to that, not least because it was true, he had indeed called him a cunt.

She then invited me to come down to the stage and have a chat with her.

Record-breaking rainfall left large parts of southern England under water. Almost all the residents of the Somerset village of Moorland had to evacuate. DAVID LEVENE

The wreckage of Malaysia Airlines Flight MH17. According to US intelligence, pro-Russian separatists in Ukraine shot the plane down, killing all 298 people aboard. MAXIM ZMEYEV / REUTERS

Residents of the besieged Palestinian camp of Yarmouk queue for food in Damascus, Syria. AP

A supporter of the Islamic State in Iraq and the Levant (ISIL), also known as ISIS, in Raqqa, Syria. REUTERS

Ukrainian riot police move in on thousands of anti-government protestors in Independence Square, Kiev. At least 13 people died and hundreds more were injured. SERGEY DOLZHENKO / EPA

Adir Ali returns to her devastated home after Israel's bombardment of Gaza. More than 2,000 Gazans died during 'Operation Protective Edge', and more than 10,000 were injured. SEAN SMITH

Tear gas rains down on a woman standing with her arms raised after a demonstration over the killing of Michael Brown, an unarmed black teenager, by a police officer in Ferguson, Missouri. SCOTT OLSON / GETTY IMAGES

President Barack Obama, British PM David Cameron, and Danish PM Helle Thorning-Schmidt pose for a selfie during the memorial service for Nelson Mandela. Michelle Obama didn't join in. ROBERTO SCHMIDT /AFP

A black rhino is airlifted by helicopter to its new home in a South African reserve in an attempt to conserve the critically endangered species. GREEN RENAISSANCE / BARCROFT MEDIA

A swarm of giant ants take over an entire room of the Saatchi Gallery, thanks to Colombian artist Rafael Gómezbarros. DAVID LEVENE

Nigel Farage celebrates after Ukip stormed to victory in the European elections in May – the first time since the general election of 1906 that a party other than Labour or the Conservatives topped a British national election. FACUNDO ARRIZABALAGA / EPA

On 11 March, Bob Crow, general secretary of the Rail, Maritime and Transport Workers union, died suddenly, aged 52. Only three days later, another lifelong socialist, Tony Benn, died. He was 88. LINDA NYLAND

A bad year for Nigella Lawson, whose acrimonious split from her husband Charles Saatchi was very publicly aired during the trial of their personal assistants. The PAs were found not guilty of defrauding the couple.
BEN STANSALL / AFP

A good year for British film-maker and artist Steve McQueen, whose *12 Years a Slave* won the Oscar for Best Picture – making McQueen the first black person to win the much-coveted award. GILES PRICE

Dejected England fans can hardly bear to watch as Uruguay's win shatters their World Cup hopes. TOM JENKINS

Alex Salmond campaigned tirelessly for a yes vote in the Scottish referendum – a week after this picture was taken, the vote was lost and Salmond resigned as first minister. MURDO MACLEOD

She was so warm, friendly and engaging that it was impossible to pick a fight with her. You couldn't beat her in an argument but she was so immensely likable that it felt a privilege to lose.
Kizbot

Georgina, you've created a second family and given people a voice they never realised that they had. What an achievement and may you rest in eternal peace.
AlanMcInally

Thanks for creating *CIF* and you were too young to die and it isn't fair.
P_P Proudhon

How sad, but what a great legacy ... don't screw it up, *Guardian*!
joshthedog

14 FEBRUARY

Katie Hopkins interview: 'Can you imagine the pent-up rage?'

DECCA AITKENHEAD

Two million people watched Katie Hopkins' latest TV appearance last week, but I'm not sure how many of them would even recognise the woman I meet a few days later at her London hotel. The snarling aggressor we saw on Channel 5's *Big Benefits Row* has become a friendly Sloane who squeals 'Lush!' at the waiter, teaches me how to talk about sex in 'girl code' (a sort of exaggerated whisper that sounds like Miranda Hart playing a boarding-school girl on her 'PER-I-OD!'), jokes around, laughs at herself and is great company.

Viewers who have followed her TV career are unlikely to have formed this impression. Having distinguished herself as *The Apprentice*'s most notoriously rude and ruthless contestant ever, the former business consultant has built a media career as a 'social commentator', and is a regular fixture on TV-studio sofas, scandalising audiences with a set of opinions typically held by mean girls bitching in the playground. When not on telly, she can be found calling Nelson Mandela a 'cantankerous old git' in her weekly *Sun* column, or tweeting prolifically about her disgust for people who are fat, or unemployed, or badly dressed. Most famously, she has declared ginger-haired babies 'harder to love', and forbidden her children to have friends called Tyler or Chardonnay, as these names are 'lower class'.

If you managed to miss all of that, you would get an idea of her style from her reply when I ask if she'd call herself a snob. 'Oh, definitely, yeah, 100 per cent. I think it's really important to be snobby. Do I think social-mobility policy will ever work? Absolutely not. Is social class a much more efficient way of getting people to the top? Absolutely. Social class has worked for years. Born into the right family, go to the right schools, even if you're not super-bright to start with, you'll turn out bright. You go to the right university, you get the right job, you have the right connections, you'll make it to the top. Job done, very efficient.'

Efficient at what? 'Efficient at getting smart, well-connected people to the top. It is efficient, because what public money was required to move those people to the top? None.' That would depend on whether we want the best people at the top, surely, or just the cheapest way to get some people to fill up the top? 'Oh, for goodness' sake,' she exclaims impatiently. 'It's this whole state-school thing: "Oh, there are a couple of bright sparks, let's invest £50m trying to get the two or three who might achieve to the top." Or, shall we take really clever people and not have to spend any money on them, and get them to the top because they're connected and went to brilliant schools and their families will support them and they're fantastic? So why bother with social mobility? Why does it matter? Why? Why? I don't understand the obsession with it.'

We could easily spend the interview arguing. I think Hopkins would quite like that – she tries to pick a couple of fights when I haven't even disagreed with her. In between the jokes and giggles she is coiled to spring from what she calls 'girly chitchat' into TV-studio rottweiler mode, but whenever she does, she stops listening, so it seems pointless. We already know what she thinks. I'm more interested to know why.

'But a lot of women think the sort of things I say,' she protests. 'You know, "Oh God, she's put on so much weight, she looks dreadful." Well, I just say it.' But that still doesn't explain why an apparently cheerful and successful woman would want to make herself a national hate figure. Rubbished all over the internet and booed by studio audiences, Hopkins seems to relish her reputation as a pantomime monster.

Some critics claim she doesn't believe a word she says, and peddles controversy for money. Others think she must be secretly horrified that so many people hate her. I don't detect an ounce of truth in either theory. It turns out Hopkins has never watched herself on television, never cries, is essentially immune to most human emotion, confuses public insults with compliments, and has kept secret the fact that she is hospitalised on average once every 10 days. The curious puzzle of Hopkins only begins to make sense when she describes the first 23 years of her life.

Now 39, Hopkins grew up in 'a regular middle-class family' in a small Devon town, the youngest of two daughters to an electrical engineer and a housewife. Both girls attended a private convent school from the age of three to 16. 'I don't mean some notion of a grammar school convent school, I mean proper nuns, nunned up to the max. The headmistress was called Sister Philomena, and she,' Hopkins adds admiringly, 'was mean.' The nuns tied Hopkins' left hand behind her back to try and force her to be right-handed, and school life was highly regimented. 'Oh, beyond! Whistle blows once: don't move. Whistle blows twice: into lines. Whistle blows three times: into class. Can you imagine,' she laughs, 'the pent-up rage?'

I can imagine, but it appears Hopkins can't. 'Yuh, very exciting. I had a hoot at school, it was a blast, it really was St Trinian's – we were all girls together and it was really good fun.' She can't recall any bullying or teasing, lost her virginity at 14 to a boyfriend 'who looked like Tom Cruise', and had no teenage insecurities at all, on account of always getting As, mastering grade-eight piano and violin by 14, and being picked for all the sports teams. 'I suppose I was one of those girls that was just fine.' Her parents were strict about exams and homework, but didn't need to be, because 'I wasn't going to come second. One of the frustrating things with my children now is that I understood very quickly what you had to give the teacher to get a top mark. It's not rocket science, is it? It frustrates me that mine can't see that yet.' Her three children are nine, eight and five.

She knew exactly what she wanted to do. 'I was going to be the colonel of the forces. I loved the military. I loved the discipline, the rigour, the big shouty men. I love monosyllabic orders. "George: bed! George: shoes!" That's how I talk to my children, yeah, and I love it. Love it!' She still likes to address her girlfriends by their surnames, 'So you'd be "Heads"', and the very thought of a man in uniform barking acronyms sends her into a schoolgirl froth. 'Yes! Someone hot. With muscles. That you can clearly see, despite thick cotton. Definitely!'

After A-levels she signed a 35-year contract with the intelligence corps, who sponsored her through an economics degree at Exeter University, where she spent her weekends with the Territorial Army – 'really fun, lying around in forests with guns having a brilliant time' – before arriving at Sandhurst. 'And someone starts shouting at you the minute your parents drive away. Put in a little tiny room and told to clean it with a toothbrush, that kind of stuff.' Literally? 'Yeah!' Her eyes gleam. 'And you had to iron your pants into six-inch squares. I can still do it now. Everything in your wardrobe had to be a certain way. Brilliant!' She looks visibly excited by the memory. 'Yeah I am, really excited.'

Significantly, she was at her happiest when being publicly insulted on the parade square. 'The drill sergeant majors are enormously funny individuals, with brilliant lines. To the girl with sticky-out teeth: "You could eat an apple through a tennis racket with those teeth!" I can't even be half as witty, and everyone loves the guys, these are massive men who've earned their stripes, they're 6ft 4in, usually Welsh, brilliant! Utterly brilliant men.' They mocked her ceaselessly for the size of her nose, but she never took offence, 'because it's almost more like kudos – you're in the club and they know you can take it.' No insult was off limits. 'There is no line, no barrier, no nothing.' She thinks every young person should have to go through something similar. 'Wouldn't it be great? Do you not think we'd all learn a little bit of discipline?'

But Hopkins' military career came to an abrupt end days before the passing-out ceremony. If I didn't slow her down she would have glossed briskly over the details, but it transpires that she had an epileptic seizure on the parade square. 'It's not something I talk about,' she says quickly, 'because I see it as a failing. So it does annoy me a little bit when people say "she failed at the forces", but of course I never respond. I never say why, because it sounds like an excuse, and I won't have that. I won't have an excuse.'

She didn't cry when the army discharged her. In fact, in her whole life she 'genuinely can't remember ever crying', and says she doesn't even know what fear feels like. The only failure she can identify was her first marriage, which ended within a year. 'That was bad. But am I over it? Yes. Did it really matter? No.'

Hopkins joined a business consultancy after Sandhurst, moved to Manhattan and began going out with the boss. When their first daughter, India, was born in 2004, she took two weeks' maternity leave, and was away on business most of the time, seeing her daughter only at weekends. The couple moved back to the UK and got married before the arrival of their second daughter, Poppy, the following year. Her husband was present for the birth, but Hopkins had to get herself and Poppy home from the maternity ward 48 hours later, because by then he had left her for his secretary. Neither Hopkins nor her daughters have ever spoken to or seen him again.

She relays all this with the pragmatism of someone describing a little HR restructuring – and looks pleased when I say so. 'Well, it sort of was like that, only in a life way.' She says she doesn't experience 'emotional stuff', has never known a moment's maternal guilt, and were I to ridicule her children in this article, 'I would go, "You know what, I put myself out there, so I have to accept what happens."' Nothing anyone has ever said or written has hurt Hopkins, or caused her to reconsider, because no one else's feelings or opinions matter to her in the slightest, apart from her close family's. For Hopkins, being in the public eye is exactly like being on the army parade square. Anything is fair game, and anybody who gets upset is as pathetic as the women in her old platoon who couldn't hack Sandhurst and quit.

Deaf to distress, her indifference towards anyone else's feelings makes sense. But I'm confused about how she reconciles her contempt for emotional messiness with a private life so colourful that she once listed 'stealing husbands' as her hobby on her CV. Her first husband was just one of a string of married fathers whom Hopkins seduced away from their families, including her second husband, the father of her five-year-old son.

How can someone so impatient with indisciplined self-indulgence justify wreaking havoc in so many lives, in – of all things – the name of love? 'Oh, spare me the oestrogen tears,' she groans. 'We've all got skeletons in our closets. I couldn't be disingenuous enough to say I'm sorry for those women or children, because lots of us have done things wrong. When you look at the statistics for men and women having affairs, it's huge.'

Lots of women are a size 18, but in Hopkins' book that's inexcusable. So why is poor impulse control acceptable in sexual behaviour, but not anything else? 'For me there are certain standards of life. Intrinsic to my life are work, fitness, discipline.' So if I was fat she'd call me disgusting, but if I tried to steal her husband she'd say: 'Fair enough'? 'Yeah.'

It must surely have struck Hopkins that her arguments about how everyone should be – slim, fit, punctual, organised, smartly dressed, hard-working – are just descriptions of her own preferences. We'd all like everyone else to abide by our personal rules, but most of us see that our rules are wildly inconsistent and wholly subjective, whereas she has invested hers with the certainty of universal truths. How can she be so sure her standards are objectively right? 'Because when I look at the things I think are important, they're all things that don't ask anything of anybody else. If you are healthy and not obese you're not asking the NHS for anything. I'm not asking the taxpayer to fund my benefits. Because I'm not asking anything from anyone, I think that that gives me the right to say: "This is how it should be."'

I had put Hopkins' horror of being weak and needing help down to nothing too terrible ever having happened to her. But the horror is too visceral for that, and the real explanation is a revelation. She can see how some people have suffered awful things, 'but I just don't connect with that, because I still have my thing going on'. It takes a moment to realise she is talking about epilepsy. All of a sudden she speaks very quickly, as if the words were burning coals.

'When I have a fit at night, my arms come out. They dislocate. So I have to go into hospital to have them relocated. That's happened 26 times in the last nine months. So we all have crap to deal with in our lives. I'm hard with myself. Get on with it. Move on. Get your arms put back in.' She never talks about it, she says, and as soon as she has told me she looks as if she wishes she hadn't.

Has anyone ever suggested, I ask, that she is profoundly disconnected from her emotions? 'No, I think I'm just very male.' I think her emotional disconnect is quite extreme. 'Do you?' She looks surprised. 'I don't think it is.' But being 'very male' wouldn't explain her violent disgust for others' failure to live up to her standards, nor why women's failings upset her so much more than men's. It doesn't explain why she never watches herself on TV, not even her debut on *The Apprentice*. 'Yes, that is odd,' she concedes, when this curious fact emerges. 'I hadn't actually thought that before, but I suppose it is.' And it doesn't explain why the only response she seems unable to deal with is sympathy. If I glowered at her she would be quite impervious – but a sympathetic look is a kind of agony for Hopkins, making her literally squirm, and I think this has distorted her entire perspective on other people's problems.

Had she been born to a drug-addicted prostitute and an alcoholic pimp, and suffered unspeakable violence and neglect from infancy, would she expect herself to be as self-sufficient as she has been? 'Look, there's always an argument for why people don't make it. Whereas I look at myself and go, you know what, I've had a fair amount to overcome. But I haven't allowed it to get in my way.' So she would expect the same of someone born into addiction and abuse? 'Yes. And I'm sorry, but they lose. They lose. The truth is, life is just not fair.'

Isn't it interesting that people who say that are always at the top of the pecking order? 'Yes, but isn't it interesting that people who work hard do really well? Isn't it interesting that people who get up at 5.30 a.m. to go running aren't fat?' Not really, I say. Those are just examples of logical cause and effect. The child I've just described didn't do anything to cause its circumstances – so why is it right for that human being to lose?

'I really don't have an answer for it,' she admits. 'But if you're the sort of parent who can't give a toss, then I can't give a toss about your child either.'

17 FEBRUARY

How we ended up paying farmers to flood our homes

GEORGE MONBIOT

It has the force of a parable. Along the road from High Ham to Burrowbridge, which skirts Lake Paterson (formerly known as the Somerset Levels), you can see field after field of harvested maize.

In some places the crop lines run straight down the hill and into the water. When it rains, the water and soil flash off into the lake. Seldom are cause and effect so visible.

That's what I saw on Tuesday. On Friday, I travelled to the source of the Thames. Within 300 metres of the stone that marked it were ploughed fields, overhanging the catchment, left bare through the winter and compacted by heavy machinery. Muddy water sluiced down the roads. A few score miles downstream it will reappear in people's living rooms. You can see the same thing happening across the Thames watershed: 184 miles of idiocy, perfectly calibrated to cause disaster.

Two realities, perennially denied or ignored by members of this government, now seep under their doors. In September the environment secretary, Owen Paterson, assured us that climate change 'is something we can adapt to over time and we are very good as a race at adapting'. If two months of severe weather almost sends the country into meltdown, who knows what four degrees of global warming will do?

The second issue, once it trickles into national consciousness, is just as politically potent: the government's bonfire of regulations.

Almost as soon as it took office, this government appointed a task force to investigate farming rules. Its chairman was the former director general of the National Farmers' Union. Who could have guessed that he would recommend 'an entirely new approach to and culture of regulation ... Government must trust industry'? The task force's demands, embraced by Paterson, now look as stupid as Gordon Brown's speech to an audience of bankers in 2004: 'In budget after budget I want us to do even more to encourage the risk-takers.'

Six weeks before the floods arrived, a scientific journal called *Soil Use and Management* published a paper warning that disaster was brewing. Surface water run-off in south-west England, where the

Somerset Levels are situated, was reaching a critical point. Thanks to a wholesale change in the way the land is cultivated, at 38 per cent of the sites the researchers investigated, the water – instead of percolating into the ground – is now pouring off the fields.

Farmers have been ploughing land that was previously untilled and switching from spring to winter sowing, leaving the soil bare during the rainy season. Worst of all is the shift towards growing maize, whose cultivated area in this country has risen from 1,400 hectares to 160,000 since 1970.

In three quarters of the maize fields in the south-west, the soil structure has broken down to the extent that they now contribute to flooding. In many of these fields, soil, fertilisers and pesticides are sloshing away with the water. And nothing of substance, the paper warned, is being done to stop it. Dated: December 2013.

Maize is being grown in Britain not to feed people, but to feed livestock and, increasingly, the biofuel business. This false solution to climate change will make the impacts of climate change much worse, by reducing the land's capacity to hold water.

The previous government also saw it coming. In 2005 it published a devastating catalogue of the impacts of these changes in land use. As well as the loss of fertility from the land and the poisoning of watercourses, it warned 'increased run-off and sediment deposition can also increase flood hazard in rivers'. Maize, it warned, is a particular problem because the soil stays bare before and after the crop is harvested, without the stubble or weeds required to bind it. 'Wherever possible,' it urged, 'avoid growing forage maize on high and very high erosion risk areas.'

The Labour government turned this advice into conditions attached to farm subsidies. Ground cover crops should be sown under the maize and the land should be ploughed, then resown with winter cover plants within 10 days of harvesting, to prevent water from sheeting off. So why isn't this happening in Somerset?

Because the current government dropped the conditions. Sorry, not just dropped them. It issued – wait for it – a specific exemption for maize cultivation from all soil-conservation measures.

It's hard to get your head round this. The crop that causes most floods and does most damage to soils is the only one that is completely unregulated.

When soil enters a river we call it silt. A few hundred metres from where the soil is running down the hills, a banner over the river Parrett shouts: 'Stop the flooding, dredge the rivers.' Angry locals assail ministers and officials with this demand. While in almost all circumstances, dredging causes more problems than it solves, and though, as even Owen Paterson admits, 'increased dredging of rivers on the Somerset Levels would not have prevented the recent widespread flooding', there's an argument here for a small amount of dredging at strategic points.

But to do it while the soil is washing off the fields is like trying to empty the bath while the taps are running.

So why did government policy change? I've tried asking the environment department: they're as much use as a paper sandbag. But I've found a clue. The farm regulation task force demanded a specific change: all soil-protection rules attached to farm subsidies should become voluntary. They should be downgraded from a legal condition to an 'advisory feature'. Even if farmers do nothing to protect their soil, they should still be eligible for public money.

You might have entertained the naive belief that in handing out billions to wealthy landowners we would get something in return. Something other than endless whining from the National Farmers' Union. But so successfully has policy been captured in this country that Defra – which used to stand for the Department for Environment, Food and Rural Affairs – now means Doing Everything Farmers' Representatives Ask. We pay £3.6bn a year for the privilege of having our wildlife exterminated, our hills grazed bare, our rivers polluted and our sitting rooms flooded.

Yes, it's a parable all right, a parable of human folly, of the kind that used to end with 300 cubits of gopher wood and a journey to the mountains of Ararat. Antediluvian? You bet it is.

20 FEBRUARY

Blair emails

STEVE BELL

Steve Bell responds to the news that Tony Blair had advised Rebekah Brooks shortly before her arrest in the phone-hacking scandal. The cartoon never appeared in print as the trial was ongoing. Brooks was acquitted in June.

23 FEBRUARY

What the hell is Obama's presidency for?

GARY YOUNGE

A few days after John F Kennedy's assassination, Lyndon Johnson sat in his kitchen with his key advisers working on his first speech to Congress. It was the evening of Kennedy's funeral – Johnson was now president. The nation was still in grief and Johnson, writes Robert Caro in *The Years of Lyndon Johnson: The Passage of Power*, was not yet able to move into the White House because Kennedy's effects were still there.

He had been a hapless vice-president; now he had to both personify and project the transition from bereavement to business as usual. In the midst of the cold war, with Vietnam brewing, the Kennedy administration had been trying to get civil rights legislation and tax cuts through Congress. There was plenty of business to attend to. Johnson's advisers were keen that he introduced himself to the nation as a president who could get things done.

For that reason, writes Caro, they implored him not to push for civil rights in this first speech, since it had no chance of passing. 'The presidency has only a certain amount of coinage to expend, and you oughtn't to expend it on this,' said 'one of the wise, practical people around the table'. Johnson, who sat in silence at the table as his aides debated, interjected: 'Well, what the hell's the presidency for?'

'First,' he told Congress a few days later, 'no memorial oration or eulogy could more eloquently honour President Kennedy's memory than the earliest possible passage of the civil rights bill for which he fought so long.' Over the next five years he would go on to sign the Civil Rights Act, the Voting Rights Act, launch the war on poverty and introduce Medicaid (medical assistance for low-income families) and Medicare (for seniors). That's what his presidency was for.

Barack Obama has now been in power for longer than Johnson was, and the question remains: 'What the hell's his presidency for?' His second term has been characterised by a profound sense of drift in principle and policy. While posing as the ally of the immigrant he is deporting people at a faster clip than any of his predecessors; while claiming to be a supporter of labour he's championing trade deals that will undercut American jobs and wages. In December, even as he pursued one whistleblower, Edward Snowden, and kept another, Chelsea Manning, incarcerated, he told the crowd at Nelson Mandela's funeral: 'There are too many leaders who claim solidarity with Madiba's struggle for freedom, but do not tolerate dissent from their own people.'

If there was a plot, he's lost it. If there was a point, few can remember it. If he had a big idea, he shrank it. If there's a moral compass powerful enough to guide such contradictions to more consistent waters, it is in urgent need of being reset.

Given the barriers to democratic engagement and progressive change in America – gerrymandering, big money and Senate vetoes – we should always be wary of expecting too much from a system designed to deliver precious little to the poor. We should also challenge the illusion that any individual can single-handedly produce progressive change in the absence of a mass movement that can both drive and sustain it.

Nonetheless, it was Obama who set himself the task of becoming a transformational political figure in the mould of Ronald Reagan or JFK. 'I think we are in one of those fundamentally different times right now where people think that things, the way they are going, just aren't working,' he said. It was he who donned the mantles of 'hope' and 'change'.

It was obvious what his election was for. First, preventing the alternative: presidential candidates in the grip of a deeply dysfunctional and reactionary party. His arrival marked a respite from eight years of international isolation, military excess and economic collapse. He stood against fear, exclusion and greed – and won. Second, it helped cohere and mobilise a new progressive coalition that is transforming the electoral landscape. Finally, it proved that despite the country's recent history Americans could elect a black man to its highest office.

So his ascent to power had meaning. It's his presence in power that lacks purpose. The gap between rich and poor and black and white has grown while he's been in the White House, the prospects for immigration reform remain remote, bankers made away with the loot, and Guantánamo's still open. It's true there's a limit to what a president can do about much of this and that Republican intransigence has not helped. But that makes the original question more salient not less: if he can't reunite a divided political culture, which was one of his key pledges, and his powers are that limited, then what is the point of his presidency?

This should not deny his achievements. He scaled down one major war, is winding down another, and helped save the US car industry. If he's on the hook for growing inequality, then he can take credit for the deficit shrinking and unemployment falling. But together, this amounts to an extended period of triage before sending the patient back out into the world without any plan for long-term recovery. The underlying impulses, policies, priorities and structures that made the wars and economic collapse possible are still in place.

Finally, there's health care reform. The brouhaha over its botched roll-out will scarcely be remembered a few years hence.

But with roughly 31 million people set to remain uninsured and little changing for many, its undeniable benefits are not likely to be remembered as transformational. All in all, there's precious little that Obama has done that any of his primary opponents would not have done.

Occasionally, he either gives a lead – like after the shootings at Newtown when he advocated for gun control – or follows one, as in his support for gay marriage or preventing the deportation of young undocumented immigrants, which helps to set a tone or establish a moral marker. But these interventions are too rare, and their remedies too piecemeal, to constitute a narrative.

'If you're going to be president, then I guess you obviously want to be in the history books,' said Susan Aylward, a frustrated Obama supporter in Akron, Ohio, shortly before the last election. 'So what does he want to be in the history books for? I don't quite know the answer to that yet.' Sadly, it seems, neither does he.

3 MARCH

Lupita Nyong'o:
a Hollywood star is born

BIM ADEWUNMI

'Nee-Yongo.' 'En-Yong-Go.' 'Nwon-go.' 'Nye-ongo.' Nobody on any of the red-carpet feeds seemed able to pronounce the surname of the woman who won the Oscar for best supporting actress on Sunday night. It didn't matter, though. Lupita Nyong'o has arrived. And while most of us seem glad of it, some of us are inevitably more glad than others.

Although *12 Years a Slave* is her first Hollywood movie – her first job out of Yale Drama School, even – Nyong'o is no ingénue. She's 31, abundantly talented – having worked on the production crews for Hollywood movies such as *The Constant Gardener* – and almost extravagantly charming. At the Oscars, she never had that look of being cowed or overawed by all the pomp and pageantry. Dazzled, sure (who wouldn't be?), but never looking out of place with it. There was always a confidence, borne out by her wonderful and gracious acceptance speeches and interviews. It helps that she looks beautiful too, with her super-short hair (a fade! On a black woman! On the red carpet!) and dark brown skin, but even that beauty seems independent of the circus around her. Of course that is not the neat reality, as she explained in her speech at the *Essence* Black Women in Hollywood luncheon in February: 'I remember a time when I too felt unbeautiful. I put on the TV and only saw pale skin, I got teased and taunted about my night-shaded skin. And my one prayer to God, the miracle worker, was that I would wake up lighter-skinned.'

Her portrayal of Patsey, a slave forced to bear the worst conditions on a daily basis, already had the critics taking notice. Her Wikipedia page lists no fewer than 45 wins for the role (the outcome of three nominations are still pending, including a couple at the *Guardian* film awards), plus 28 other nominations. Over the promotional cycle, she showcased a rainbow of stunning dresses (look up the United Colours of Lupita meme), each one more fabulous than the last. The world swooned (that red cape! That flower neckline!), but again, some of us a little harder than others.

It all came to a head on Sunday night, though, when she appeared on the red carpet in an ice-blue number with a delicate gold-and-diamond headband, and a froggy ring on the little finger of her right hand. The frog, she explained, was a family totem. And the dress? 'Well, this is Prada,' she told red-carpet presenter Ryan Seacrest. 'And it was made for me.'

It might not seem like a big deal; after all, the big designers tend to dress the big stars at these award ceremonies. But this is Prada, a fashion house that did not use a single black model in its runway shows between 1993 and 2008, and only last year cast a mixed-race (Kenyan-born) model in its campaign advertisements – the first in almost 20 years.

And then Lupita explained her choice: 'It's a blue that reminds me of Nairobi. I wanted to have a little bit of home,' she told Seacrest. Over on the AP feed, she smiled and repeated the line, adding it also reminded her 'of champagne bubbles'. See? Extravagantly charming. Incidentally, is this the point where we all start referring to that shade as 'Nairobi blue'? We live in hope.

What does it all mean? A star is born, clearly. But the post-Oscars career slump is fairly well-documented. It would be amazing if Nyong'o cleared that hurdle and went on to have a Meryl Streepesque career that goes from strength to strength. She deserves it and, just as importantly, so do we. Some of us are willing her on just a little harder than others.

4 MARCH

A month in Ambridge

NANCY BANKS-SMITH

Many of the children in Ambridge have a somewhat opaque parentage. There is Daniel born by IVF, and Henry by artificial insemination. Not to mention George, Phoebe, Rich and Ruairi, who are just the innocent products of complicated plots. *Who Do You Think You Are?* (a programme that abhors the commonplace and discarded even Johnny Vegas as too humdrum) would fall on the Archer family tree with delight, whooping like baboons.

Only Henry, conceived in a fertility clinic, can't take even a sporting guess at his father. However – prepare to be amazed – I think Rob Titchener, the dapper dairy manager who has swept Helen Archer off her feet, despite the misgivings of her family and friends, is secretly Henry's sperm donor. And He's Up To Something. How else can we account for his gnomic phone calls to his wife, a children's social worker, and his inexplicable fondness for a tiresome toddler? Also (and this is the clincher) Helen, who has the incisive intellect of a marsupial, is fatally attracted to bounders. I may be wrong, but I'm not as wrong as Rob, a man who clearly cannot walk from A to B in a straight line.

Currently Ambridge is under water, and not before time, you may feel. The Bull is flooded, and Brookfield – not the best name for a farm in the present climate – is awash with refugee sheep. 'There's a flood alert on the Am! The water's still rising!' 'Oah! Noah!' (Aficionados of Ambridge accents will recognise Ruth's voice here.)

In the great scheme of soaps, Ambridge is a pond not a torrent, but lately life seems to be lapping round our ankles. It may be that, under its new producer, Ambridge too is experiencing a climate change. Jennifer's insistence on replacing her 'old-fashioned, inefficient and extraordinarily out-of-date kitchen' with something ever-so-very-in-vogue sounds like a metaphor for a new, improved Archers.

Which is all fine and dandy, but will the lemon drizzle cake taste as good?

5 MARCH

The clash in Crimea is the fruit of western expansion

SEUMAS MILNE

Diplomatic pronouncements are renowned for hypocrisy and double standards. But western denunciations of Russian intervention in Crimea have reached new depths of self-parody. The so far bloodless incursion is an 'incredible act of aggression', US secretary of state John Kerry declared. In the 21st century you just don't invade countries on a 'completely trumped-up pretext', he insisted, as US allies agreed that it had been an unacceptable breach of international law, for which there will be 'costs'.

That the states which launched the greatest act of unprovoked aggression in modern history on a trumped-up pretext – against Iraq, in an illegal war now estimated to have killed 500,000, along with the invasion of Afghanistan, bloody regime change in Libya, and the killing of thousands in drone attacks on Pakistan, Yemen and Somalia, all without UN authorisation – should make such claims is beyond absurdity.

It's not just that western aggression and lawless killing is on another scale entirely from anything Russia appears to have contemplated, let alone carried out – removing any credible basis for the US and its allies to rail against Russian transgressions. But the western powers have also played a central role in creating the Ukraine crisis in the first place.

The US and European powers openly sponsored the protests to oust the corrupt but elected Viktor Yanukovych government, which were triggered by controversy over an all-or-nothing EU agreement that would have excluded economic association with Russia.

In her notorious 'fuck the EU' phone call leaked last month, the US official Victoria Nuland can be heard laying down the shape of a post-Yanukovych government – much of which was then turned into reality when he was overthrown after the escalation of violence a couple of weeks later.

The president had by then lost political authority, but his overnight impeachment was certainly constitutionally dubious. In his place a government of oligarchs, neoliberal Orange Revolution retreads and neo-fascists has been installed, one of whose first acts was to try and remove the official status of Russian, spoken by a majority in parts of the south and east, as moves were made to ban the Communist party, which won 13 per cent of the vote at the last election.

It has been claimed that the role of fascists in the demonstrations has been exaggerated by Russian propaganda to justify Vladimir Putin's manoeuvres in Crimea. The reality is alarming enough to need no exaggeration. Activists report that the far right made up around a third of the protesters, but they were decisive in armed confrontations with the police.

Fascist gangs now patrol the streets. But they are also in Kiev's corridors of power. The far-right Svoboda party, whose leader has denounced the 'criminal activities' of 'organised Jewry' and which was condemned by the European parliament for its 'racist and anti-Semitic views', has five ministerial posts in the new government, including deputy prime minister and prosecutor general. The leader of the even more extreme Right Sector, at the heart of the street violence, is now Ukraine's deputy national security chief.

Neo-Nazis in office is a first in postwar Europe. But this is the unelected government now backed by the US and EU. And in a contemptuous rebuff to the ordinary Ukrainians who protested

against corruption and hoped for real change, the new administration has appointed two billionaire oligarchs – one who runs his
business from Switzerland – to be the new governors of the eastern
cities of Donetsk and Dnepropetrovsk. Meanwhile, the IMF is
preparing an eye-watering austerity plan for the tanking Ukrainian
economy which can only swell poverty and unemployment.

From a longer-term perspective, the crisis in Ukraine is a
product of the disastrous Versailles-style break-up of the Soviet
Union in the early 1990s. As in Yugoslavia, people who were
content to be a national minority in an internal administrative
unit of a multinational state – Russians in Soviet Ukraine, South
Ossetians in Soviet Georgia – felt very differently when those
units became states for which they felt little loyalty.

In the case of Crimea, which was only transferred to Ukraine by
Nikita Khrushchev in the 1950s, that is clearly true for the Russian
majority. And contrary to undertakings given at the time, the US
and its allies have since relentlessly expanded Nato up to Russia's
borders, incorporating nine former Warsaw Pact states and three
former Soviet republics into what is effectively an anti-Russian
military alliance in Europe. The European association agreement
which provoked the Ukrainian crisis also included clauses to inte-
grate Ukraine into the EU defence structure.

That western military expansion was first brought to a halt in
2008 when the US client state of Georgia attacked Russian forces
in the contested territory of South Ossetia and was driven out.
The short but bloody conflict signalled the end of George Bush's
unipolar world in which the US empire would enforce its will
without challenge on every continent.

Given that background, it is hardly surprising that Russia
has acted to stop the more strategically sensitive and neuralgic
Ukraine falling decisively into the western camp, especially given
that Russia's only major warm-water naval base is in Crimea.

Clearly, Putin's justifications for intervention – 'humanitarian' protection for Russians and an appeal by the deposed president – are legally and politically flaky, even if nothing like on the scale of 'weapons of mass destruction'. Nor does Putin's conservative nationalism or oligarchic regime have much wider international appeal.

But Russia's role as a limited counterweight to unilateral western power certainly does. And in a world where the US, Britain, France and their allies have turned international lawlessness with a moral veneer into a permanent routine, others are bound to try the same game.

Fortunately, the only shots fired by Russian forces at this point have been into the air. But the dangers of escalating foreign intervention are obvious. What is needed instead is a negotiated settlement for Ukraine, including a broad-based government in Kiev shorn of fascists; a federal constitution that guarantees regional autonomy; economic support that doesn't pauperise the majority; and a chance for people in Crimea to choose their own future. Anything else risks spreading the conflict.

17 MARCH

Telling a young person to 'Just get a job' is like going to the Sahara and yelling 'Just rain!'

ERICA BUIST

In a society where it's considered rude to answer 'yes' to the question 'Does anyone want the last scone?' (especially if they're at the next table, I've learned), it's amazing how many people will happily go up to a young jobseeker, pick up their last shred of self-esteem and dunk it in their tea until it disintegrates into soggy clumps. My year spent blogging about joblessness landed me a job, and a doctorate-level knowledge of what not to say to a jobless youngster.

'Get a job'

Today's youth has spent years chasing qualifications no one ever asks us about. The notion that algebra would ever be useful seemed fishy, but the grown-ups insisted: education, no matter how apparently arbitrary, leads to jobs.

But the minute we graduated, something switched in employers' heads. The same generation who had us sit SATs and the 11-plus and the 12-plus and SATs again and mock GCSEs and real GCSEs and AS-levels and A-levels and BAs and MAs and MSCs and PhDs decided education is an afterthought. Experience is what's really important. Which none of us had, because we'd been busy pretending Romeo and Juliet weren't just horny teenagers and Pythagoras wasn't the most tedious bastard that ever existed.

We were told that education was a ticket to employment, when really it's more like vague directions to the station.

We've all watched the Gen Y horror show unfold. We all know many entry-level positions are now filled with cycles of interns, that underemployment is cleverly hidden by internships or zero-hours contracts, that an unprecedented number of jobs created are part-time. By October last year, long-term youth unemployment had risen to four times the 2004 figures (oh, and tripled in the first three years of the coalition).

So telling a young person, 'Just get a job' is not tough love. It's like going to the Sahara, looking up and yelling 'Just rain!' Which is weird. Stop it.

'YOU THINK YOU'RE TOO GOOD FOR A JOB AT COSTA'

Graduates expect too much. That's the line – often stated as if it came out of the blue. After our American-dream-style 'You can do anything!' upbringings, apologies if it takes us a while to recover from the disappointment of realising it was all, well, a dream.

The 'job snobs' snub acknowledges that traditionally competitive industries are double-locking their doors, while ignoring the fact that low-skilled jobs are as rare as a worm concussion; a branch of Costa in Nottingham received 1,701 applications for eight positions. Not to be outdone, Asda got over 2,500 applications for 300 jobs. They should give scratchcards out with applications to double your chances of a win.

It's not arrogance; it's the embers of optimism. Do you think snobbery comes easily to someone who's rejected for a cleaning job for 'not having enough experience'? (I knew I shouldn't have put my mum as a reference for that one.)

Lest we forget, our parents and teachers asked what we wanted to be when we grew up, then demanded a ransom of education, good grades, experience and a charming interview manner. We've done what you asked, society! Release the jobs!

'YOU'LL NEVER GET A JOB IF YOU THINK NEGATIVELY'

Does anyone actually believe this hippy hogwash? That 'positive thoughts' are a mystical good-things magnet? Sorry to shoot down those bluebirds that dress you in the morning, and put them in a pie, but positive feelings don't attract positive events. They're a result of them. Only actions matter – as long as jobseekers tweak their CVs for every job and turn up to interviews prepared and smiling, it really doesn't matter if they're dead inside.

Empathise. Don't leap around shouting, 'Be positive!' like an inappropriate funeral director.

'APPLYING FOR ASDA? BUT YOU HAVE A DEGREE!'
Damned if I do, job snob if I don't. And thanks for reminding me that I've spent thousands of pounds to beg someone to let me stack their yoghurts.

'HAVE YOU TRIED DOING AN INTERNSHIP?'
Yes, I did partake in a few rounds of 'Who can earn the least for longest?' but I had to fund my expensive habit of paying for things. Don't prod a spot this sore. An internship is not a job, it's a barricade dressed as a stepping stone. Plus you're bringing back bad memories – the excruciating awkwardness of parachuting into an office for a two-week internship can't be overstated. Inside jokes whizz around you like Dementors, and any attempt to join in with a conversation is met with stares, as if you've just said, 'Guys, look at this rash on the inside of my cheek! Look by TOUCHING!'

'DO SOMETHING FUN WITH ALL THAT FREE TIME!'
Free time? When your life is a cycle of applying for jobs, listening to crickets and crying into sponges, you don't get to clock off.

Also, what fun is there for the jobless? Perhaps taking some sort of revenge on the employed? Deliberately getting to the front of the Starbucks queue at 08:56 and saying, 'Umm ... what's actually in a latte?' Going to a pub on a Friday night and joining in some random work drinks, claiming to work in accounting and watching them pretend to remember the time we met at the water cooler?

Well, I did, and I just felt silly.

20 MARCH

I am a gay Ugandan about to go home

FRANK MUGISHA

Growing up in Uganda, homosexuality was not something we talked about much. I knew I was gay from a young age, and I came out to those close to me when I was a teenager in the early 90s. Some in my family accepted it, while others refused to acknowledge it. Homosexuality wasn't always accepted but it was, largely, ignored.

There were characters from my youth whom I remember as openly gay, such as a local barber – everybody in our close-knit neighbourhood knew them for who they were. There were snide comments and rude names – it was far from social equality – but I did not experience hatred. To be gay in Uganda back then was a fairly unremarkable thing.

As a Catholic, I always knew the church and religious leaders were openly homophobic. They preached the well-known mantra that homosexuality is a sin, and goes against God's wishes, but, again, that was where it ended. There was no hate-speak, so I didn't feel too much like I would be judged when I was honest about my sexuality.

Today's Uganda is a different story. As the director of Sexual Minorities Uganda, the country's leading lesbian, gay, bisexual and transgender (LGBT) rights organisation, I have been on an advocacy trip in Europe and the US, encouraging the international community to speak out against the recently passed anti-homosexuality act, which myself and a core group of Ugandans who support human rights are now challenging in the constitutional court. As I prepare to return home, I know a law has been passed that will tyrannise my life and those of many Ugandans I know. The outlook is bleak. As a gay Ugandan, I know I am one of thousands. But as someone who has chosen to be 'out' and is still living in Uganda, I am in a minority of fewer than 20 people.

A day after the anti-gay law was passed, the Ugandan tabloid *Red Pepper* published my name and picture in a list of the 'top 200 homos'. The last time a similar article was published, in 2010 by the now-defunct *Rolling Stone*, it listed the name of my friend and colleague David Kato. He and others successfully sued the paper for this, but weeks later David was bludgeoned to death at home, almost certainly as a result of his sexuality.

Uganda has always been a conservative society in which certain things are not discussed, but it never used to be a cruel environment for gay people. Twenty years ago we were not pursued by mobs, tortured by police, or run out of our homes. When I came out as gay the sort of hysteria that has since overwhelmed my country was unthinkable. If I were a gay 13-year-old in Uganda today, I probably wouldn't tell anyone.

Many people I have met with over these past few weeks, including Britain's foreign secretary, William Hague, have asked me: what has changed so dramatically? It is true that same-sex sexual acts between consenting adults have been illegal in Uganda ever since the British introduced their penal code at the beginning of the 20th century. But this recent era of expanded criminalisation and virulent homophobia has been another gift from the West, this time from the United States.

There is no question that the well-funded US evangelical movement has aided economic development in Uganda, building and running many hospitals, schools and orphanages. But there is also no doubt, as illustrated in the 2013 documentary, *God Loves Uganda*, that they have relentlessly stoked a loathing and disgust of sexual minorities. Now we are told that Uganda will not bow to the 'gay agenda' – a phrase I had never heard until a few years ago when American evangelicals introduced it to the political rhetoric.

Among them was the firebrand pastor Scott Lively, who first came to Uganda in 2002 and began peddling his distinctive variety of hot-headed and active homophobia. He addressed congregation after congregation, fuelling a type of public outrage that was entirely new to Uganda. His profile gave him direct access to leading government and media figures. I believe so strongly that his influence made a difference – and led to the anti-homosexuality act – that I am one of the claimants suing him for crimes against humanity under the alien tort act in the US. There is also evidence that he has helped to engender the same sort of hatred and persecutory atmosphere elsewhere, in particular Russia, which adopted its own draconian anti-gay legislation last year.

Yet Ugandan supporters of the anti-gay law say they are countering foreign influences and the international pressure to support homosexuality. In signing the law, President Museveni wanted 'to demonstrate Uganda's independence in the face of western pressure and provocation', as though this were an act of resisting neocolonial power.

It is simply untrue that homosexuality is un-African. Same-sex sexual conduct existed in various forms throughout Africa before the colonial period; same-sex relationships were known among several groups in Uganda, including the Bahima, the Banyoro and the Baganda. King Mwanga II, the last precolonial ruler of what is now Uganda, was said to have engaged in sexual relations with male courtiers.

I am a gay man. I am also Ugandan. There is nothing un-African about me. Uganda is where I was born, grew up and call my home. It is also a country in which I have become little more than an unapprehended criminal because of whom I love. I want my fellow Ugandans to understand that homosexuality is not a western import and our friends in the developed world to recognise that the current trend of homophobia is.

I am plagued by a fear of dying

MICHELE HANSON

I was walking round the block with the dog yesterday, when suddenly I felt a big 'pop!' inside my head, like a bursting balloon. 'Brain haemorrhage,' I thought, straight away, because that's what my mother had in her 50s, and very nearly pegged out, and I seem to be taking after her in lots of ways. Why not that one? It would be just my luck to drop dead on the pavement, confusing the dog and not having time to give Daughter final vital instructions. Luckily, I didn't. But there's always tomorrow.

It set me thinking through my possible hereditary options: stroke and heart attack from my father, and more stroke, haemorrhage and cancer from my mother. Grim. This is the trouble with living with a parent to the very end. You know exactly what's going to happen on the long and grisly way out: the hoists, nappies, hernia, commodes, aphasia, swallowing problems and being spoon-fed slop. Help. And I have the starter signs already: sore feet, bowel turmoil, falling over, cataracts, wind, bloating and choking. Just like my poor mother. And I can't swallow a pear unless I'm sitting up very straight.

Last year, Fielding went to seven funerals. He's losing his musculature and gnashers, going blind in one eye, guzzling statins and remembering his ulcerated mother. We can't help but have death on our minds. Most mornings I wake up in a sunny mood, just for a couple of seconds. Then wham, the sudden terrors again, about nothing in particular. Or everything. Those few seconds may well be the only truly carefree moments in my day. I have no desperate problems at present. But you never know, do you?

'Don't be so ridiculous,' says Olga briskly. 'There's no point worrying about all that. You could be run over tomorrow, blah, blah ...' Oh, thank you, just before I drive across London to visit another chum. Will I crash on the shiny wet Westway in a sudden shower?

No, I didn't. Here I still am. If my hereditary theory is correct, I may have 27 years' intense anxiety to go. My mother lasted to 98.

26 MARCH

Pass notes: 'conscious uncoupling'

TIM DOWLING

NAME: Conscious uncoupling.

AGE: Recently emerged.

APPEARANCE: Wholeness in separation.

THAT DOESN'T MAKE ANY SENSE. You ain't heard nothing yet, mate.

WHAT IS CONSCIOUS UNCOUPLING? It's something that Coldplay's Chris Martin and acting's Gwyneth Paltrow are trying out just now.

IS IT A MEDIATION TECHNIQUE? A NEWFANGLED THERAPY? It's more of a divorce.

NO! Or at least a separation.

BUT THEY SEEMED MADE FOR EACH OTHER, LIKE ARTICHOKES AND QUINOA RIGATONI. They're consciously splitsville, according to a statement on Paltrow's website Goop.

I THOUGHT GOOP WAS FULL OF WEIRD RECIPES AND SILLY DETOX DIETS. That stuff is still there. But the newest post is an announcement headed 'Conscious Uncoupling' that begins: 'It is with hearts full of sadness that we have decided to separate.'

WHAT ELSE? They've asked for their privacy to be respected as they 'consciously uncouple and co-parent'.

CONSCIOUS UNCOUPLING – IT SOUNDS LIKE SOMETHING SHE MADE UP. Apparently it's a thing. She has also posted a long treatise on the subject from Dr Habib Sadeghi and Dr Sherry Sami.

SO HOW IS IT DIFFERENT FROM A NORMAL, COMPLETELY ACRIMONIOUS SEPARATION? 'Conscious uncoupling brings wholeness to the spirits of both people who choose to recognise each other as their teacher. If they do, the gift they receive from their time together will neutralise the negative internal object that was the real cause of their pain in the relationship.'

OK. WHO GETS THE CAR? That's not spelled out, but there's something about constructing an internal cathedral with spiritual trace minerals of self-love and self-forgiveness.

OH, RIGHT. THAT CLEARS THAT UP THEN. CHRIS AND GWYNETH WERE TOGETHER FOR A LONG TIME, WEREN'T THEY? Ten years. The general reaction on Twitter seems to be that if they can't make it work, no one can.

BUT BY THE SAME TOKEN, IF THEY CAN GET DIVORCED, SO CAN I! Are you even married?

I'VE ALWAYS KEPT THAT PART OF MY LIFE PRIVATE. Sorry.

DO SAY: 'Drink plenty of water, cultivate your feminine energy, keep building that spiritual endoskeleton and don't forget to try the blueberry-and-almond smoothie.'

DON'T SAY: 'After I got divorced I went out and did a lot of unconscious coupling, and that sort of worked too.'

29 MARCH

Ask a grown-up: what would happen to the Earth if everyone in the world jumped at the same time?

DR RADMILA TOPALOVIC

The astronomer at the Royal Observatory, Greenwich answers nine-year-old Angus's question.

If you were to jump right now, you'd move away from the Earth and the Earth would move away from you: because every force exerts an equal and opposite force, your action leads to a reaction from the Earth.

There are 7 billion people on our planet – that's a 7 with nine zeros after it. Our Earth has a mass 600,000 billion times greater than all those people combined. If everyone in the world jumped at the same time, we'd all make the Earth move in different directions and all these effects would cancel out, so there would be no overall change in the Earth's motion.

If we all squeezed together into one giant person with a mass of 350 million tonnes and jumped up half a metre from one spot, the Earth would move by only 100 millionth of the width of a strand of hair. This is equivalent to a ladybird jumping on something as heavy as two Great Pyramids of Giza.

Go ahead and jump!

Spring

Sketch: Maria Miller's apology

JOHN CRACE

Blink and you missed it. Shortly before 12.30 p.m. Maria Miller rose from the backbenches to make her apology to the House for not co-operating with the standards committee over her expenses claim. Seconds later she was back in her seat amid a chorus of 'hear, hears' to be smothered in the warm embrace of Jeremy Hunt and other Tories who had delayed their usual Thursday early getaway to show their support. The Labour benches were nearly empty.

Just how many seconds Miller's apology lasted was a matter of some argument. Some timed it at 34, others at 28. I guess it rather depends on when you think her apology started. Was it the moment her muscles first contracted to lift herself out of her seat? Or was it when she engaged her vocal chords? Let's split the difference and call it 31 seconds. Either way, it wasn't the shortest parliamentary apology on record: that honour falls to Nadine Dorries after trousering her *I'm a Celebrity ... Get Me Out of Here!* fee, with 24 seconds. But Miller ran her close.

It was also arguable whether what Miller said actually constituted an apology. She gave the appearance she was doing everyone a huge favour by interrupting her lunch. Her speech confirmed this initial impression. 'I wish to make a personal statement in relation to today's report,' she said in a brusque monotone. 'The report resulted from an allegation made by the member for Bassetlaw. The committee has dismissed his allegation. The committee has recommended that I apologise to the

House for my attitude to the commissioner's inquiries, and I of course unreservedly apologise. I fully accept the recommendations of the committee, and thank them for bringing this matter to an end.' If Miller had spoken less formally, she could have got her statement down to a single word. 'Whatever.'

The one part of Miller's cameo that did ring true was her gratitude to the standards committee. She has a great deal to be grateful for. The commissioner, Kathryn Hudson, had said: 'I have established beyond reasonable doubt that between June 2005 and April 2006 Mrs Miller claimed for mortgage interest against a mortgage significantly larger than the one required to buy her property,' along with several other damning conclusions. Somehow or other the committee interpreted this as 'don't bother your pretty little head with all these mortgage thingy things. They are awfully complicated and it's terribly easy to end up with an extra £45,000 in your bank account. Just try not to do it again, but if you do, please be a little less stroppy with the commissioner. She's got terrible self-esteem issues.'

Having done the bare minimum, Miller left the chamber with the air of a woman cruelly wronged. A smirk might have been a more appropriate response, as it looked for all the world as if the minister in charge of making sure the press behaves itself had just been handed an unexpected £45,000 bonus by her colleagues. I know George Osborne is doing his best, but I'm not quite sure these were the kind of tax breaks for hard-working families he had in mind in his budget. Still, Westminster is a law unto itself. And Miller has David Cameron's full backing. So she's probably safe. For now.

10 APRIL

Why *Frozen*'s 'Let It Go' is more than a Disney hit – it's an adolescent aperitif

DORIAN LYNSKEY

I don't yet know what my song of the year is, but I can tell you without hesitation what the song I've heard the most is, albeit not always in its recorded version: the Oscar-winning 'Let It Go'. Technically, the song from *Frozen* is sung by Broadway star Idina Menzel in the role of Elsa the Snow Queen, but as far as my seven-year-old daughter – who has been singing it several times a day for weeks – is concerned, it's hers.

Like the snow in *Frozen*, 'Let It Go' is everywhere, and it's not disappearing without a fight. It's the main reason why the *Frozen* soundtrack has been the number-one album in the US for nine weeks and counting – Beyoncé only managed three – and a significant reason why the film became the highest-grossing animated movie of all time. On YouTube, where it sits along-side countless amateur cover versions, spoofs, supercuts and fan-made videos, the 'Let It Go' sequence uploaded by Disney last December has attracted almost 180m views. Still, these mind-boggling statistics strike me less forcefully than my daughter's unprecedented obsession. To her, an older sister at an age where boys are beginning to become a source of intrigue rather than irritation, and conventional Disney princesses are a prissy drag, it's more than a song. It's a glimpse of the future, a vessel for secret knowledge.

Critics are often accused of overthinking mainstream hits, but the songs that outstrip all expectations (Disney didn't anticipate that Menzel's original would eclipse Demi Lovato's tamer pop version) always demand a closer look. One test of a truly great song is an ability to listen to it dozens of times without screaming. I'm not a musicologist, but anyone can understand why 'Let It Go' is a bravura piece of musical storytelling: the nervous minor chords of the first verse, jumping to an emphatic major key with the line 'Well now they know!'; the frantic, pulse-quickening syncopation of the bridge; the explosive leap of the chorus, mirrored in the animation's rapid ascent; and the final imperious shrug of 'The cold never bothered me anyway'. It's uncommonly fast for a power ballad, too – 137 beats per minute – which is why it's been recommended as a workout song and remixed, badly, into a club banger.

'Let It Go' is so undeniable that it changed the direction of the movie. When Kristen Anderson-Lopez and Robert Lopez were commissioned to write 'Elsa's Badass Song', the Snow Queen was a more conventional villain, but the song's emotional power forced a rethink. 'The minute we heard the song the first time, I knew that I had to rewrite the whole movie,' said director Jennifer Lee. That's pretty potent songwriting.

In the film, 'Let It Go' is a moment of dark irony. Elsa's liberation doesn't just mean lifelong solitude but eternal winter for everybody else – although she doesn't yet know it. Even before she realises the damage she's done, her excitement is gleefully irresponsible: 'No right, no wrong, no rules for me.' In one popular YouTube parody Elsa sings 'Fuck it all,' which is pretty much the gist of it. The viewer knows she's wrong but gets carried away anyway.

I think this is why the song is so addictive for girls a few years away from puberty, already chafing a little at the parental reins. It serves as an aperitif for adolescence. Elsa's leaving home and finding a place of her own (buck the house-price boom by building your own ice palace in minutes!), marking her rejection of social and familial pressure by swapping formal palace-wear for ice-minx couture.

Slate's movie critic Dana Stevens, who also has a *Frozen*-addicted daughter, has written about her 'familiar sense of deflation every time that pulse-racing song culminates in a vision of female self-actualisation as narrow and horizon-diminishing as a make-over'. Like her, I usually dislike the makeover trope, but here it's not designed to impress a man – it's purely for Elsa. And this sequence isn't a happy-ever-after resolution. It's a moment of transition and upheaval which conveys the giddy, reckless buzz of expressing yourself without considering the consequences. At such moments, teenage girls are not famed for acting like feminist paradigms. Disney's first movie without an unambiguous villain produces its first song to describe how young people really do behave rather than how they should behave.

I suspect girls like my daughter sense that the song's emotional landscape is adolescent – somewhere over the horizon, not yet visible, but faintly palpable. The Lopezes have said they were 'thinking from an emo kind of place', inspired by the likes of Aimee Mann and Adele, when they wrote it. And, as *Indiewire*'s Sam Adams notes, thrilling yet terrifying superhuman powers have been used as metaphors for hormonal uproar elsewhere, for example in *Carrie* and *X-Men*.

Outside the film, 'Let It Go' is also a coming-out anthem for lesbian, gay, bisexual and transgender people: 'Conceal, don't feel, don't let them know/ Well now they know!' The lines 'It's funny how some distance/ Makes everything seem small/ And the fears that once controlled me/ Can't get to me at all' could almost be from an It Gets Better video. 'I was really excited to write an anthem that said, "Screw fear and shame, be yourself, be powerful,"' said Anderson-Lopez.

The titles of various international versions speak volumes about the different potential emphases: 'Let Out Your Secret' (Arabic), 'Let It Be' (Estonian), 'Let Go and Forget' (Russian), 'Doesn't Matter' (Ukrainian), 'It Ends Now' (Serbian), 'I Have This Power' (Polish), 'I'm Free' (Portuguese), 'Freed, Released' (French) and, somewhat literally, 'Ice Heart Lock' (Cantonese). If Pharrell's 'Happy' can be weaponised as a protest song, I wouldn't be surprised if 'Let It Go' found its mutinous calling one day, studded as it is with the language of refusal: 'not', 'couldn't', 'can't' (twice), 'no' (three times), 'never' (four) and 'don't' (five).

To me, it means something else. Whenever I hear my daughter singing it, swept up in its vertiginous intensity, belting out the chorus as loudly as someone trying to call for help in a high wind, I feel a tiny premonition of loss. She doesn't know it yet, but some day she will rebel, fight for her independence, do brilliant things, do stupid things, learn about her power and the dangers of power, and what she'll be letting go of, as she should and must, is her parents.

15 APRIL

'Making the nation as one man': the birth of the BBC (extract)

CHARLOTTE HIGGINS

The manse on Lynedoch Street, Glasgow, is a handsome double-fronted house with nine steps up to its front door. It clings to the flank of its sandstone church, whose brace of tall, pencil-straight towers are linked by an elegant classical pediment. The manse –

which still exhales an air of four-square Victorian respectability – occupies the high ground above the green spaces of Kelvingrove Park, in which, before the first world war, its son John Reith would walk, feeling the winds of destiny brushing his cheek as they blew down from the Campsie Fells – or so he said. Even when a teenager, Reith, a very tall man, had a face with something of the Easter Island carving about it: graven, austere, immense-jawed. In the first world war, part of the left side of his face was blown off, leaving a jagged scar. As he aged, the dark bushy eyebrows became more wayward and independently active, the white hair wilder. There is footage of him being interviewed in 1967 by Malcolm Muggeridge. When the terrifying, wolfish smile comes, the face looks as if it has been forced open by a hammer and chisel.

The church has now been converted into the premises of an accountancy firm and a business consultancy, which would horrify the intensely religious Reith: in his youth it resounded to sermons given by his father George, a Free Presbyterian minister whom he worshipped second only to God: 'His sense of grace was apostolic; his sense of righteousness prophetic ... his eyes would flash; the eloquence of his indignation was devastating.'

The church 'was one of the wealthiest, most influential, most liberal in Scotland'. Its congregation ran the social scale from 'merchant princes, great industrialists, professors' to a 'considerable element of the humble but equally worthy sort'. Reith the younger was to outdo his father: his own congregation would consist of the whole population of Britain.

On 13 October 1922, having had a good war but in need of a job, Reith scanned the situations vacant. One advertisement read: 'The British Broadcasting Company (in formation). Applications are invited for the following officers: General Manager, Director of Programmes, Chief Engineer, Secretary. Only applicants having the first-class qualifications need apply. Applications to be addressed to Sir William Noble, Chairman of the Broadcasting Committee, Magnet House, Kingsway, WC2.' His interview consisted of 'a few superficial questions', he recalled in his memoir, *Into the Wind*. He added: 'I did not know what broadcasting was.'

He was duly appointed general manager, and for the next few days, still in utter ignorance of the nature of his new job, tried to 'bring every casual conversation round to "broadcasting"' until an acquaintance enlightened him. On 22 December 1922 he turned up at the offices (deserted, as it was a Saturday). He found 'a room about 30 foot by 15, furnished with three long tables and some chairs. A door at one end invited examination; a tiny compartment six foot square; here a table and a chair; also a telephone. "This," I thought, "is the general manager's office."' ('Little more than a cupboard,' remembered Peter Eckersley, the first chief engineer.) Including Reith, there were four members of staff.

The BBC today, with its workforce of 21,000 and its income of £5bn, is such an ineluctable part of British national life that it is hard to imagine its birth pangs, comparatively recent as they are. In only its 10th decade, the BBC looms larger in most of our daily lives than properly long-lived British institutions such as the monarchy, the army and the church. Its magical moving pictures, its sounds and words are not just 'content', but the tissue of our dreams, the warp and weft of our memories, the staging posts of our lives. The BBC is a portal to other worlds and lives, our own time machine; it brings the dead to life. Once a kindly auntie's voice in the corner of the room, it is now the demonic voice in our ear, a loving companion from which we need never be parted. It is our playmate, our instructor, our friend. Unlike Google and Amazon, which soothe us by presenting us with the past (their profferings predicated on our web 'history'), the BBC brings us ideas of which we have not yet dreamed, in a space free from the hectoring voices of those who would sell us goods. It tells seafarers when the gales will gust over Malin, Hebrides, Bailey. It brings us the news, and tries to tell it truthfully without fear or favour. It keeps company with the lonely; it brings succour to the isolated. Proverbially, when the bombs rain down, the captain of the last nuclear submarine will judge Britain ended when Radio 4 ceases to sound.

The year the BBC was born was also the year Northern Ireland seceded from the Free State; it was the year James Joyce's *Ulysses* was published; and its creation was sandwiched between the first general election in which women voted (1918) and universal suffrage (1928). The BBC took its place as an expression of, and a power in, new ideas about nationhood, modernity and democracy. With the coming of the BBC, it became possible for the first time in these islands' history for a geographically dispersed 'general public' to be able to experience the same events simultaneously.

Broadcasting knows no scarcity; it cannot run out: 'It does not matter how many thousands there may be listening; there is always enough for others,' as Reith put it in his 1924 book *Broadcast Over Britain*. Nor is it a respecter of persons: 'The genius and the fool, the wealthy and the poor listen simultaneously ... there is no first and third class.' Broadcasting, said Reith, had the effect of 'making the nation as one man'.

This is an extract from 'The BBC Report', Charlotte Higgins's nine-part series on the past, present and future of the BBC.

21 April

What would a 2014 Beveridge report say?

LARRY ELLIOTT

Five giants bar the road to progress: want, ignorance, idleness, disease and squalor. So said William Beveridge in the report commissioned by the wartime coalition published in 1942 which shaped the politics of postwar Britain, most especially the Attlee administration of 1945–51 but also the Conservative governments that followed.

Want was tackled through a cradle-to-grave welfare state; ignorance through the tripartite education system (grammar schools, secondary moderns and technical colleges); idleness through the commitment to full employment; disease via the creation of the NHS; and squalor through a programme of mass house-building and higher standards of provision.

Confronting the five giants remains the meat and drink of politics, as a quick flick through the *Observer* shows. 'Labour considers raising national insurance to fix £30bn NHS "black hole"', says one headline. 'Christian charity hits back over Tory attacks on food banks,' says another. A third referring to the mental health problems caused by flexible work patterns is headlined: 'Supermarket shifts "cause anxiety and insecurity"'.

So let's assume that a far-sighted government took the view that a new Beveridge report was needed in response to the problems thrown up by the Great Recession of 2008–09, just as the original was a response to the poverty and economic stagnation of the period between the first and second world wars. What would it say?

It would start by recognising that great progress has been made. Britain is a richer, healthier, better educated and more tolerant country than it was 70-odd years ago. Life expectancy has risen by well over a decade; university education is no longer for a tiny elite; incomes adjusted for inflation are four times higher than they were at the end of the second world war; the number of people in owner-occupation has more than doubled; people no longer live in substandard homes without baths and inside toilets.

But a new Beveridge would also say that there is still much wrong with Britain that needs to be put right. The life expectancy of someone born in Glasgow is 10 years lower than someone born in East Dorset; the UK is sliding down the league table of educational attainment; almost a million people are using food banks; almost four million families could not pay their rent or mortgage for more than one month if they lost their job.

Next, it would ask which of the five giants remain the most formidable barriers. Two are still alive and kicking, a third once assumed to have been slain could come back to life.

The dormant giant is disease. Spending on the NHS is 10 times higher than it was when it was founded; over the past 60 years the average increase in the budget for health has been just under 4 per cent. So while the ring-fencing of the NHS since 2010 looks generous against the deep cuts in, say, the Home Office or the Ministry of Justice, it represents the biggest squeeze on resources since 1948. This is against the backdrop of a population that is living longer and where technological advance means that prices in health care rise more rapidly than the cost of living generally. Britain loves the NHS and has no desire to move away from a free-at-the-point-of-use system. But unless the public is prepared to pay more, the quality of care will deteriorate. Labour's proposed solution is an increase in national insurance contributions specially designated for health and care costs.

That leaves the two giants that already loom large. The first of these is want, as is clear from the vigorous debate about living standards in the UK. Are they going up? Is there a cost-of-living crisis or not? Who is benefiting from a growing economy?

What's happened is this. In the past decade, pay rates have been historically low. Real pay was struggling to keep up with inflation even before the financial crisis of 2007, and has fallen sharply since. Wages buy 10 per cent less now than they did at their pre-recession peak.

Even now, it is questionable whether they are actually rising. The government's measure of average earnings is a mean. If pay increases are skewed to those in the better-paid jobs, the mean can increase while most workers' pay increases less quickly than inflation. Average earnings excluding bonuses (which tend to go to those on higher incomes) are rising by 1.3 per cent a year, which is still below the official inflation rate of 1.6 per cent.

Some increase in earnings is to be expected as the economy grows and unemployment comes down. But the structure of the labour market means that the pick-up in real pay growth will be slow and it is likely to take until the end of the decade – and perhaps longer – to get back to pre-recession levels.

It would not take a new Beveridge report long to find the reason for the squeeze on living standards: the imbalance of power in the workplace. Over the past 25 years, the trend has been towards an atomised and casualised workforce that has little or no bargaining power. The Britain of today is a land of secure workers on good incomes but also of gangmasters, zero-hours contracts, domestic servants and the self-employed scratching a living. Under the Labour government of 1997–2010, tax credits were used to top up low pay, but austerity means they have become less generous. There are now more people in poverty who are in work than there are who are workless.

Unless the state is willing to act as the guarantor of a living wage through the tax-and-benefit system, there are only two possible outcomes. One is that the labour share of national income will continue to fall, leading either to a reduction in aggregate demand and/or higher indebtedness. The other is that the bargaining power of labour is increased through full employment, stronger trade unions and collective bargaining.

The other giant is housing. Owner-occupation, which rose steadily in the 20th century, is in decline. House-price inflation coupled with low earnings growth means that a quarter of young people aged between 20 and 34 live with their parents. In the more prosperous parts of Britain, there is a mismatch between housing supply and demand.

This is not a new problem. A decade ago, the report prepared by Kate Barker for Gordon Brown said 210,000 new homes a year were needed in England to avert a housing crisis. Since then 115,000 homes a year have been built.

Result? A housing crisis, for which the only solutions are a successful regional policy that moves people to where the empty homes are, or builds lots more houses where the jobs are.

The final thing the new Beveridge would say is this: cracks can only be papered over for so long. In all the key areas – the NHS, living standards and housing – it is time for action.

24 APRIL

Nigel Farage: a pustule of resentment on the body politic

SUZANNE MOORE

There is for ever an England where Ukip is nothing more than a joke on Twitter, the *Daily Mail* is something that no one you know actually reads, where Christianity is a misguided thought process, where everyone understands that taxation is absolutely the right price to pay for the things we value. Maybe you live in that England. Lucky you. I visit it, of course, but I don't come from it. My family were that not-so-rare breed, working-class Tories. Turkeys not only vote for Christmas, I soon realised, they enthusiastically talk about the various ways in which they will be stuffed, every day of the week.

So I was very young when I understood that simply telling people that they are stupid and wrong does not make them suddenly embrace socialism. Nor is everything easily divisible into right and left. Right now it is 'ordinary people' versus the 'trendy metropolitan elite' (people who live in London and enjoy a wide range of dining opportunities).

The reality is, of course, not so simple. While everyone claims to speak for 'ordinary people', many of our institutions do not speak to them. The right is honest about its condescension – we are governed by those born to rule – but the certainties of a left-wing mindset can be equally patronising. How often do I hear the opinion that if someone votes for a different party, or reads a different newspaper or doesn't like a particular comedian, then they are basically a terrible person? Actually, quite a lot.

Parts of the left have always mystified me, as they seek to represent those they so obviously despise. It is not spelled out, it's implicit. Thus we have to import a spadtastic American such as David Axelrod for Labour to explain itself to 'ordinary people'. Something has gone wrong here.

It is this gap between Little England and Big England that Nigel Farage exploits so well. He and his ever-changing cast of semi-barking compadres are not simply a joke. Labour has been complacent in thinking Ukip could simply split the Tory vote – it also appeals to Labour punters. Once you get to Kent or East Anglia, Farage is not so funny. He can present himself as a rebel with a cause because people feel very insecure, economically and emotionally. Change has come too fast and furious for many. To voice this is not inherently racist and yet for every problem to be blamed on Europe and immigration is ridiculously simplistic.

What Farage taps into is this sense of people not feeling in control of their own lives, of rules being made elsewhere, of things not being fair. He even rebuts the logic of the market, ignoring the fact that Europe is our biggest trading partner.

All these sentiments should be the natural territory of the left, not the right. In simple terms, ordinary people feel they have no power; in jargon, a neoliberal agenda is concentrating wealth at the very top and all the main parties are signed up to this, as though this agenda is a natural, not a man-made force. All across Europe, such alienation combined with nationalism fuels the right. It is dangerous.

If the left is to be meaningful it has to speak both to and about this alienation. But politicians are loath to do so as it would mean admitting they are not in full control. Instead, figures such as Farage pop up as pustules of resentment on the body politic. His discourse is emotional, angry, unanchored, which is why Clegg's mannered reasonableness and narcoleptic intoning of facts and figures was fairly useless against it.

The difference between the language of a managerial political class and the way that many people speak is huge. Half-hearted visions need to be translated into robotic nonsense such as the 'squeezed middle'. Phrases have to be invented, as there are not enough words to convey the passions of Cameron or Miliband. Where there cannot even be a common language, there is no way of expressing common interests. We are linguistically divided.

This is about more than great oratory; it is about a kind of fear. The unmediated voices of ordinary people are a worry for every part of the establishment, including much of the media. They say the wrong things. They are ignorant of what is important. They are overemotional. They can only appear on Radio 4, for instance, in oddly written dramas or asking experts about pensions. They remain unheard. Even social media serves mainly to amplify the already powerful.

So it is easy for Farage to play the underdog, the ventriloquist of pub wisdom, the ordinary bloke. And it is significant that the most strident criticism of the Ukip posters has come from the military, who do not want the flag messed around with. This is potent imagery and we should not be dainty about it.

To tackle this stuff head-on we must do so in the same language of morality. What is right, wrong and fair. For it is completely out of touch to say Farage has lowered the tone of political debate. This tone was already there. One would have had to have tin ears never to have heard it. Or perhaps never stepped outside of the real Little England, the one that seeks to represent ordinary people without ever talking to them.

3 MAY

Max Clifford: the rise and fall of the UK's king of spin

SIMON HATTENSTONE

A few weeks before the Max Clifford case came to court, I visited him at his home in Surrey. The *Guardian* hoped to make a film about his trial, to be shown at its conclusion, but he declined the request on the grounds that he wasn't the emotional type and wouldn't provide the tears and tantrums he thought we wanted. He gave a pacy run-through of the charges he faced: 11 counts of indecent assault against seven teenage girls, aged 14 to 19, between 1966 and 1984. They were all rubbish, he said. It was obvious from one woman's description of his office that she had never been there; another said that he had abused her in his car at a time when he had no car and hadn't even learned to drive ... And on it went.

There could be only one motive, he thought: the promise of publicity and money. After all, nobody understood the world of kiss-and-tell better than he did. As far as he was concerned, it wasn't a question of *if* he got cleared, but when. And when he was, boy, was he going to give Operation Yewtree – the police investigation into historic sex offences committed by Jimmy Savile and others – a piece of his mind.

Clifford's house, on a private road in Hersham, was so pristine; it looked like a show home. He showed me the outdoor heated swimming pool where he swims every day, introduced me to his housekeeper (he was taking her for dinner that evening to celebrate her birthday). He was rough-hewn charm itself. His second wife and former PA, Jo Westwood, was 'away in the country'.

Halfway through our two-hour meeting, his phone rang. It always rings in meetings with him, partly because he is a busy man and partly because it gives him a chance to show off. It's normally Simon (Cowell) or Kerry (Katona) or Louis (Walsh), calling for advice. (There is no way of knowing if it really *is* Simon or Kerry or Louis, short of snatching the phone from him.) 'Don't thank me, thank Beyoncé. Yes, darling, it's a pleasure. Yes, of course, darling, I'll tell Beyoncé how grateful you are.' He got off the phone and resumed our conversation as if nothing had happened.

'What was all that about Beyoncé?' I asked.

'Oh, nothing,' he said. This was classic Clifford: keep them hungry. When pressed, he explained that he'd helped the woman caller out financially. So what did it have to do with Beyoncé? 'Well, I've just been paid by Beyoncé for some work I've done for her, and I used some of that to help this lady.'

But Beyoncé doesn't know anything about it? 'No, of course not. But it makes her feel good to think it came from Beyoncé. And where's the harm in that?'

Clifford seemed resilient. But then he started to talk about the £1m-plus he had lost since his arrest, as the clients tailed off, and how he had learned to distinguish between true friends and the phoneys. He talked about the various charities of which he is patron – the children's hospices and cancer hospitals – and showed genuine emotion as he explained they had asked him to keep his distance until the trial was over. Nothing personal, you understand.

He quickly gathered himself before giving me a lift to the station in his silver Rolls-Royce Ghost (registration number 100 MAX). There was one thing I felt confident of: this was an Operation Yewtree fishing expedition – for all his lies and braggadocio, Max Clifford was an innocent man.

And then the trial started. As witnesses came forward by the dozen to give evidence at Southwark crown court, the pugnacious, barrel-chested bullyboy of the PR industry started to look like an old man. His jackets were spotless, his shoes shined, his sense of outrage was obvious, and yet he often seemed defeated – shuffling into court, shaking his head, wearing a hearing loop that looked like a dog collar (at the end of one morning, he admitted he had struggled to hear any of the evidence). As the weeks went by, he stopped stifling his huge yawns as the case was made against him.

The trial ranged from Greek tragedy to *Carry On* farce. At times, it felt too strange to be true – or, as the prosecution argued, too strange not to be true. Max's Angels, as Clifford's all-female office team are known, attended on a shift basis, one at a time, sitting loyally in the public gallery as their boss was labelled an exhibitionist and an abuser. They were joined by a handful of civilians (largely retired, portly men), there on a regular basis to enjoy the spectacle. Occasionally, eccentrics walked into court: one man took umbrage when asked by the clerk to stop filming; a drunk woman sidled up to me and whispered that she had a story to sell. The air fizzed with schadenfreude.

In the dock, we saw Clifford's many sides: the loving father who straightened his back when his daughter Louise came to give evidence, giving her a don't-worry-about-me smile; the caged jaguar, prowling the dock impatiently before the day began; the belligerent victim who turned his head to stare out one hostile witness as he left court; the irrepressible chancer winking at old friends who provided good character witness statements.

Most of the women who testified against him were around 50, well-spoken and eerily similar: immaculate long hair, beautifully turned out, the air of former models. Their stories provided intricate Venn diagrams of overlapping evidence. All had been teenagers when Clifford told them he could arrange for them to meet the Walker Brothers, or star in *Dynasty*, or in films with Charles Bronson and David Bowie, or in the James Bond film

Octopussy. We heard from women who said they had visited Clifford in his office, then been sent out to receive calls purportedly from James Bond producer Cubby Broccoli, or Bronson, or *Dynasty* producer Aaron Spelling – all of whom appeared to be a poorly-disguised Clifford. Two women said they had been phoned by a man with an effeminate voice called Terry Denton. One girl was told by 'Denton' that he didn't like Clifford, and could she find out whether it was true that he had a small penis? Another was told Denton was jealous of her because he fancied Clifford and was sure the publicist would make her a star. Clifford admitted he had used the name Terry Denton (a late friend) as a means of testing potential clients' trustworthiness. We heard from women who said they were abused in his office, in toilets, in his car, in a cab, on holiday in a Jacuzzi.

Clifford's barrister, Richard Horwell, ripped into these complainants with steely eloquence. He pointed out their inconsistencies with theatrical relish: the woman who claimed to have been abused in Clifford's office, yet described a room that bore no resemblance to 109 New Bond Street; the witness who claimed Clifford had encouraged her to go for a part in *Octopussy* two years after the film came out; the woman who said she was abused in Torremolinos when he wasn't there. The evidence, Horwell suggested, was unreliable at best, dishonest at worst.

Then Horwell pulled out his trump card: Clifford's penis. He reeled off the contradictory evidence: it was tiny, two and a half inches erect, according to some; according to another complainant, it was huge. In fact, Horwell argued, it was average, at five and a quarter inches flaccid. This bombshell was introduced with a Cliffordian flourish: the PR man's perfectly ordinary penis had been measured by a medical expert called Dr Coxon.

There were other moments of manic humour. The witness who described Clifford's penis as huge rationalised her apparently contradictory evidence by pointing out that she had a small mouth: 'My dentist always said so.' At which point the jury had to be temporarily dismissed for giggling. There was the defence witness who constantly referred to him as Sir Max and believed he was the editor of the *Daily Mail*; when told he didn't have a knighthood, she said she was just being respectful. Clifford himself was sometimes deliberately funny (when talking about his education through Diana Dors sex parties), sometimes unwittingly so ('Why would I need to name-drop when I represented the Beatles?'). The penis evidence was vital, Horwell argued, because it showed that the complainants had never seen it. Prosecution barrister Rosina Cottage counterargued that size was in the eye of the beholder – and anyway, it wasn't the size of Clifford's penis that mattered, but what he did with it.

This was courtroom drama at its finest: two contrasting QCs at the top of their game – the calm, meticulous Cottage stitching together disturbing patterns of behaviour; the waspish Horwell playing to the gallery. Cottage labelled Clifford a 'master in the art of intimidation', who used his celebrity connections to 'bully and manipulate' young women, treating his office as his 'sexual fiefdom'.

Horwell rubbished this. He said he'd hand his wig to any member of the jury who could make sense of one particular scenario, and rejected some allegations as 'grubby voyeurism ... fifth-rate fiction not even Mills & Boon would countenance'. The reasons most of the women had given for not fighting back or going to the police at the time (they were scared, or shocked, or naive) were an insult to women the world over, he said: 'Women *are* not stupid, *were* not stupid.' Cottage's approach, he suggested, had been to 'speculate like mad and hope the jury buy it'.

This case was about more than the fall of one man. Barely two miles away, at the Old Bailey, two former *News of the World* editors were on trial, accused of conspiracy to hack phones. Clifford had fed the *News of the World* and other tabloids many of their larger-than-life stories: 'Commons call girl' Pamella Bordes dishing the dirt on Conservative minister for sport Colin Moynihan in 1989; actress Antonia de Sancha getting her revenge on Tory national heritage minister David Mellor (in his Chelsea strip) in 1992; Rebecca Loos settling a score with David Beckham in 2004. For decades, Clifford (and the red-tops) thrived on a cocktail of sport, sleaze and scoops. (The Old Bailey has heard that News International offered Clifford a £200,000-a-year retainer to represent the *Sun* in exchange for him calling off his lawyers in a phone-hacking civil claim.) Between Southwark and the Old Bailey, were we witnessing the death rattle of an era, of the kiss-and-tell, the 'cheeky' sexism that runs through tabloid and entertainment culture – from Page 3 to the 'old-school misogyny' Rebekah Brooks detailed in her evidence?

This was also a vital case for the Crown Prosecution Service, after a number of trials for historic sexual abuse had collapsed. *Coronation Street* actors Bill Roache and Michael Le Vell were cleared of sexual abuse charges including rape, as was Conservative MP Nigel Evans. It was an important case for Operation Yewtree in particular, after a series of high-profile arrests had resulted in discharge. In February, Dave Lee Travis was found not guilty on 12 charges of indecent assault – though later this month he will stand trial again, after the jury failed to reach a verdict on two charges; he also faces one new charge of indecent assault. Had Clifford been cleared this week, more questions would have been asked about the wisdom and practicality of prosecuting alleged assaults going back decades.

At times over the past year, it has felt as if a whole generation of minor celebrities are being tried for the sins of Savile, who is believed to have committed hundreds of sexual crimes in his life-time without facing a single charge. Are these cases laying down a marker for the future by convicting old men for behaviour once commonplace? (Most of the claims against Travis were for groping.) Yet many of the alleged offences were far more serious.

I first met Max Clifford in 2001, at his New Bond Street office, where I interviewed Ted Francis, the man whose evidence helped jail Jeffrey Archer. Francis had provided a false alibi for Archer in 1986, used as evidence that he hadn't been with a prostitute; 13 years later, with Clifford's help, Francis went to the *News of the World* to admit he had lied. (He claimed he had not known the alibi was intended for use in court, and was cleared of perverting the course of justice.) Francis was a foolish, rather sad man, and Clifford felt protective towards him. But he didn't sit in on the interview, and didn't suggest what I should write, as many publicists do. This was the kind of story with which Clifford liked to associate himself: broadsheet-worthy, with political resonance, giving Clifford a certain gravitas.

We next met a year later, when I interviewed Simon Cowell at the same offices. Clifford was his publicist – or svengali, as he would have liked us to believe. Cowell was already famous for *Pop Idol*, but nowhere near as famous as he would go on to be. Back then, he obediently turned up for interviews at Clifford's office, lifted his top to show his high trousers and hairy stomach, while Clifford watched on proudly and told me that his main job was keeping Cowell out of the papers. When Cowell was asked by Piers Morgan on the television series *Tabloid Tales* for the best career decision of his life, he replied, 'Hiring Max Clifford.'

For years, Clifford had a prurient finger in every pie, from footballers' wives to royal affairs. In his memoir, he wrote that he had been hired by James Hewitt to keep him and Princess Diana out of the papers, before casually claiming Hewitt had confided in him that their affair had started two years before the birth of Prince Harry. Clifford often claimed there was a higher purpose to his sex scoops: for instance, his revelations about Conservative MPs in the 90s exposed the hypocrisy of John Major's family-values campaign, and helped bring down the government.

In 2002, I had arranged to interview the film-maker Louis Theroux. I wanted to follow him around as he worked, but he insisted on a formal meeting at his office. I knew Theroux was making a programme about Clifford, so I phoned Clifford's office and asked if I could meet up with him when Theroux was filming. A few days later I received a call: could I meet Max at Sainsbury's in Surbiton? Not long after I got there, I walked into him being followed by Theroux and his camera crew.

Theroux was irritated and the whole episode ended in farce, but it was typical Clifford: generous, manipulative, keen to impress me, keen to get one over on everybody.

The next time we met was almost a decade later, when I interviewed his new client Mark Kennedy, the police officer who had infiltrated a group of environmental activists and been exposed for having long-term relationships while undercover. Clifford was in clover: he knew it was a great broadsheet story – one that brought the integrity of the Metropolitan police into question and caused political embarrassment, and one that had sex at its heart. There was a camera crew in his tiny office, and Clifford bossed the room. But after a couple of hours he told us it was time to leave. 'Right, that's enough. You can all fuck off now.'

Maxwell Frank Clifford was born in Kingston upon Thames, Surrey, in 1943, the youngest by nearly 10 years of four children – a war baby and a 'mistake'. His father worked as an electrician and gambled away the family money. His mother was a huge, loving presence. Nobody tells the Clifford tale better than he does. How he left school at 15 with no qualifications; got sacked from his first job as an apprentice salesman at Elys department store in Wimbledon, for being rude to a customer; how his printer brother used his trade-union contacts to get him a job as an editorial assistant on the *Eagle* comic. By 18, he was a trainee reporter and writing a music column for the *Merton & Morden News*. He loved the music industry – the celebs, the glamour, being at the hub of happening London. He also loved journalism: he keeps his NUJ life membership certificate on the mantelpiece, awarded for 40 years' continuous service in the trade union.

He was headhunted by EMI in 1962 to work in the press office, and likes to tell the story of how he was given an unknown band to work with for six months. But even Clifford admits he had little to do with the Beatles' subsequent success. In 1970, he formed his own company, Max Clifford Associates, and before long had rewritten the rules of public relations, not only providing stories, but often making them up. In court, Cottage referred to him as a ringmaster and control freak – the very words he'd used to describe himself in his revealing and ultimately self-incriminating autobiography, *Read All About It*.

The book was meat and drink for the prosecution. Was he a sex-obsessed philanderer? 'I was too greedy to be faithful,' he wrote. 'Almost anything went, including having two girls at a time. Having sex with girlfriends' mothers and watching others have sex.'

Clifford admitted to the jury that he'd had four long-term relationships while married to his first wife; as for the sex parties, he claimed to be just an obliging host. His book told it differently: 'I became the ringmaster, a role I liked to have in many aspects of my life ... The parties became my circus and various people performed in different ways.'

Did he promise girls success in exchange for sex? 'Often they were both beautiful and randy, and because some of the male guests were TV and film producers, they saw the parties as a way of getting an Equity card ... Fortunately I knew one or two agents who would issue false contracts in return for sexual favours,' he wrote. Did he lie to the girls about who some of the men were? 'Sometimes I'd invite a mate along as a treat. One was a plumber, but I pretended to the girls at the party that he was a film producer. I made sure he had a wonderful time with a couple of them who thought they might get a part in his next film.'

At times, he portrays himself as running a protection racket – keeping stories out of the news by making the victim of an exposé pay the girls more than they would get from the papers; or getting one man so drunk that Clifford was able to replace the woman in his bed with a man, then film it and tell him he had been with an underage teenager. At other times, he comes across as a pimp: 'Sexual procuring has never bothered me as long as the people involved have been old enough to know what they're doing.' As for the specialist tastes of some clients, *Read All About It* boasts that he provided a safe environment in which they could indulge their perversions.

In court, Clifford insisted he would never exploit women sexually, or take photographs of them topless for a kick. But again his memoir tells a different story, boasting of a bet he had with Freddie Starr (another Operation Yewtree arrest) that he could make the first woman he stopped in the street come to his office and agree to a revealing photo; he won when a traffic warden happily took off her top and told him she wanted a career in TV. For Clifford, these were dares and pranks.

He also wrote of his contempt for paedophiles. He said of Jonathan King, 'I'm delighted to have played a small part in his arrest and trial. I even have a letter from the Surrey chief of police thanking me for my help in bringing him to justice. King and Glitter are typical paedophiles, manipulative and arrogant. Their arrogance is necessary for them to squash their guilty conscience. And they need to be manipulative to undermine their victims. The only difference between them and other paedophiles is that they like the spotlight, whereas most prefer to stay hidden away.'

In 2011 I interviewed Clifford. He said he had never discussed the affairs or sex parties with his first wife, Liz. He had found it easy to get away with them because of his job and his lifestyle. He said he had always loved sport, and considered sex another sport, admitting it was not so much him that women found irresistible as his power. 'Not only was I in the sweet shop, I owned it ... For 30-odd years I was making people famous, looking after stars, going to the most glamorous places in the world, so the Hunchback of Notre Dame would have been incredibly successful sexually.'

It was a Friday evening, and Clifford was meeting his daughter Louise for a charity do. As he stood up at the end of the interview, his trousers fell down, revealing a pair of sparkling white pants. He had sat behind his desk with his trousers unzipped and unbuttoned throughout. In court, Cottage repeatedly made the point that his office was his 'sexual fiefdom'. I'm pretty sure it wasn't that day – it was just his fiefdom. But he saw no reason why he shouldn't sit there comfortably unbuckled.

If the tabloids were ever to do him over, I asked then, what would be the worst thing they could say about him? 'Well, they can't say I'm alcoholic because I don't drink.' He paused, before finally saying: 'They might have said I'm perverted because of a lot of the things I got up to.'

For all the unintentional hilarity, there was a sadness at the heart of Clifford's trial. For decades, he'd had the Midas touch when it came to muck-raking; now everything he touched turned to dirt. Witnesses called him a 'repulsive geek', and remembered his bad breath, his desperate fumblings, his diminished manhood.

Many of the witnesses he called to his defence failed him. The brother Clifford said had taught him to drive couldn't remember doing so. The pop-flop singer who had won *New Faces* gave an initial statement saying that they were on holiday together in Spain at a time that potentially incriminated Clifford. He then said he had got the month wrong. When it was suggested by the crown that he was lying to help Clifford, he said he wouldn't lie, couldn't lie, and if Clifford had done any of these things, he deserved everything coming his way. A former PA (and lover) remembered the yellow Jaguar that Clifford had such trouble recalling, and in which he was alleged to have abused one of the complainants. They were trying their best, but no one could tell Clifford's story as convincingly as he could.

Saddest of all was his daughter Louise, now 41, in the witness box. A young girl who suffered debilitating juvenile arthritis, she had belatedly taken herself off to university to get a degree and ended up working alongside her father. She told the jury what a wonderful father he had been, how he and her mother had had a great relationship, despite the affairs, how many sacrifices he had made for her. Yet even Louise's evidence was called into question: she insisted that she had only ever visited a Jacuzzi in Spain – where Clifford was accused of abusing a 12-year-old girl – with her parents, only to be contradicted by the Jacuzzi boss, who said Louise had sometimes taken friends. (The case was not among the charges, because the alleged incident happened abroad.) After giving evidence, Louise turned up most days to support her father from the public gallery. Clifford's wife, Jo, remained conspicuous by her absence.

One day, a member of Clifford's staff rang me. 'How do you think it's going?' she asked. I told her I thought it could go either way. She sounded disheartened. 'Do you really think I'd have spent six years working for a pervert?' She said they were stressful times. 'All our livelihoods are at stake.'

At the start of the trial, Horwell had said we would hear from a number of Clifford's famous friends, and warned that the defence had no intention of turning the trial into a celebrity circus. They were as good as their word. They called car experts, arthritis experts, penis experts, and still we waited for the celebrities. Clifford had been well and truly abandoned – there was not so much as a whisper of a guest appearance from Simon Cowell. Who did that leave Clifford to call on?

In the end, actress Pauline Quirke and singer Des O'Connor came forward to vouch for him. Both knew him through charity work and as friends, and said he was utterly trustworthy, a good man who loved to help others. We heard from numerous people who talked about his charity work, as if altruism and indecent assault were mutually exclusive. Even here, Clifford had lost his touch: when we were told how 'he makes dreams come true for the children', it was impossible not to think of Jimmy Savile.

Occasionally, Clifford would try to assert his former authority with journalists. One day he popped into the waiting area to tell us, strictly off the record, why one of the jurors had been dismissed. Another time, after giving evidence about his sex parties, he poked his head in to jokingly ask a couple of female journalists if they were free that night. When he saw me standing near the women's toilet, he benignly threatened, 'You look dodgy, Simon. You're loitering. I'm going to get one of the journalists to write up a piece on you. From the *Independent*.' Yes, it was a joke, but it all felt so inappropriate, as if he had forgotten where he was and what he was being tried for. Much of the time, he didn't have the energy or will to put up a front. Waves of tension rippled through his back as he sat in the dock. At times he was breathing so heavily, you feared he might have a heart attack.

The most powerful witness was the woman who gave evidence from behind a screen, the first complainant who had come forward. She said she had met Clifford on holiday with her family when she was 15, and claimed to have been groomed by him. Her evidence was quietly convincing, as she related Clifford's befriending of her parents, his claim that she could be the new Jodie Foster, the way he told her to take off her top in his office, took her on trips in his yellow Jaguar and sexually assaulted her. When Clifford told her that a photographer had hidden in a bush and snatched photographs of her performing a sex act on him – 'so close he could see your freckles' – and that the photographer was now threatening to publish, she said she became suicidal. Clifford told her he was doing his best to protect her. Most haunting of all was an anonymous letter the complainant had written to Clifford three years ago – significantly, before Savile's crimes came to light. The letter – calm, detailed, despairing – was read out in court by Cottage:

I wondered if you remembered as I do the child sexual abuse you engaged in, befriending my parents, flattering their daughter, talking of an acting/modelling career, offices near Bond Street. They were impressed even though no one had heard of you. Conversations about your friend Tommy Steele – wasn't it squash you played? Julie Christie and the new *Star Wars* film that was soon to hit the cinema. Lots of famous names, places and yet still down to earth. A local lad done good. Recommending restaurants, funny stories, little secrets you fed them to gain their trust.

The abuse started in your office. You sat behind your desk, eventually persuading me to strip, convincing me that my protesting was ridiculous and very childish. 'Don't you want to be grown up?'

You took pleasure in degrading me, visiting me at home, taking me out to meet fictitious people, abusing me instead and returning me with a story so my parents didn't become suspicious. Names of people we had met, places we had been to, so they would be fooled that their daughter was in safe hands and not those of a paedophile. A+ in grooming children. How proud you must be.

What chance did I have? You made my life a living hell, up until the point when I even contemplated suicide.

You repulsed me then as you do now, wearing the mask of someone who has values, hiding behind charity work, trying to cleanse yourself of the guilt you must feel perhaps and stating that you don't have sympathy for paedophiles.

You say you can't bear hypocrisy and that is what spurs you on, when you yourself are a hypocrite worse than any of those you seek to shame. A paedophile who publicly condemns other paedophiles to divert attention. A double bluff ...

Part of the reason I'm writing to you is that my counsellor has recommended it as part of my therapy. I'm undecided how much it will help or where we go from here.

When the police searched Clifford's house after the woman made a complaint, the letter was found in his bedside drawer. Unsurprisingly, the prosecution suggested that this was significant. Clifford told the jury he had shown the letter to both Louise and his wife (who, it emerged in court, had secretly made a photocopy of it). If he'd had anything to hide, he said, he would have destroyed the letter. He kept it because he thought it might be a precursor to blackmail.

He had a point. Even the victim's therapist had told her the letter's conclusion might read like a threat. But she never did blackmail him. Instead, a couple of years later, she went to the police. Her parents had recently died and this was a factor in her coming forward – she had been ashamed of what had happened, and did not want to hurt them. Clifford said he thought it was a 'tragic' letter, but dismissed it as having been written by somebody who was disturbed.

By now the trial was taking its toll on everybody. The jury was already down to 11 (one member had been dismissed because she knew the casting director of *Octopussy*), when another juror abruptly announced in court that she would definitely take Judge Anthony Leonard's directions seriously. It was a strange outburst – was she ridiculing him or just being friendly? Two days were lost when the juror went sick before being dismissed.

Meanwhile, Clifford's Angels were looking increasingly worn. One shook her head even more vigorously than Clifford as the judge summed up. Louise looked inconsolable. When the court closed for Easter, I wished her a good holiday. She looked at me as if she couldn't quite believe what I had said.

Clifford was also getting nervous. In the canteen, he bit his nails as his friends talked around him. He was overheard on the phone saying, 'I'm hoping for the best and preparing for the worst.' By the time we left for Easter, he had recovered his colour. I passed him as he was stepping into the lift with a big silver-haired man. Clifford stopped the lift to address me.

'Simon, if you really want a scoop, you ought to do something on this fella. You could investigate him. He's the one who holds the Ukip Christmas party.'

It turned out to be Richard Hunt, who had indeed hosted the 'Ukip Christmas ball' at his Hampshire home. (Despite calling himself a lifelong socialist, Clifford had done work for Ukip, claiming he made them electable.) For a moment, he seemed to be the old Clifford, insouciant, embarrassing, showing off that he could still throw me the bone of a story.

A week later, and the jury was still sitting. With the verdict sweepstake long done and conversation exhausted, journalists were quietly losing it in the press room. *Sun* reporter Chris Pollard had started a Clifford Fashion Watch to keep himself amused. The member of staff who had told me she would not have spent six years working for a pervert said she was stressed: 'I'm beginning to fear the worst of all options – a hung jury and a retrial.' She just wanted it over, one way or another.

Only Clifford looked as if he was thriving. The longer the jury deliberated, the more he returned to his old ebullient self. As I left court on Friday last week, with no decision in sight, he called out, 'Oi, Simon, you've been here every day for seven weeks and you've not written a word. Some job that is. I buy my *Guardian* every day, and not a word.'

It was on Monday during the lunch break that everybody was recalled to court. We'd already had one false alarm that day – when the jury accidentally pressed the light used to confirm they had reached a verdict, only to announce that they needed a cigarette break. This time round, the clerk told us they were just back for a point of information. In fact, Judge Leonard announced that the jury had reached a decision on all but one count – and that was enough for him. By now the court was full, tense and airless.

Louise was dressed all in black as if preparing for the worst. Clifford wore a royal-blue sports jacket with gold buttons. The clerk asked the head of the jury for the verdict on each of the 11 counts of indecent assault. Count one – no decision. Count two – not guilty. We could see the way this was going.

Then came the four counts of indecent assault on the 15-year-old victim who had written the anonymous letter. Guilty. Guilty. Guilty. Guilty. There was no expression on Clifford's face as the first few guilty verdicts were announced. Then he inflated his cheeks and released his breath slowly.

He was found guilty on eight of the 11 counts. Judge Leonard addressed him in a brusque manner we had not seen before: 'Mr Clifford, stand up.' He told him sentencing would be delayed until Friday; he was being granted bail but that was no indication that he would not go to jail.

As Clifford walked out, he put his arm around Louise's shoulders. It looked as if he needed the help, not her. Only then did the significance begin to sink in. The King of Spin was no more. Maybe Clifford will appeal, but whatever happens his reputation is in tatters. Britain's best-known publicist is likely to be remembered as an abuser and a groomer. Meanwhile, Operation Yewtree is celebrating its first significant victory. What once looked like little more than a trawl of half-forgotten gropers from long ago had successfully prosecuted serious sexual abuse.

Doubtless in prison Clifford will hand out pearls of wisdom to his fellow inmates, do deals, make friends and influence people. But public relations will never be the same in the UK – and nor will the red-top press.

It's a world that was changing even before he was sent down. Post-hacking, post-*News of the World*, with pressure on the press to rein in its excesses, kiss-and-tell is never going to be what it once was. Perhaps there was an inevitability about Clifford's fall. Live by the sleaze, die by the sleaze.

Outside court, Clifford posed for the cameras with Louise. She raised her head to the sky, her eyes shut. 'Max, will you appeal?' shouted the reporters. 'Max, you said it was a witch-hunt, do you still feel like that?' 'Max, have you anything to say to the women?' 'Max, is it time to say sorry?'

For once, the man who prided himself on always having the perfect soundbite to hand had nothing to say.

Clifford was sentenced to eight years in prison on Friday 2 May.

7 MAY

Review: Miley Cyrus – loud, lewd, but still laudable

ALEXIS PETRIDIS

Miley Cyrus's *Bangerz* tour arrives in London trailing in its wake precisely the kind of spluttering outrage that's marked pretty much every turn in the 21-year-old singer's career over the last year or so.

Horrified accounts from the US leg of the tour described the former Disney poppet taking the stage in a costume apparently made entirely of marijuana leaves and pretending to fellate a man wearing a Bill Clinton mask. The latter reference to a decades-old sex scandal rather raises the question of which piping-hot political controversy the singer might address next: Watergate? The 1971 Industrial Relations Act? The repeal of the Corn Law?

In a sense, the outrage Cyrus has caused feels a little confusing. She's not really doing anything that hasn't been done before: virtually every former squeaky-clean teen star, regardless of their sex, seems to find it necessary to clangingly broadcast that they're now an adult and in possession of a set of fully-functioning genitals sooner or later.

That said, as tonight's show amply proves, few of them have been quite as relentless about it as Cyrus. She takes the stage sliding down a huge tongue, then variously spanks her backing dancer's buttocks, pretends to masturbate, addresses the audience as 'you bunch of fucking sluts', appears in a black-and-white film naked, with a bunch of roses sticking out of her bum, and yanks at the crotch of her bodysuit as if trying to give herself a wedgie. Watching it feels a bit like being repeatedly bludgeoned over the head, and just as erotic.

But that's not to say Cyrus's live show isn't entertaining. Quite the opposite: it's so gleefully, dementedly, cartoonishly vulgar that it's almost impossible not to be entertained.

Other stadium-sized pop artists tend to try to signpost their maturity with arty films or clanging visual references to Warhol: Cyrus dances onstage with a pantomime horse. The recent death of her beloved dog Floyd is commemorated by a 30-foot statue of a dog being lowered on to the stage: it shoots lasers out of its eyes. The ballads are seldom the high point of a huge pop show, but in Cyrus's case, a degree of interest is added by the fact that she sings one of them while being pursued around the stage, for reasons that aren't entirely clear, by a giant fluorescent-orange fluffy bird.

A cynical observer might suggest that all this detracts attention from the music, and a cynical observer might have a point. At her best – 'Wrecking Ball', 'Can't Be Tamed' – Cyrus's brand of production-line pop is pretty fizzy, but live it invariably seems secondary to the visual chaos.

That said, an acoustic section highlights the more straightforward Nashville entertainer she might have chosen to become. 'Do y'all like Bob Dylan?' she asks. The ensuing silence suggests she may have sorely overestimated the average Miley Cyrus fan's familiarity with *Highway 61 Revisited* and *The Basement Tapes*, but her version of 'You're Gonna Make Me Lonesome When You Go' shows off her voice – more earthy and interesting than your average manufactured pop starlet – to considerable effect.

Then she sings Dolly Parton's 'Jolene', altering the words so they're laden with expletives, having the time of her life. The audience roar their approval and you can see why: better this – shambolic, tasteless, childish and occasionally baffling as it is – than a perfectly choreographed, antiseptic pop show.

15 MAY

Chibok: the village that lost its daughters to Boko Haram

CHIKA ODUAH

Asabe Kwambura is getting tired of waiting. Sitting under a young mango tree alongside the charred remains of her school, the headteacher looks around nervously. It's not safe to be out here in one of the most dangerous parts of north-eastern Nigeria, but the government has promised to send a team to investigate the kidnapping of more than 200 pupils from her school and she wants to greet them in person.

'These are *our* girls,' she says. 'They are from Chibok.' She punctuates her words by pointing to the ground. 'They are from here.'

Around her are abandoned desks and burnt-out classrooms destroyed when Boko Haram militants stormed the Chibok government girls' secondary school a month ago, loading the girls into lorries and driving them away.

Kwambura's face is drawn and tired. The kidnapping has left its mark on everyone in this remote settlement, which has been living under a state of emergency since Boko Haram stepped up its attacks more than a year ago.

Mohammed Dunoma, the chairman of the local parent-teacher association, says many villagers are now reluctant to allow their daughters to go to school. Boko Haram, whose name means 'western education is sinful', is an ever-present threat, he says: 'We don't know when they will come.'

This is a close-knit community, and it is in mourning. Esther Yakubu's 15-year-old daughter, Dorcas, is one of the missing girls. She is furious with the government for failing to come to her aid.

'What about us living in Chibok? Are we not people too?' she asks. 'They abandoned us. Just because we live in the villages.'

Asked if she believes the rumours that the girls may have crossed the border into Cameroon and been forced to marry their abductors, she shakes her head vehemently. 'No, no. They are in Nigeria,' she says, holding a photo of Dorcas wearing a blue dress. The picture, taken the day before she was kidnapped, was supposed to be a gift to Dorcas for completing secondary school.

Dorcas's sister, Happy, says she is not afraid of Boko Haram. 'I just want my sister to come back,' she says.

Away from Chibok, the social-media campaign to #bringback-ourgirls has generated more than one million tweets and swelled into a global outcry, with famous figures including Angelina Jolie, Malala Yousafzai and Michelle Obama joining the calls for Nigeria's government to recover the remaining girls. But here there is no electricity or internet access, and little awareness that the world's attention is focused at its door.

The oldest man in the village, Bitrus Dawa, known locally as Badalu, has not heard about the global search effort for the girls he describes as 'my daughters'. Dawa, who says he was born in 1910 and can remember the first time he saw white men in 1923, shakes his head as he laments a government 'fraught with corruption' that has not been able to eliminate Boko Haram.

Beyond the village, the wide trunks of baobab trees cast shadows across the Sahelian landscape where the Sambisa game reserve stretches ominously. Many Chibok residents believe their daughters are in one of Boko Haram's encampments in the Sambisa bush.

'We went inside the Sambisa to look for them,' says Lawan Zanna. Hoping to find his 18-year-old daughter Aisha, the 45-year-old father of nine said he had joined more than 100 others three days after the abduction. Along the way, villagers from nearby areas told them they had seen Boko Haram militants with the girls. Zanna said he wanted to continue following the abductors' tracks, 'But they told us, "Don't follow them. They will kill you."'

Despite Boko Haram's threats, Zanna says he will keep his seven daughters in school. 'Even the Qur'an tells us that knowledge is obligatory.'

Since the abduction, Chibok's local government has introduced a curfew, outlawing all driving after 6 p.m. The village has deployed its own civilian force of fighters to defend the area. Bulus Mungo Park, a 38-year-old civil servant who says two of his nieces are among the kidnapped, is one of them. A volunteer in the national vigilante association, Mungo Park says the local force is about 300-strong. 'We must fight this Boko Haram and we will win,' he says.

With a hunting gun strapped around his tall shoulders, Mungo Park escorted a convoy of girls who escaped from Boko Haram to the state capital of Maiduguri on Tuesday. Local authorities had invited them to watch the latest video released by the militants to help identify the girls shown.

The journey to Maiduguri from Chibok is an 80-mile (130km) stretch of abandoned villages razed by Boko Haram's insurgency. Drivers on this road are careful to avoid stopping between the regular military checkpoints inspecting all passers-by. At the checkpoints, soldiers and civilian fighters call out suspicious-looking men and ask them to stand in a line. One by one they lift the men's fingers, looking for tell-tale signs of heavy gun usage.

'This is the situation we are in now because of the Boko Haram,' says Mungo Park.

The road runs alongside the Sambisa bush, and locals say Boko Haram fighters often cross this way, shooting at cars as they go.

For 18-year-old Lydia Pogu, her brush with Boko Haram ended with a dramatic getaway. With a friend, Lydia managed to jump out of one of the lorries after it succumbed to mechanical failures. 'I escaped. They didn't know I jumped,' she says. She ran into the bushes, leaving behind Aisha Zanna, Dorcas Yakubu, Deborah Solomon and more than 200 other classmates.

But now she's too afraid to go back to school. She says she wants to be a farmer and tend to a small plot of land with her mother, a sturdy woman who speaks little English and smiles often at her daughter.

Lydia says she will not be happy until her classmates return. She locks the doors of the small family home as Chibok settles for the night. Storefronts are closed. Chickens and goats retreat into wooden stalls.

Kwambura and her colleagues give up their wait for the day. Another day has gone by, the girls are still missing and the government delegation has not come to help.

At the time of going to press, the girls are still missing.

20 MAY

What do you call a tough female boss? (Answer: boss)

HADLEY FREEMAN

Look, I've been thinking about this a lot and I've decided there's only one thing for it: we're going to have to invent a new language. We need a subsidiary language, an offshore language, if you will, to deal with certain elements of life that English has proved incapable of handling.

There are many things beyond English's grasp, and many of these are handled with aplomb by the German language. The best one, of course, is '*Kummerspeck*', which is translated as 'excess weight due to emotional overeating', but I prefer the literal translation of the term, which is 'grief bacon'. Who among us in the English-speaking world has not been in need of some grief bacon?

But grief bacon, sadly, is not our subject today. Rather, it's how women in authority – or, specifically, female bosses – are discussed, because English is incapable of dealing with this crazy female phenomenon, as demonstrated by the palaver following the sacking last week of Jill Abramson as the executive editor of the *New York Times*.

I have no hot exclusive insight whatsoever into whether Abramson's sacking was to do with the *New York Times*'s sexism (as many initially claimed) or her mismanagement of staff (as the *New York Times* has insisted). But then, plenty of other folk with a similar lack of insight have argued that one can't cry 'sexism' every time a woman is sacked. Absolutely: let's not play the Defcon 1-like feminist card here before necessary. But I can say with utmost certainty that the language used to describe her has long been enthrallingly sexist. Maybe Abramson's behaviour was outrageous, but it's notable how the complaints keep returning to the personal, and how eager they were to do so from the start, as they always do with women who are bosses and almost never do with men.

Abramson, it has been reported, was 'brusque', 'pushy', 'mercurial'. Take a minute to think if you have ever heard any of those words applied to men, let alone in a way that suggests a sackable offence. Spoiler alert! No, you haven't. One source complained that Abramson 'has this disapproving look on her face all the time', raising the thrilling possibility that Abramson was sacked for having Bitchy Resting Face. The publisher of the *New York Times*, Arthur Sulzberger, issued a statement over the weekend furiously denying that Abramson was sacked because she was a woman and that it was instead due to her 'arbitrary decision-making, a failure to consult and bring colleagues with her, inadequate communication and public mistreatment of colleagues'.

It feels almost too obvious to point out that all of those complaints can be aimed right back at Sulzberger, specifically in relation to his generally astonishing, notably brusque and especially brutal firing of Abramson. But as my colleague Emily Bell wrote, 'No one will castigate him for being insufficiently warm and friendly, because no one expects him to be.' No word yet on the state of Sulzberger's Bitchy Resting Face.

As it happened, the editor of *Le Monde*, Natalie Nougayrède, was sacked on the same day as Abramson, and she also happened to be a woman. She, like Abramson, was criticised for poor communication skills ('very difficult to talk to'), her bossiness ('authoritarian') and her brusque nature ('Putin-like'). Fancy the coincidence! As former national news editor at the *Washington Post* Susan B Glasser wrote this weekend: 'Just about every single thing that was said about Jill Abramson and Natalie Nougayrède was said about me. That I was difficult and hard to understand and divisive ... I have never read a story that I can recall about [a male editor's] "temperament" ... Do you really believe that all these women were temperamentally incompatible with their positions?'

That women in positions of authority face a double bind – be tough and get called bitchy, or be soft and accused of being weak – is not news. But it's easy to forget how tight this double bind is. On Monday the *New York Times* – yes, back to them again – reported that the Democratic party (you know, the liberal one) had never elected a single female governor in the north-east (you know, the liberal part of the country). Plenty of Democratic women have been elected to the Senate, but senators are part of a collective body, whereas governors stand alone.

'Convincing voters that women can serve where the buck stops is still a hurdle,' said one academic. Not only are voters and companies generally less convinced of women's buck-stopping abilities (women make up only 17 per cent of board directors of the FTSE 100 companies, remember), but a report found that those few who are hired as CEOs are also far more likely to be swiftly fired. A company will hire a woman when it needs saving (as the *New York Times* did), because it reflects well on the company to have a woman in charge (as it did with the *New York Times*), but they will then be pushed off 'the glass cliff' first, as women are still seen as 'outsiders'.

'We tend to like those that are most like us,' one of the report's authors said. 'Sadly, company boards are still mostly men, and they're more inclined to pull the trigger on women if things aren't working out.'

So, as you can see, a change is needed. To be honest, I'm not really convinced that changing a language can fix systemic sexism – playing around with words in such situations often feels like putting up new wallpaper over damp and calling the problem solved – but, hell, it's a start.

Term for 'tough – I don't want to say bitch exactly, but, you know, bossy. Insists on having things done her way, which can be a drag': boss.

Term for 'not always happy and smiling, which, personally, I find aesthetically upsetting': boss.

Term for 'female boss who doesn't always talk in the sweet dulcet tones of angels with the patience of a bank of saints': boss.

Term for 'boss who is not a man': boss.

Term for 'excess weight due to emotional overeating': grief bacon.

Summer

The Mr Men inhabit
a godless universe

CHARLIE BROOKER

I moved house recently and was once again stunned by how much dead media I'm lugging around. First it was vinyl. Then CDs. Now the DVD collection has joined the VHS collection in my personal poorly curated Museum of Obsolete Clutter.

I can chart my history with each format. The surviving remnants of my VHS era, for instance, commence with an off-air recording of series one of *The Young Ones* transferred from Betamax in my teens, and conclude with a review copy of an *Apprentice* episode dating from about seven years ago. The DVD wing comprises box sets, rushes, rough cuts, and a Christmas edition of *The Black and White Minstrel Show* I had to watch for a TV programme I was doing. Beyond that point, I don't really own anything. It's all in the cloud these days.

Same with books. My bookshelves chiefly function as a snapshot of what I was reading prior to the invention of the Kindle. The only physical, actual, by-God-it-exists books I buy these days are children's books. In fact, the only books I read these days are children's books.

Each night I read stories to a two-year-old to distract him from reality, which, being two, he hasn't learned to despise yet. He earnestly believes everything is brilliant. Yesterday he discovered the timeless magic of throwing a fork under the sofa again and again and again. He laughs at the sight of a squirrel. Sometimes he spins on the spot and throws his arms out, shrieking with boundless delight for no reason. What a moron.

He wants to cling to every crumb of conscious existence, so it's tough to convince him to let go long enough to fall asleep. Bedtime stories ease the transition.

We began with the classics. 'Goldilocks and the Three Bears' is simple enough to recount from memory in the dark. Simple and boring. I regularly drifted off while reciting it aloud, and sometimes added new bits in a dreamlike daze. I once caught myself saying baby bear's head had fallen off because his nose was made of hair. It was hard to steer the narrative back on course after that.

I tried reading fairy tales off an iPhone, but that didn't work. For starters, it's impossible to hold an iPhone in the same hectare as a toddler without prompting an instant, bitter struggle for possession that makes the battle for Ukraine look dignified. Besides, fairy stories exist in a peculiar medieval realm. Reading about tunics and spindles off a glimmering smartphone screen just feels wrong. You need a hand-me-down Ladybird book to really do them justice. A book filled with creepy paintings to match the creepy text. In 'Snow White and the Seven Dwarves', the handsome prince falls in love with a corpse in a glass box. It's right there in black and white. No trigger warnings or anything.

Still, fairy tales were just a gateway drug to a wider world of kiddywink fiction. Quickly we moved from *Peepo!* to *Goodnight Moon* to *The Gruffalo* and beyond. Brilliant though *The Very Hungry Caterpillar* is, it's only about 20 words long. You could tweet the whole thing while falling downstairs. And the storyline is full of holes.

Out of selfish nostalgia I bought a complete box set of Mr Men stories, which turned out to be the most satisfying purchase I've made in about a decade. The stories themselves aren't especially remarkable. They follow a fairly rigid template. In each story Mr Titular wakes up, has breakfast (usually eggs, consumed in a manner that vividly illustrates his character), goes for a walk, encounters a worm or a wizard or a shopkeeper, learns a harsh moral lesson and then crawls home, a changed man, hopelessly broken by experience.

The Mr Men inhabit a godless universe. They chiefly fall into two camps – those with character defects (e.g. Mr Greedy) and those with afflictions (e.g. Mr Skinny). They all suffer in some way, except those too mad (Mr Silly) or too stupid (Mr Dizzy) to comprehend what suffering is.

There is justice in their realm, but it's applied inconsistently at best. Mr Nosey, for instance, has all his inquisitiveness literally beaten out of him when the townsfolk conspire against him. He hears an interesting noise behind a fence and pokes his nose round it, only to be smashed in the face by a man with a hammer – who laughs about it afterwards. But Mr Nosey's only crime was excessive curiosity, whereas Mr Tickle – a 1970s children's entertainer with wandering hands who runs around town touching strangers inappropriately from dawn till dusk – goes unpunished.

Most of those with afflictions are bluntly informed that their conditions are untreatable. Messrs Bump, Bounce, Forgetful, Quiet, Small and Tall, for instance, simply have to lump it. Mr Sneeze is cured, but only after a wizard turns his wintry homeland into a suntrap, in an early example of man-made climate change.

It's a brutal existence, albeit a cheerfully rendered one. And in revisiting the books I was surprised to discover that despite forgetting most of the storylines, the visuals felt so familiar, they can't have ever left my mind. When I was young, I wanted to be a cartoonist. As a teenager, I even managed to make a career of it for a few years. Back then I figured I'd formed this ambition thanks to the comics I'd read when I was about 12. Now, looking back at some of my ham-fisted drawings of the time, I realise the Mr Men must have kicked off the yearning years before that. I was unconsciously sampling and regurgitating whole sections of Roger Hargreaves' visual repertoire. The way Roger Hargreaves drew a shoe is still the way a shoe looks when I picture it. Same with a house. Or a hat. Or a butcher. Or a wizard. Or a cloud.

And when I thought about that, a sad thought occurred to me: that these children's books may well be the only physical books my son will ever own. Because when he gets past about six, all his books will be in the cloud, surely. Not on a shelf. Not in a library. In a cloud. A cloud I can only picture in the shape of Mr Daydream.

Not that my son cares. Like I said, he's still astounded by squirrels and forks. Monumental idiot.

10 JUNE

Sleeve tattoos are now a hipster habit – and the permanence of mine pains me

BIDISHA

'You know this is permanent?' the sceptical tattooist says. It's 1999 and I'm in a tattoo parlour in Mill Hill armed with a copy of British *Vogue* to anaesthetise my brain. I'm having a full sleeve done.

Sadly, the word 'permanent' has no resonance when you're 20. Barbed-wire effect around the wrist? Hokusai-style wave design resembling the marbling in medium-strength Castello cheese? Big black paisleys pieced together like a children's jumbo jigsaw into a faux armour plate? Indigo slashes over smeared blocks of red, purple, pink and green? I have them all. On one tattoo.

I now think of my sleeve as a form of socially legitimised self-harm, done at a time when I was agonising about my career. A self-sabotaging former child prodigy and writer whose physical prowess is part of the package, and whose best days are behind them by their 20s? The sleeve had to be done. And since then more and more people have made the same decision, although probably for very different reasons. Fifa has just released photos of the England World Cup squad, revealing that four players have had the mental acuity to pick up on the sleeve trend just five years after it first peaked, inspired by David Beckham. Justin Bieber has, inevitably, completed a sleeve too.

But I no longer belieb. Underneath my ink smears are raised scars; the whole thing bubbles up and itches in summer. Even in a tailored suit it peeps out like mould. Blue ink has seeped between the layers of skin and spread into my armpit. My generation will be at the NHS at 80 getting our gammy legs seen to while doctors try to find a vein under the faded, stretched, misshapen detritus of our unartistic body art; a postmodern mash-up of badly translated Chinese words, bungled Latin quotes, dolphins, roses, anchors, faces of favoured children or pets, and Japanese wallpaper designs.

Nearly all world cultures have had tattoos. They represent adulthood rites, warrior marks, artistry and beauty, tribal identification, victories won, journeys undertaken. They have represented both belonging and marginality; individuals on the edge, pillaging, hustling, grifting. Now they are a hipster habit, a sheeplike folly, a permanent pretension. You can stumble into a Magaluf tat parlour in a drunken stupor and have Snoopy inked on your minge.

My sleeve took three sessions of nine hours each and felt like what it was: a needle loaded with ink jamming into my skin at high speed. It vibrates exhilaratingly through your bones, zings into the flesh, numbs you out, exhausts you later, sweats blood, swells up. A one-inch tattoo across the nervy, fatty pad at the bottom of my spine hurt a million times more than the sleeve.

At the parlour the man next to me was having the Rizla logo put on his shin. 'Why?' asked the tattooist. 'Cos I'm a puff 'ead, in't I?' he roared. Then he went, 'Woah. Head rush,' and fainted. 'Only blokes faint,' the tattooist said. The puff 'ead couldn't stand his own humiliation and decided to project it on to the nearest female: me. 'I bet I scared you, didn't I?' he said.

Women with full sleeves are common now, as in plentiful. In my day we were common as in trashy. 'That's your warrior side,' my female friends said. No – for my martial spirit comes from within.

A few years ago I went to the Royal Free hospital to talk about removal. The doctor was unwilling. 'You did a big, bold thing in getting it done,' he said. 'Now be big and bold in living with it.'

16 JUNE

Sorry, David Cameron, but your British history is not mine

OWEN JONES

The government's crusade to embed 'British values' in our education system is meaningless at best, dangerous at worst, and a perversion of British history in any case. It's meaningless because our history is the struggle of many different Britains, each with their own conflicting sets of values.

For example, the values of many post-Thatcher Conservatives are predominantly neoliberal, drawn from an ideology that champions the extraction of commercial value from everything and that has little respect for national boundaries. Indeed, its founding fathers are the likes of the American economist Milton Friedman and the Austrian Friedrich Hayek. At a Conservative research department meeting, Thatcher once slammed down a copy of Hayek's *The Constitution of Liberty*, declaring: 'This is what we believe!'

My own values, on the other hand, are inspired by a variety of Welsh, Scottish, English and foreign socialists. Where modern Tories promote dog-eat-dog individualism, ruthless competition and the supremacy of private profit, I believe in solidarity, collective action and a fundamental redistribution of wealth and power. My opponents would characterise their own values rather more sympathetically and mine less so, but the point of agreement should surely be that there is a chasm between us. It will be said that we are united by a common belief in democracy, but this is hardly a specifically British value – and, in any case, my perception of a democracy that is continually imperilled by Tory-backed corporate and private interests is rather different to theirs.

Where the government's agenda becomes dangerous is if one side claims its values are those of the nation as a whole. This is an age-old strategy of authoritarian regimes and movements, used to exclude, ostracise or suppress dissidents. The instrument of McCarthyism to persecute the US left, after all, was the House Committee on Un-American Activities. But we've seen this at work in our own country recently. The *Daily Mail* declared that Ralph Miliband was the 'man who hated Britain' because he was a Marxist who opposed institutions such as the monarchy, the Church of England and the army. Not deferring to the status quo, in its view, is not just un-British, but anti-British.

It is an agenda based on the twisting of British history too. Magna Carta – an English, rather than British document – will be the centrepiece of the values campaign. David Cameron wants 'every child' to learn about it. Given that speaking English normally heads lists of skills required by those who like to define the British way of life, it is amusing that a document originally written in Latin, before it was translated into French after four years, is being exalted like this. Here was a charter imposed by powerful barons – hardly nascent democrats – on the weak King John to prevent him trampling on their rights: it didn't satisfy them, and they rose in revolt anyway. It meant diddly-squat to average English subjects, most of whom were serfs.

Only in the 17th century did it begin to win its central place in English mythology: it suited Levellers and other radicals to portray themselves as reactionaries, attempting to turn the clock back and reassert ancient rights that had supposedly been trampled on. After all, the word 'revolution' comes from the Latin *revolvere*, or to 'turn back'.

But here's the point. There is a history of Britain that is about empire, aristocracy, monarchy, the established church, exploitative employers, and so on. The Tory view of history is founded on the myth of a benevolent elite granting carefully managed change out of goodwill and generosity. But there is another history, of struggle from below against those in power – often at great cost and sacrifice – by ordinary people who are airbrushed from history. These different histories inform a schism in values that lasts to this day.

This other history goes back to the Peasants' Revolt of 1381, when ordinary folk rose in rebellion at a poll tax. It wasn't just led by men: women such as Johanna Ferrour played a key role (court documents damn her as 'chief perpetrator and leader of rebellious evildoers from Kent'). Tens of thousands of people – ranging from roofers and bakers to millers and parish priests – marched on Blackheath, where the Lollard priest John Ball publicly questioned the class system: 'When Adam delved and Eve span, who was then the gentleman?' Widespread defiance against the ruling elite would re-emerge in the 17th century: we had our own revolution a century and a half before the French stormed the Bastille. The king was deposed, and radical movements like the democratic Levellers and socialistic Diggers flourished.

Resistance to authority is a value threaded through our history. When six Dorset labourers were transported to Australia in the 1830s for organising a primitive trade union, 800,000 signed a petition demanding freedom for the Tolpuddle Martyrs. In the following years, the Chartists emerged – the world's first great working-class political movement. Today the suffragettes are treated as vindicated heroes, but they were force-fed in prisons and demonised as terrorists and anarchists in the early 20th century. Those who fought sexism, racism and homophobia – as at the first LGBT demonstration in London in 1970, when 150 protesters were outnumbered by police officers – were demonised and persecuted in their time.

The welfare state, the NHS, workers' rights: these were the culmination of generations of struggle, not least by a labour movement that had set up the Labour party – controversially at the time – to give working people a voice. The values and interests of Britons have always been pitted against each other.

It is this history – of a very different Britain to that championed by this government – that underpins my values. It helps drive me to oppose the values underpinning Cameron's administration, which justify policies that kick the poor – such as the bedroom tax – while shovelling even more wealth into the hands of the richest, through tax cuts and privatisation. It's also why I think people should be inspired by the values and traditions of our ancestors who fought back, and emulate their example.

So if the coalition wants a divisive struggle over 'values', fine – bring it on. But if the government's rationale is that 'values' will unite the nation, it had better think again.

18 June

Further military intervention in Iraq? It beggars belief

SIMON JENKINS

What is going on? Until recently Britain's foreign secretary, William Hague, parroted Washington's thesis that Iran was an axis of evil. No epithet was too harsh for the ayatollahs and their minions, and 'all options' were on the table for punishing Tehran. Now, the UK government is in a spot of bother in Iraq, and suddenly it is: please Iran, dear Iran, best-beloved Iran – this is your real friend, William, calling.

This has been a bad week for consistency. Iraq's Nouri al-Maliki, until recently blessed as architect of Anglo-American nation-building, is now blamed for nation-demolishing. The Sunni 'reawakening councils', created at vast expense to help America and Britain get out of Iraq, are now aides to its insurgents and invaders. Syria's Bashar al-Assad was a vicious war criminal, though perhaps for the time being he is a force for stability and order.

Meanwhile, we condemn the Isis militants for committing war crimes by executing Iraqi soldiers in cold blood with AK47s, and then we discuss executing them in cold blood with drone bombs. A former US general even explains that the drones will need 'execution-level intelligence' to work. Quite so.

There is scant morality in western military intervention these days. Tony Blair returned this week from beyond the grave and showed no concern for justice, reason or even national interest. He is a confirmed Iraq disaster-denier. Civilisation may advance in leaps and bounds over millennia, but politics remains stuck in Homer's day, in human vanity and tribal loyalty.

Each week Hague sits in his Whitehall office drinking in the pictures of Britain's imperial past on his walls. Then up he jumps and declares, 'What we want to see in Iraq ... ' Or it could be Iran or Afghanistan or Congo. Does he ever wonder at his reference for that first-person plural?

Hague is now suffering from what philosophers call agency confusion. He does not distinguish between wanting something 'to happen' and wanting something 'to be done', possibly by him. We can all wish for the best in Iraq. That does not mean we have to act to bring it about. Nor does not acting render us guilty of 'standing idly by'.

On the other hand, doing something imposes substantive obligations. In the case of Saddam Hussein, we wished him gone (a happening) and got rid of him (a deed). We then vaguely wished it would all turn out well in the end (a happening). This confusion holds the key to the immorality of the Iraq invasion. Its apologists cannot excuse themselves by claiming the invasion was fine and only the aftermath bungled. Invasion and aftermath were a single act. They involved death, destruction, a collapse of order and a flight into tribalism. Blair was blinded by Thatcher's Falklands victory and wanted one of his own, without thought of consequences. Others were no less culpable in supporting him.

Ten years ago, soon after the 2003 invasion, I had dinner in Baghdad with a man I took to be a British spy. Like many spies at the front, he was shrewd and unconcerned with diplomatic nicety. I had been shocked by visits to Fallujah and Basra, and he convinced me that the longer the chaos lasted the sooner Iran would come in to protect the Shias from Sunni revanchists. The most likely outcome would be an Iraq divided into three autonomous provinces, for Kurds, Sunnis and Shias. I wrote accordingly.

Ten years and 180,000 Iraqi corpses later, that prediction is coming true. And still a British cabinet is itching 'to see something happen in Iraq'. There are plenty to the right of Hague (such as Blair) ready to interpret this not just as a wish but as a statement of agency. They dream of more war, always starting with 'just some bombing from the air', always 'to make the streets of Britain safe'.

Now Hague is meddling with the Iranians. Even I can hardly imagine a British foreign secretary so cynical as to be in cahoots with Iran's dreadful and corrupt revolutionary guards. These are the troops against whom a certain Saddam Hussein fought in the 1980s, with British support. They have since kept in practice by torturing Tehran dissidents. But then disaster makes strange bedfellows. Who would have thought Washington would back the 'plucky' Taliban in toppling the Russians in Afghanistan in 1989, and then topple them in turn in 2001? The maxim that my enemy's enemy is my friend is an old standby.

Of course, western intervention was not entirely to blame for plunging so many south-west Asian states into chaos. Turkey, Iran and Egypt have been upheaved without western help. But the West crucially misread the importance of the Ba'ath party and other secularists, from Nasser to Saddam, in keeping Islamist fundamentalism at bay. The Ba'athists stalled what the US historian Bernard Lewis called 'new causes for anger, new dreams of fulfilment, new tools of attack'. We opposed them as enemies of democracy, and got ayatollahs and al-Qaida instead.

For western leaders emerging from victory in the cold war to make this category error must rank as a catastrophe of modern history. As the Pulitzer Prize-winning historian Barbara Tuchman said of leaders who pursue folly, the most inexcusable are those who were warned at the time but went ahead for short-term gain. Thus was Iraq.

The forces that drive democracies to war are as incorrigible as ever. Barack Obama is now abused as weak, David Cameron as vacillating. The media drive them on, demanding resolution and firmness, always professing a belief in the efficacy of air power and the need to 'deter the men of violence'.

It beggars belief that further military intervention by the West in Iraq is now being considered. Yet the yearning to intervene, to bomb someone even if just to 'send a message', shows how thin is the veneer of sanity cloaking great power aggression. War still has the best tunes. How glorious it must seem to certain politicians to somehow turn 10 years of disaster in Iraq into a final victory.

That is why the causes and effects of 2003 must be nailed to the wall, time and again. Trillions of dollars were spent and tens of thousands of people died, for no good reason then and no good reason now. It was a total disgrace.

25 JUNE

Phone-hacking trial was officially about crime; but in reality, it was about power

NICK DAVIES

This was no ordinary trial.

It was unusual in its sheer scale: more than three years of police work; 42,000 pages of crown evidence; seven months of hearings; up to 18 barristers in court at any one time; 12 defendants facing allegations of crime spreading back over a decade.

But what made it most unusual was what it represented. First, this was a long-delayed showdown between the criminal justice system and parts of Fleet Street, in which the reputations of both were at stake. Beyond that, however, this was a trial by proxy, in which Rebekah Brooks stood in the dock on behalf of a media mogul and Andy Coulson acted as avatar for the prime minister, with the reputations of Rupert Murdoch and David Cameron equally in jeopardy. Officially, the trial was all about crime; in reality, it was all about power.

And just as the main players were absent from the court, so the real issues which for years had inflamed public opinion were not mentioned on the indictment – the perception that some news organisations were all too happy to invade privacy and ruin lives in order to sell more papers; that they regarded themselves as not only above the law but above the government, which would do their will or suffer for it; that they had poisoned the mainstream of public debate with a daily drip-feed of falsehood and distortion.

On the afternoon of 30 October 2013, as the prosecuting counsel, Andrew Edis QC, first rose to his feet, I looked across at the 12 jurors who had just been empanelled – mixed gender, mixed race, mixed age – and thought that they represented arguably the most ancient form of democracy (centuries older than the idea of voting); that this was the moment when all the wealth and influence of the Murdoch network finally confronted a form of popular will that they could not compromise. It was not as simple as that.

Somebody called it the trial of the century. That worked well enough as an indication of its scale and of the highly unusual status of some of those in the dock. But it was more accurate in another sense: that, as the weeks went by, this trial came to embody the peculiar values of this particular century – its materialism and the inequality that goes with it, the dominance of corporation over state.

The judge, Mr Justice Saunders, was outstanding – clever, considerate, surprisingly funny, displaying never a flicker of fear or favour towards the ambassadors of the power elite who sat before him in the dock. The jurors were a tribute to the jury system. Their facial reactions each day showed that their concentration scarcely wavered during the marathon (though one had the initially alarming habit of listening with her eyes shut). Often, they sent written notes to the judge which were extraordinarily astute, spotting glitches in the evidence that had been missed by every single one of the highly paid counsel in front of them. But ...

Rupert Murdoch's money flooded that courtroom. It flowed into the defence of Rebekah Brooks, because he backed her; and to the defence of Andy Coulson, because Coulson had sued and forced him to pay. Lawyers and court reporters who spend their working lives at the Old Bailey agreed they had never seen anything like it, this multimillion-pound Rolls-Royce engine purring through the proceedings. Soon we found ourselves watching the power of the private purse knocking six bells out of the underfunded public sector.

In the background, for sure, there was a huge publicly funded police inquiry, forced by the stench of past failure to investigate thoroughly the crime that had been ignored and concealed for so long. But when it came to handling the police evidence in court, Brooks and Coulson had squads of senior partners, junior solicitors and paralegals, as well as a highly efficient team monitoring all news and social media. The cost to Murdoch ran into millions. Against that, the Crown Prosecution Service had only one full-time solicitor attached to the trial and one admin assistant. They worked assiduously. One prosecution source said it was surprising they had not simply collapsed under the strain. The effect was clear.

Defence barristers would pause, turn and find a solicitor to feed them information while crown counsel often found an empty seat. The defence produced neatly laminated bundles of evidence, while the crown hastily photocopied material into files which sometimes proved to be incomplete.

Towards the end of the trial, Edis decided the jurors needed an electronic index to be installed on a computer in the jury room to help them find their way through the avalanche of paperwork that had descended on them. With the CPS struggling for cash, Edis offered to pay for it out of his own pocket, and, in the absence of CPS manpower, two junior crown counsels had to create the index themselves. Over and again, the defence teams had the resources to find some helpful stick with which to beat a potentially dangerous witness – a misremembered date, a forgotten detail, even on one occasion the fact that the witness had once had coffee with Nick Davies from the *Guardian*. So they were able to create complication, confusion, doubt.

An expert witness claimed to be able to track the movements of defendants by analysing their use of mobile phones: the prosecution failed to notice that his conclusions were contradicted by his own data; he was chopped to pieces by the defence and admonished by the judge. The jury was told that the *News of the World* had hacked phones to obtain a story about Paul McCartney having a row with his then wife Heather Mills and throwing their engagement ring out of a hotel window: the prosecution failed to take account of evidence in the possession of the police which indicated the paper had bought the story from someone who worked in the hotel.

These weaknesses were exploited by the kind of high-octane cross-examination that could raise reasonable doubt about whether the witness is breathing. ('When did you start this breathing? ... You can't remember?! ... How often do you breathe? ... You don't know?!') Here the disparity in funding was striking but not so important. There were masterclasses in the skills of advocacy from Edis as well as from some of those acting for those in the dock. It simply stuck in the craw that Edis was earning less than 10 per cent of the daily fees enjoyed by some of his opponents.

Finally, the crown was hampered by the rules of court that allow it to make an opening statement but require it then to present items of evidence without any comment as to why they matter, a rule policed with ferocious efficiency by the Rolls-Royce defence teams. In a normal case, where the prosecution might spend only three or four days presenting its case, that would not matter: the evidence would be relatively simple; it would be clear how each piece fitted into a picture. In a seven-month trial, the rule combined with the crown's scarce resources to produce a kind of chaos.

When Brooks's barrister, Jonathan Laidlaw QC, rose to open her defence after nearly four months of prosecution evidence, he told the jury, with his trademark combination of gentle delivery and vicious effect, that it had not been 'the easiest case to follow'. The crown had jumped from topic to topic, he said. It had made 'something of a mess' of timelines for the key hacking victims, which were incomplete and potentially misleading. It had flashed up documents on the courtroom screens and forgotten to give them to the jury: 'If there is a sense of confusion about the evidence and what it is supposed to relate to, that would be entirely understandable ... There are categories where we simply don't know or understand the point that is being made.'

It may have been patronising, but he had a point. The crown had spent months effectively throwing random bricks at the jury with little or no explanation as to how they fitted together.

Laidlaw set about building the prosecution's house for them, attempting to persuade the jurors that, when they saw it in its final form, they would see it was full of holes.

This is not to say that the defendants had no problems. In pre-trial hearings, Brooks lost her lead barrister, John Kelsey-Fry QC, because the former royal editor, Clive Goodman, said he wanted to call him as a witness to the cover-up at his own trial for hacking in 2007. The judge agreed to delay the trial for seven weeks while she instructed Laidlaw – and that meant Coulson lost his barrister, Clare Montgomery QC, because the new timing overlapped with a case she had to conduct in Hong Kong.

The trial opened against a backdrop of public hostility to Brooks and Coulson, not only because of the high-profile hacking saga, but also because of their careers. Brooks's lawyers tried and failed to persuade the judge to ban all trade-union members from the jury on the grounds that they were bound to be antagonistic.

Throughout the trial, the defendants were thrown off course as the crown, struggling to keep up, served new evidence that should have been presented before the trial started. Even as the final evidence was being put to the jury in April, the prosecution suddenly announced it had 48,000 email messages which the FBI had obtained from News Corp in New York; they had been with police in London for 16 months.

All this made the trial a peculiarly unpredictable contest. From the start, the crown case was weak, particularly against Rebekah Brooks. There was no direct evidence at all to implicate her in phone hacking. Indeed, there was simply a lack of any direct evidence about her of any kind. That was partly because of the passage of time: she stopped being editor of the *News of the World* in January 2003, so naturally paperwork and other evidence had been lost. Some had been destroyed. Over the years, News International had deleted some 300m emails from their systems, only 90m of which were retrieved, including only a handful from Brooks's editorship. The hard drive had been removed from her computer for safekeeping, then lost.

But there was no doubt at all that the *News of the World* had been involved in crime on a massive scale. Before the trial opened, three former news editors and the specialist phone-hacker Glenn Mulcaire had pleaded guilty to conspiring to intercept voicemails. By the time it finished, News International had paid compensation to 718 victims of the hacking – an average of nearly three agreed victims for every week during the five years for which patchy evidence of Mulcaire's work has survived. Hundreds more alleged victims were still being identified by police.

The hacking case against Brooks and Coulson was based on a platform of inference. How could they not have known about the beehive of offending around them, the crown asked. How could they not have known about Mulcaire's speciality when he was one of only two outside contributors with a full-time contract and was being paid more than any reporter, at one point more even than the news editor? How could they not have known the origin of all those stories whose accuracy they had to test? How could they have been ignorant when a humble sports writer described Mulcaire, a former footballer, as 'part of our special investigations team' in a story published by the *News of the World* when Brooks was editor? Brooks and Coulson insisted they had known nothing of Mulcaire's criminality. They had not even heard his name until he was arrested in August 2006, they told the jury.

The attack on this platform of inference included a striking example of the impact of Murdoch's money. The evidence that lies at the core of the hacking scandal is the collection of notes found by detectives when they first arrested Mulcaire in August 2006: 11,000 pages of his barely legible scribble and scrawl and doodle. The original police inquiry took one look at it and decided it simply did not have the resources to go through it all. When Operation Weeting in 2011 finally did the job properly, it took it the best part of a year. Brooks's Rolls-Royce did it in three months and then had the resources to produce a brilliant analysis.

The notes showed that Mulcaire was tasked some 5,600 times during the five years that he worked on contract for the *News of the World*, an average of more than four for every working day. As a crude average, that would imply that between September 2001, when he was contracted to work for the paper, and January 2003, when Brooks left, he was commissioned around 1,400 times. But Brooks's legal team set aside all those notes where it was not 100 per cent certain they had been written during that time; and all those where it was not 100 per cent certain that Mulcaire had been tasked to intercept voicemail as opposed to 'blagging' confidential data. Since a considerable mass of his notes were incomplete and/or ambiguous on either date or task, this allowed Laidlaw to tell the jury that there were only 12 occasions when it was 100 per cent certain that Mulcaire had hacked a phone while she was editor – an eye-catching point to be able to deliver in answer to the crown's inference.

Where Brooks was concerned on the hacking charge, there was very little extra evidence to add to that platform of inference. Three witnesses came to court and recalled social occasions when she had discussed hacking with apparent familiarity. Brooks told the jury that she had read about hacking in newspaper stories; she had talked about it casually because she had not realised it was illegal; but she would never have sanctioned it because it was such a severe breach of privacy. One of these three witnesses – the former wife of the golfer Colin Montgomerie, Eimear Cook – was cut to pieces by a particularly destructive cross-examination.

Cook told the jury she recalled a conversation at lunch in September 2005, when Brooks had not only warned her that her own phone might be hacked but had described the ease with which it could be done. Cook added that during the same lunch, she thought Brooks had discussed the famous incident when she had been arrested for assaulting her then partner, the actor Ross Kemp. Laidlaw gently pawed her into position, confirming without doubt the date of the lunch, challenging the strength of her memory until she insisted she was absolutely certain and then, like Hannibal Lecter in a horsehair wig, softly and courteously, he cut out her heart: the incident with Kemp had happened six weeks after the lunch. Her story could not possibly be right.

Then there was Milly Dowler. This was almost spooky. It was the *Guardian*'s disclosure of the hacking of the missing Surrey schoolgirl's phone that finally broke open the scandal. That was purely about the emotional impact of the story – that this was no celebrity victim, but an ordinary civilian, a child, and one who had been abducted and murdered by a predatory paedophile. Now, in court, once more, it was Dowler who presented the threat, not because of any emotional impact, but because it just so happened that this was the one example of hacking under Brooks's editorship where there was some hard evidence. This was, as the judge said in a ruling, 'the high point of the prosecution case'.

Having picked up a voicemail which seemed to suggest that Dowler was alive and working in a factory in Telford, the *News of the World* not only hid that information from police but later, when they had failed to find her, they contacted Surrey police and demanded that they confirm the story for them – and quoted the voicemail, in phone calls and even in email. The records of those calls and messages survived in the Surrey police archive. Brooks must have been consulted about the high-risk decision to hide information from the police, the crown argued.

She must have been told about this potentially huge scoop – and about its origin, they said. She must have known that seven journalists were working on it, including her news editor, Neville Thurlbeck, and her managing editor, Stuart Kuttner, who had both personally contacted Surrey police and quoted the intercepted voicemail. If it was not secret from the police, why would it be a secret from the editor? From the editor who was running a national campaign to protect children from predatory paedophiles?

Brooks's answer was that she had been on holiday that week, in Dubai, and simply had not been told about any of this. Even here, the Dowler case proved special. She had been using a News International phone, and the itemised bill had survived in the company's vaults. If she had been in London, there would have been no record of her conversations, but the phone bill showed she had called the desk occupied by her deputy, Coulson, for 38 minutes on the Friday of that week, as reporters crawled over the big story, and again for 20 minutes on the Saturday, as they pressed the police to confirm it. She had texted him too. However, the prosecution had failed to realise that the records of some of those calls and texts were linked to the time in Dubai, not London, a three-hour difference which allowed Laidlaw to pour justifiable confusion over the evidence.

In addition, she and Kemp had been joined on the holiday by a British tourist, William Hennessy, who told the jury that she had spent a lot of time on the phone, explaining on one occasion that she had to make a call 'about the missing Surrey girl'. Hennessy was sure of the timing: he had bought a watch in Dubai and kept the receipt, which was dated. Brooks said she had no memory of that. She had remained oblivious to the whole saga, she said, even when she returned to the office the following week, never reading the story which the paper had published quoting the voicemail verbatim, never knowing that managing editor Stuart Kuttner was still hectoring Surrey police to confirm the tale.

Kuttner, also on trial, was himself found not guilty of conspiring to hack phones.

Coulson always had more to deal with. While evidence of his three years as Brooks's deputy was hard to find, there was a wealth of phone records, emails, voicemail recordings and Mulcaire notes about the hacking that happened when he was in charge, from January 2003 to January 2007. And Coulson had got himself dangerously close to the action.

Searching Mulcaire's home and the *News of the World* office, police found hundreds of voicemails left by David Blunkett for his lover, Kimberly Quinn. Coulson startled the court by admitting that his chief reporter, Thurlbeck, had played some of them to him. He had then personally confronted the then home secretary with the allegation of his affair, telling him: 'I am certainly very confident of the information ... It is based on an extremely reliable source.' Blunkett taped that meeting, and the tape survived. Coulson argued that this might show that he was aware of one instance of hacking but not that he was part of the conspiracy to make it happen.

Mulcaire then hacked the voicemail of a Labour special adviser, Hannah Pawlby, attempting to prove a false allegation that she was having an affair with the next home secretary, Charles Clarke. Coulson personally called Pawlby, saying he needed to talk to Clarke about 'quite a serious story'. Mulcaire actually hacked his own editor's message from Pawlby's phone, and the recording was found by police when they searched his home. Coulson said simply that he wanted to talk to Clarke about a different story which was also serious; he had known nothing about the hacking of Pawlby's phone.

When they were investigating Calum Best, *News of the World* executives feared that one of their journalists might be leaking information to him, warning him about what they were planning. Coulson sent an email: 'Do his phone.' Mulcaire's notes showed that he did then target Best, though it was not clear whether he succeeded in hacking his messages. Coulson said his email was an order to pull the itemised phone bills of the journalist who was suspected of leaking, to see if he had been calling Best.

Unlike Brooks, Coulson also faced two live witnesses who claimed he had known about the hacking. A show-business writer, Dan Evans, who had become a specialist hacker, told the jury that Coulson had hired him from the *Sunday Mirror* explicitly because of his hacking skill. He claimed that one day in the newsroom, he had played Coulson a tape of a voicemail hacked from the phone of the actor Daniel Craig in which Sienna Miller said she was in the Groucho club with Jude Law.

Coulson's counsel, Timothy Langdale QC, a model of old-school courtesy built around a core of steel, released a swarm of questions around Evans. He stung him into describing his own criminality, his deal with the police, his history of cocaine abuse, finally pushing him into claiming to be sure of the date when he had played the Craig voicemail to Coulson – and then revealed that the editor had not been in the office on that day. When Langdale went on to query whether Miller and Law had been in the Groucho during that time frame, the prosecution was left floundering: it had failed to get evidence from the club to prove their point.

Similarly, Coulson's former friend and royal editor, Goodman, went into the witness box and told the jury that Coulson had personally approved his hacking of royal phones, for which Mulcaire was paid in cash with a false name and address on internal paperwork. He added that hacking was going on on 'an industrial scale' at the time and was often discussed in meetings with Coulson until he banned any further open mention of it.

Langdale pushed back hard, confronting him with evidence to suggest he had lied about the extent of his own involvement in the royal hacking.

A trial deals with only a limited amount of information, considering only the evidence that is available and also admissible and which relates directly to the charges on the indictment. As in any case, there was a great deal which the jury did not hear; information that could have tipped their judgment for or against the defendants.

Some 30 *News of the World* journalists provided information which helped the *Guardian* uncover the scandal. But almost without exception, they spoke off the record. One of them – Sean Hoare – spoke openly, but he died in July 2011. A senior former executive and two of those who had pleaded guilty before the trial – Mulcaire and Thurlbeck – had discussions with the police about giving evidence for the prosecution. All three negotiations failed. Evans and Goodman were alone.

The jury heard nothing about earlier police inquiries into allegations of the *News of the World*'s involvement in blagging confidential records and bribing corrupt police for information, which occurred in the late 1980s and 90s. They heard nothing of the 3,000-word feature in the *Guardian* that described in detail the alleged involvement in this blagging and bribing of a senior executive from the paper. Similarly, they were told very little of the paper's use of Steve Whittamore, who blagged information illegally, culminating in his conviction in court in April 2005.

The jury was told in detail about the information which Brooks said she had been given by an officer from the original inquiry, DCI Keith Surtees, who met her in September 2006 to tell her that her own phone had been hacked by Mulcaire. An internal email written at the time reported that, according to Brooks, police had found 'numerous voice recordings and verbatim notes of his accesses to voicemails' and that they had a list of more than 100 hacking victims (as distinct from the eight who were later named in court) and that they came from 'different areas of public life – politics, showbiz etc.' (as distinct from the royal victims who were of interest to the only *News of the World* journalist they had arrested). This information was shared with Andy Coulson.

However, the jury was not then told of the letter that Brooks wrote to the media select committee in July 2009, after the *Guardian* first reported the true scale of the hacking, in which she said that the *Guardian* had 'substantially and likely deliberately misled the British public'. Nor were they shown Brooks's famous evidence to that committee in March 2003 when she said that her journalists had paid police for information in the past. Select committee evidence is not admissible in court because of rules around parliamentary privilege.

Beyond all that, the jury was specifically not invited to consider behaviour which may not be criminal but has most offended public opinion.

As tabloid newspaper bosses, Brooks and Coulson ruined lives. They did it to sell newspapers, to please Murdoch, to advance their own careers. One flick of their editorial pen was enough to break the boundaries of privacy and of compassion. The singer's mother suffering from depression; the actor stricken by the collapse of her marriage; the DJ in agony over his wife's affair: none of their pain was anything more than human raw material to be processed and packaged and sold for profit. Especially, obsessively, if it involved their sexual activity.

With all the intellectual focus of a masturbatory adolescent, their papers spied in the bedrooms of their targets, dragging out and humiliating anybody who dared to be gay or to have an affair or to engage in any kind of sexual activity beyond that approved by a Victorian missionary. They did it to friends – like Blunkett, for example, sharing drinks and private chats with him and then ripping the heart out of his private life, sprinkling their story with fiction as they did so. And to Sara Payne: befriended by Brooks in her campaign to change the law about publication of the home addresses of sex offenders; investigated by her paper on the false suspicion that she was having an affair with a detective.

But above all, they did it to their enemies. Among the politicians who they exposed for being gay or for having affairs, the left-wingers easily outnumbered the occasional stray right-winger. In among them were the special enemies who dared to challenge News International. In the early stages of the hacking story, there was only one frontbench politician from any party who was willing to attack the *News of the World* – the Lib Dem home affairs spokesman Chris Huhne. In June 2010, when Brooks was chief executive of News International, it was her *News of the World* which exposed Huhne's affair.

The *News of the World* also targeted the private life of its most outspoken critic in parliament – Tom Watson. Brooks had loathed Watson since he took part in the 'curry house' plot in 2006, attempting to engineer Gordon Brown into Downing Street at the expense of her favourite, Tony Blair. News International reporters say that during the hacking saga, she called in reporters to ask if they had any dirt on Watson. The *News of the World* put a private investigator on his tail, hoping to catch him having an affair.

They did all this with breathtaking hypocrisy. While Coulson and Brooks were using their front pages to expose public figures for having affairs, they were themselves having an affair and keeping that information very private. Behind the scenes at the trial Brooks took the hypocrisy a step further. Although her newspapers had frequently attacked the Human Rights Act, she tried to use Article 6 – on the right to a fair hearing – to prevent her 'affair' letter to Coulson being put before the jury.

Before the trial started, Laidlaw attempted to get the whole case against Brooks thrown out on the grounds that prejudicial news-paper coverage meant she could not get a fair trial. The crown replied by citing the case of Abu Hamza, who tried and failed to stop his own trial in 2006 because of prejudicial publicity in the *Sun*, then edited by Brooks. Laidlaw went on to complain about the scrum of press photographers waiting to pounce outside the Old Bailey door.

Their willingness to ruin lives was directly linked to their political power. MPs feared that they might find their own private behaviour being monstered on News International's front pages. This is the power of the playground bully: he has only to beat up one or two children for all of them to start trying to placate him. Beyond that, government collectively feared having its agenda destroyed, its daily activity destabilised, its future terminated if Murdoch's editors turned against it. Former ministers and senior Whitehall officials all tell the same tale – that as Murdoch increased the size of his empire, governments became obsessed with newspaper coverage, particularly that of the *Sun*.

The power that Coulson and Brooks enjoyed delivered the kind of access for which unscrupulous lobbyists will pay large bundles of cash. As a tabloid editor, Brooks was courted by ministers. At the Leveson Inquiry, she disclosed 185 meetings with prime ministers, ministers and party leaders while apologising that her records were incomplete.

At the *News of the World*, Coulson showed little enthusiasm for politics, according to former Downing Street officials, one of whom remembers him being invited for breakfast with Gordon Brown and showing so little interest in policy that the two men ended up talking about newspaper circulations.

Brooks, however, was a different story. Far more than Coulson, she played the game of power, exploiting her extraordinary social skills to build an unrivalled network of connections.

Backed by fear of what her journalists could do, Brooks used her access to get her way. She could do it over small things: 'If she was going to the US and she realised she had no visa, all she had to do was to make a phone call to a minister, and they'd sort it out for her,' according to one former official. She used it to get stories. An adviser from the Ministry of Defence recalls the government being under pressure about British soldiers being killed and maimed by roadside bombs in Afghanistan: 'We were told we couldn't release all we were doing for op-sec reasons, yet the MoD went ahead and gave the information to the *Sun*.'

More than that, she used her influence to try to change government policy, not simply and legitimately by publishing stories but privately with ministers by cajoling, insisting, playing on their fear. This might be aimed at scoring a victory for her newspapers – persuading the government to order a police review of the Madeleine McCann case as part of her strategy to encourage the toddler's parents to let her newspapers serialise their book; pushing hard to end the career of Sharon Shoesmith, head of children's services in Haringey, whom the *Sun* blamed for the death of Baby P. Shoesmith was sacked, a decision that was later described by the court of appeal as 'intrinsically unlawful'. Or Brooks aimed at larger policy which suited the ideology of the *Sun* and of its owner – over crime, immigration, public spending and notoriously over Britain's membership of the European Union and its potential involvement in the euro.

This exercise of power reached a peak with the sequence of events surrounding Murdoch's attempt to buy BSkyB: the *Sun* turning on Gordon Brown in September 2009; the sustained campaign of hostile reporting apparently calculated to ensure that the electorate would force him out of office; the parallel campaign in all the Murdoch titles attacking the BBC and Ofcom; the announcement of the BSkyB bid within a month of David Cameron's election; the Cameron government imposing drastic cuts on the BBC and Ofcom; Cameron's culture secretary, Jeremy Hunt, allowing his special adviser to act as a back channel to the Murdochs while he considered the bid. Hunt duly gave a green light to the deal, which was within days of being confirmed in July 2011 when the hacking scandal erupted and moved parliament to denounce it.

And in all of this, Brooks consistently injected a highly contentious political ideology into the arteries of public debate, a toxic cocktail of crude populism and intellectual confusion. They demanded lower taxes and then damned public services for the failures inflicted on them by lack of funding. She led the cheers for stripping regulation out of the financial sector and then blamed Brussels for the ensuing crisis in the eurozone. She attacked the state when it inhibited corporate power and then promoted it when it engaged in military violence. She insisted on wars and then dared to claim to be the protectors of the soldiers who died in them (while Mulcaire, without her knowledge, hacked the phones of some of their families). She was a leader of opinion who had thought no further than the bland and self-serving simplicity of James Murdoch's theory about free media, that the only guide to independence is profit.

As a single example of the distorting impact of their work, YouGov in December 2012, working for the TUC, found that the average public perception was that 41 per cent of the welfare budget was spent on the unemployed. The reality is 3 per cent. And that 27 per cent of that budget was eaten up by fraud. The reality, as far as official figures can detect, is 0.7 per cent. So the simple, beautiful idea of all citizens voting for government became an exercise in the bland leading the blind.

And while Operation Weeting succeeded in bringing cases to court, these 'crimes' remain unchallenged. The power remains. Leveson's attempt at independent media regulation was throttled at birth, not simply by the genuine concerns of those who care about a free press but also by a Fleet Street campaign of aggressive falsehood and distortion of precisely the kind that had made the Leveson Inquiry necessary in the first place. Police officers resigned and politicians were embarrassed as the scandal erupted, but Scotland Yard – with dazzling cynicism – has reacted by trying to silence the kind of police whistleblowers who helped to expose the failures of their leaders; and ambitious politicians continue to dine with Rupert Murdoch. How long before News Corp's famous summer party is revived as a compulsory opportunity for political genuflection?

It seems to have become forgotten, conveniently by some, that before the Old Bailey trial, two former newsdesk executives, Greg Miskiw and James Weatherup, pleaded guilty, as did the phone-hacker Glenn Mulcaire and a former reporter, Dan Evans, who confessed to hacking Sienna Miller's messages on Daniel Craig's phone.

Neville Thurlbeck, the *News of the World*'s former chief reporter and news editor, pleaded guilty after the police found the tapes he had of Blunkett's messages in a News International safe.

In the trial, Coulson was convicted of conspiring to hack phones while he was editor of the *News of the World*. The jury was discharged after failing to reach unanimous verdicts on two further charges of conspiring to commit misconduct in a public office faced by Coulson and Goodman.

But Brooks was found not guilty of four charges including conspiring to hack phones when she was editor of the *News of the World* and making corrupt payments to public officials when she was editor of the *Sun*. She was also cleared of two charges that she conspired with her former secretary and her husband to conceal evidence from police investigating phone hacking in 2011.

The jury at the Old Bailey returned true verdicts according to the evidence. They were not asked to do more.

8 July

Brazil 1: Germany 7

DANIEL TAYLOR

It was the night Germany removed the crown from football royalty. They did so with their own version of the beautiful game and, by the time they had finished, Brazil had suffered an ignominy that was so extreme and implausible it felt as though a black marker pen had been taken to the pages of their football history.

No team in that famous shirt has ever suffered in the way Luiz Felipe Scolari's did during a brutal first half in which Germany scored five times in 19 minutes and played as though their opponents might as well have been invited from the beach. Brazil had not lost a competitive match at home since 1975 but they were not just removed from their own World Cup. They were embarrassed in a way that will make them look back on this tournament and want to shelter their eyes. It was football's equivalent of chewing on broken glass and they should probably just be grateful Germany did not make it even more harrowing after André Schürrle had added another two goals in the second half.

This was not a team losing. It was a dream dying. There was anger, resentment and something approaching a full-on mutiny when Scolari and his players lingered too long on the pitch at the end. Yet there was also an appreciation of what they were seeing. Schürrle's second goal prompted a standing ovation. Soon afterwards Brazil's fans could be heard shouting '*olé*' to every German touch.

Until this stage Brazil's matches had been a celebration of colour and noise. Yet now there was the eerie sound of silence and other noises, too. At times it was something approaching fear, a strange gargled sound that could be heard every time Germany elegantly broke forward, threatening more humiliation. The sight of Brazil, with all their rich football history, being dismantled this way was actually shocking.

What cannot happen, however, is for the story to be all about Brazil's deficiencies when Germany have just put on one of the all-time performances. It was a masterclass. No other word does it justice and all that is left for Joachim Löw now is to hope his team have not peaked too early. If they illuminate the final in this way, they will surely have too much expertise for Argentina or Holland.

For Brazil the inquest will be torturous. It was always going to end in tears of some sort but nobody could have imagined the television cameras would already be zooming in on the first sobs midway through the first half. That was at 3–0, and five minutes later the score had risen to five. If it had continued at that rate for the rest of the match, Brazil would have sieved 15. And there were times in that first half, crazy as it sounds, when it did seem as though Germany were genuinely in the mood for double figures.

In the process Miroslav Klose scored his 16th World Cup goal, removing Ronaldo from the record books and earning himself a standing ovation when he was substituted later in the match. Thomas Müller oozed confidence, scoring his fifth goal of the tournament and playing with the nonchalant brilliance that made it seem as though all this was perfectly normal. Mesut Özil did not score but he did enough, all the same, to turn the volume down on some of his critics. More than anyone, there was Toni Kroos – left foot, right foot – showing why Real Madrid want to take him from Bayern Munich. Kroos, with two goals of his own, was the outstanding performer, though Sami Khedira was not far behind.

And Brazil? After all the pining *in absentia* for Neymar, the brandishing of his No 10 jersey during the national anthems and the '*Força Neymar*' baseball caps, maybe they should have given more credence to the fact that Thiago Silva was also missing, without even a fraction of the hysteria. The night was a personal ordeal for Dante, Silva's replacement, while David Luiz had suddenly reverted to being a player who will always give his opponents a chance.

Brazil's defending could be neatly encapsulated in that moment, after 11 minutes, when Kroos sent over a corner from the right. Seven players in yellow and blue had joined Júlio César inside the six-yard area. But not one had bothered picking up Müller and by the time Luiz realised there was a man spare it was too late. Müller's volley punished Brazil for some of the worst marking imaginable and what followed was a full-on disintegration.

Germany sensed their opponents were vulnerable and were absolutely merciless. Kroos's beautifully weighted through-ball, then Müller's lay-off, set up Klose to beat César at the second attempt for 2–0. In the next attack Philipp Lahm crossed from the right and Müller miskicked his attempt at goal. The ball arrived on Kroos's left boot and it was a cannonball of a shot for the third goal. Brazil were in disarray and the fourth was even worse from their point of view. Fernandinho lost the ball to Kroos, who broke through the centre, exchanged passes with Khedira and then slotted his shot past a hopelessly exposed goalkeeper.

By the time Khedira made it five, aided and abetted by Özil, after carving another route straight through the centre of Brazil's defence, it was tempting to wonder whether it was ever going to stop. 'It was like we blanked out,' Scolari said afterwards, reflecting on a 'catastrophe' and 'the worst moment of my life'.

Brazil were booed off at half-time and the anger manifested itself later in the scapegoating of Fred, their non-scoring goal scorer. Schürrle stroked in Lahm's centre for the sixth goal and then whacked in a shot off the underside of the crossbar. Oscar's stoppage-time goal could never be described as a consolation. Brazil had been outclassed in every department.

15 JULY

A tale of two careers:
Gove and Iain Duncan Smith

PATRICK WINTOUR

Compare and contrast a tale of two careers. Michael Gove, consigliere of David Cameron, intellectually adept and demonic in his determination to drive through reform, but demoted as education secretary and dispatched to the officers' mess as chief whip.

Half a mile away on the other side of Victoria Street, sitting inside the Department for Work and Pensions, remains Iain Duncan Smith, a man who has seen his welfare reforms repeatedly crash against the rocks of Whitehall's information technology, a self-deluding good-news culture and the messy reality of the lives of benefit claimants.

Both men are passionate and sincere reformers, determined in their own way to give greater opportunities for the poor. One, in his own terms, has succeeded, and done exactly what he and Cameron promised in the Conservative manifesto. He created academies, established free schools and imposed his no-excuses culture in schools. Multiple eggs have been broken, but there is a recognisable omelette.

The other has failed, leaving the Treasury, the National Audit Office and the Major Projects Authority exasperated. Multiple eggs have been broken and they have largely been scraped off the kitchen floor.

Yet it is Gove that has been demoted – a state of affairs that says much about Cameron and the balance of forces inside the Conservative party.

The easy, but false, explanation is that Gove has alienated teaching unions. Previous education secretaries from Kenneth Baker and Margaret Thatcher to David Blunkett have calculated that unpopularity with the National Union of Teachers goes with the territory. A greater error may be that he lost the support of teachers as a profession. But his unforgivable sin may be that he has left too many parents convinced that he pursued reform in the name of ideology, and not education. One MP argued Lynton Crosby, the party's election strategist, has declared he wants the barnacles off the boat. 'Well, Michael Gove was the King of the Barnacles,' they said.

In truth, few politicians below the highest rank register with the public. In most front rooms politicians are a grey blur of identikit-suited men. Gove, however, is an honourable exception.

A recent YouGov poll found 66 per cent know George Osborne and 60 per cent know Theresa May. But fully 57 per cent can also identify Michael Gove as education secretary. There is then a big jump down to 36 per cent until you reach Duncan Smith as work and pensions secretary.

Now, Gove's fame may simply be a product of his lengthy four-year tenure in education. Most secretaries of state last half as long. Yet notoriety is not just caused by longevity. It is demeanour.

He regarded his reforms to education, his passion to destroy the so-called blob – the amoebic educational establishment – as part of a civil rights struggle to liberate the poor. Pictures of Martin Luther King and Lenin – and Margaret Thatcher – have adorned his office.

His other great hero has been Tony Blair. He regards the former Labour leader's autobiography, *A Journey*, as the bible for any committed public-service reformer. Blair in his book rails against 'the givens' in any public service and hails speed, as the hourglass is always against you.

In that spirit, Gove deployed a group of advisers who developed a near-blitzkrieg mentality. An education act was on the statute book within seven weeks of the coalition coming to power. The danger was that dissent from any quarter became synonymous with institutional conservatism, and so could be dismissed. Too many initiatives looked as if education had become a laboratory. Some reforms blew up even before they reached the launch pad, such as the reinvention of Britain's school exam system. Others looked better on paper, such as scrapping Building Schools for the Future, than in reality.

His advisers, such as Dominic Cummings, had a proclivity for honesty bordering on the suicidal. Not for nothing did Cameron recently describe Cummings as a career psychopath. Only someone as committed as Cummings would say: 'There's institutional power that needs to be destroyed. A lot of our job is walking along the cliff edge and stamping their fingers off.' On his Twitter feed he said Gove had spent four years subverting the Whitehall and Downing Street process, and expected to last only two years, hence the necessary pace.

But a different reading of *A Journey* shows Blair recognised the distinction between political courage and political oblivion, and between tactics and strategy. 'The leader,' Blair wrote, 'should seek to persuade and in so doing use all their powers of persuasion, argument and charm at their disposal. That's tactics and should be deployed effectively and competently. The strategy should be to point to where the best future lies.'

The personal paradox is that Gove is polite, solicitous and self-aware to a point. Few politicians know their strengths and weaknesses as well as Gove.

Everyone will have their own moment when Gove burned one too many bridges. Many say it was unwise to allow free schools to be built in areas of prosperity. But the attacks on Sir Michael Wilshaw's Ofsted, and the decision to retire Sally Morgan, the Blairite chair of Ofsted, in retrospect looks like the point of over-stretch. However fluent a secretary of state may be, he or she needs sympathetic messengers to explain reforms.

It is true that education may be only the seventh most important issue in voters' minds, according to YouGov, but none of Gove's central reforms are popular. Voters want qualified teachers in the classroom by 66 per cent to 21 per cent; they want a national curriculum in every school by 56 per cent to 31 per cent; and they oppose free schools by 47 per cent to 27 per cent. Support for the Conservatives among England's teachers has fallen off a cliff.

By contrast Duncan Smith's welfare reforms are popular. They may not, in the case of Universal Credit, the Work Programme or the Personal Independent Payment, have been effectively planned, but in the public mind, his reforms, such as the cap on welfare benefits, work.

Part of Gove's difficulty is that parents, for all the talk of aspiration, are conservative. They are mostly proud of the local school their children attend, and they respect the teachers. For most parents Britain's lowly rankings in the Pisa league tables are probably something to do with Italian football.

A rueful Nick Clegg, reflecting on the unpopularity of the coalition's health reforms, once admitted that it is best in politics to make sure the public believe there is a problem with a public service before you suggest a solution.

Gove's defenders point out that the bulk of his big reforms are now in train and irreversible. Since 2010, there have been 3,500 academies, 180 free schools, 250,000 fewer pupils in failing schools and £18bn being spent on school buildings over the parliament. So 'if you seek his monument, look around you'.

The new education secretary, Nicky Morgan, may be more emollient, and the free school programme may be slowed or be made more accountable, but Gove's legacy will not be torn up. A further 200 academies are due to open in the next two years.

Finally, spare a thought for the Conservatives' coalition partners. The Liberal Democrats, in search of identity, were preparing to run an election campaign as the Not Gove party. Now he is gone, if not forgotten.

16 JULY

Witness to a shelling

PETER BEAUMONT

The first projectile hit the sea wall of Gaza City's little harbour just after four o'clock. As the smoke from the explosion thinned, four figures could be seen running, ragged silhouettes, legs pumping furiously along the wall. Even from a distance of 200 metres, it was obvious that three of them were children.

Jumping off the harbour wall, they turned on to the beach, attempting to cross the short distance to the safety of the Al-Deira hotel, base for many of the journalists covering the Gaza conflict.

They waved and shouted at the watching journalists as they passed a little collection of brightly coloured beach tents, used by bathers in peacetime.

It was there that the second shell hit the beach, those firing apparently adjusting their fire to target the fleeing survivors. As it exploded, journalists standing by the terrace wall shouted: 'They are only children.'

In the space of 40 seconds, four boys who had been playing hide-and-seek among fishermen's shacks on the wall were dead. They were aged between seven and 11; two were named Mohammad, one Zakaria and the youngest Ahed. All were members of the extended Bakr family.

Three others who were injured made it to the hotel: Hamad Bakr, aged 13, with shrapnel in his chest; his cousin Motasem, 11, injured in his head and legs, and Mohammad Abu Watfah, 21, who was hit by shrapnel in his stomach.

A man who had been near them reached the hotel terrace first, scrambling up a steep sandy bank. A skinny man in his 30s, he groaned and held up a T-shirt already staining red with blood where he was hit in the stomach. He fainted and was carried to a taxi waved down in the street as he grew pale and limp.

The children were brought up next. Pulling up the T-shirt of the first boy, journalists administering first aid found a shrapnel hole, small and round as a pencil head, where he had been hit in the chest. Another boy, a brother or cousin, who was uninjured, slumped by the wall, weeping.

The injured boy cried in pain as the journalists cleaned and dressed the wound, wrapping a field dressing around his chest. He winced in pain, clearly embarrassed too as a colleague checked his shorts to look for unseen femoral bleeding. A waiter grabbed a tablecloth to use as a stretcher, but a photographer took the boy in his arms to carry him to the ambulance.

The Israeli military said it was looking into the incident. The Israel Defence Force told the AFP in a statement: 'Based on preliminary results, the target of this strike was Hamas terrorist operatives. The reported civilian casualties from this strike are a tragic outcome.'

The Islamist group Hamas, which controls Gaza, on Wednesday formally rejected Egypt's ceasefire proposal that had been accepted by Israel to end the nine-day-old conflict which has left at least 213 Palestinians and one Israeli dead. In a text message to the Associated Press, a senior Hamas figure, Sami Abu Zuhri, said: 'We informed Cairo today officially that we don't accept the proposal they made.'

He added that Hamas felt 'alone in the field' with little support from the Arab world and called on the Palestinian president, Mahmoud Abbas, of the rival Fatah faction in the West Bank, to support Hamas's refusal of the ceasefire deal.

Diplomatic sources told the *Guardian* that they did not believe that a serious new ceasefire proposal was likely to emerge for several days and, even then, securing a deal looked very difficult.

Hamas's rejection came as an Israeli official said Israel's defence minister had asked prime minister Binyamin Netanyahu's security cabinet to authorise the mobilisation of another 8,000 reserves. The military has said about 30,000 reservists have been called up since the Israeli offensive began last week.

Israeli experts have been predicting in recent days that any ground attack, which Israel has threatened, may involve overland raids in the Gaza Strip to destroy command bunkers and tunnels that have allowed the outgunned Palestinians to withstand air and naval barrages and keep the rockets flying. Hamas continued to fire dozens of rockets into Israel on Wednesday.

Hamas views a significant easing of the Israeli blockade as key to its survival, but does not believe Egypt's current rulers – who deposed a Hamas-friendly government in Cairo last year – can be fair brokers.

The Egyptian proposal called for a halt in hostilities by Tuesday night to be followed by talks on the terms of a longer-term cease-fire, including easing Gaza's seven-year-old border blockade by Israel and Egypt. Israeli air raids on Gaza on Wednesday saw the targeting of 30 houses, including those of senior Hamas leaders, most notably Mahmoud al-Zahar, Hamas's former foreign minister.

Alongside the air strikes, Israel told tens of thousands of residents of the northern town of Beit Lahiya and the Zeitoun and Shujai'iya neighbourhoods of Gaza City – all near the Israel border – to evacuate their homes by 8 a.m. The warnings came by automated phone calls, texts and leaflets dropped from planes.

The Israeli military said in its message that large numbers of rockets were being launched from these areas and that Israel planned to bomb these locations.

'Whoever disregards these instructions and fails to evacuate immediately endangers their own lives, as well as those of their families,' the message said.

At the al-Shifa hospital on Wednesday afternoon, Hamad Bakr was conscious and waiting for surgery to remove the shrapnel from his chest and drain fluid from his chest cavity. 'My father has a fishing boat there. We were playing hide-and-seek when we were hit. I didn't hear the first one which killed one of us but I heard the second as we were running along the beach. That one killed three more.'

His mother Taghrid, 35, came into the room. 'Why did you go out of the door?' she demanded of Hamad. She said that his brother, Younis, who was with Hamad while he was being treated, 'is so scared that he is shaking'.

Suddenly angry and grief-stricken, she said: 'They killed my nephew. Who does that? Who fires on children?'

As the reporters left, Mohammad Abu Watfah was wheeled out of a lift after surgery to remove the shrapnel in his stomach. As relatives gathered not far from the Al-Deira hotel to bury the four dead boys, barely 90 minutes after the attack on the beach, the boys' uncle, Abdel Kareem Bakr, 41, said: 'It's a cold-blooded massacre. It's a shame they didn't identify them as kids with all of the advanced technology they claim they're using.'

18 JULY

I, spy: Edward Snowden in exile

ALAN RUSBRIDGER
AND EWEN MACASKILL

Fiction and films, the nearest most of us knowingly get to the world of espionage, give us a series of reliable stereotypes. British spies are hard-bitten, libidinous he-men. Russian agents are thickset, low-browed and facially scarred. And defectors end up as tragic old soaks in Moscow, scanning old copies of *The Times* for news of the test match.

Such a fate was anticipated for Edward Snowden by Michael Hayden, a former NSA and CIA chief, who predicted last September that the former NSA analyst would be stranded in Moscow for the rest of his days – 'isolated, bored, lonely, depressed ... and alcoholic'.

But the Edward Snowden who materialises in our hotel room shortly after noon on the appointed day seems none of those things. A year into his exile in Moscow, he feels less, not more, isolated. If he is depressed, he doesn't show it. And, at the end of seven hours of conversation, he refuses a beer. 'I actually don't drink.' He smiles when repeating Hayden's jibe. 'I was like, wow, their intelligence is worse than I thought.'

Oliver Stone, who is working on a film about the man now standing in room 615 of the Golden Apple hotel on Moscow's Malaya Dmitrovka, might struggle to make his subject live up to the canon of great movie spies. The American director has visited Snowden in Moscow, and wants to portray him as an out-and-out hero, but he is an unconventional one: quiet, disciplined, unshowy, almost academic in his speech. If Snowden has vices – and God knows they must have been looking for them – none has emerged in the 13 months since he slipped away from his life as a contracted NSA analyst in Hawaii, intent on sharing the biggest cache of top-secret material the world has ever seen.

Since arriving in Moscow, Snowden has been keeping late and solitary hours – effectively living on US time, tapping away on one of his three computers (three to be safe; he uses encrypted chat, too). If anything, he appears more connected and outgoing than he could be in his former life as an agent. Of his life now, he says, 'There's actually not that much difference. You know, I think there are guys who are just hoping to see me sad. And they're going to continue to be disappointed.'

When the *Guardian* first spoke to Snowden a year ago in Hong Kong, he had been dishevelled, his hair uncombed, wearing jeans and a T-shirt. The 31-year-old who materialised last week was smartly, if anonymously, dressed in black trousers and grey jacket, his hair tidily cut. He is jockey-light – even skinnier than a year ago. And he looks pale: 'Probably three steps from death,' he jokes. 'I mean, I don't eat a whole lot. I keep a weird schedule. I used to be very active, but just in the recent period I've had too much work to focus on.'

There was no advance warning of where we would meet: his only US television interview, with NBC's Brian Williams in

May, was conducted in an anonymous hotel room of Snowden's choosing. This time, he prefers to come to us.

On his arrival, there is a warm handshake for *Guardian* reporter Ewen MacAskill, whom he last saw in Hong Kong – a Sunday night after a week of intense work in a frowsty hotel room, a few hours before the video revealing his identity to the world went public. Neither man knew if they would ever meet again.

Snowden orders chicken curry from room service and, as he forks it down, is immediately into the finer points of the story that yanked him from a life of undercover anonymity to global fame. The Snowden-as-alcoholic jibe is not the only moment when he reflects wryly on his former colleagues' patchy ability to get on top of events over the past year. There was, for instance, the incident last July when a plane carrying President Evo Morales back to Bolivia from Moscow was forced down in Vienna and searched for a stowaway Snowden. 'I was like, first off, wow, their intelligence sucks, from listening to everything. But, two, are they really going to the point of just completely humiliating the president of a Latin American nation, the representative of so many people? It was just shockingly poorly thought out, and yet they did it anyway, and they keep at these sorts of mistakes.' It was as if they were trying not to find him. 'I almost felt like I had some sort of friend in government.'

He is guarded on the subject of his life in exile. Yes, he cooks for himself – often Japanese ramen, which he finds easy to sling together. Yes, he goes out. 'I don't live in absolute secrecy — I live a pretty open life – but at the same time I don't want to be a celebrity, you know. I don't want to go somewhere and have people pay attention to me, just as I don't want to do that in the media.'

He does get recognised. 'It's a little awkward at times, because my Russian's not as good as it should be. I'm still learning.' He declines an invitation to demonstrate for us ('The last thing I want is clips of me speaking Russian floating around the internet'). He has been picking his way through Dostoevsky, and belatedly catching up with series one of *The Wire*, while reading the recently published memoir of Daniel Ellsberg, the Pentagon Papers whistleblower.

In October last year, he was photographed on a Moscow tourist boat. 'Right. I didn't look happy in that picture.' And pushing a loaded shopping trolley across a road? 'You know, I actually don't know, because it was so far away and it was blurry. I mean, it could have been me.' Does he go out in disguise? He is deadpan: 'Before I go to the grocery store, I make sure to put on, you know, my Groucho Marx glasses and nose and moustache ... No, I don't wander around in disguise.' The only props in evidence today are an American Civil Liberties Union baseball cap and dark glasses, tossed on to the bed. Some disguise.

He is not working for a Russian organisation, as has been reported, but is financially secure for the immediate future. In addition to substantial savings from his career as a well-compensated contractor, he has received numerous awards and speaking fees from around the world. He is also in the process of securing foundation funding for a new press freedom initiative, creating tools that allow journalists to communicate securely.

But push Snowden further on his life in Moscow and he clams up. There are all sorts of plausible reasons for his reticence. He thinks it reasonable to assume he is under some form of surveillance, by both the Russians and the Americans. There is a small chance that he could be harassed, or worse, if his routine or whereabouts became known. Nor does he want to be 'Russianised': pictures of him in Red Square would not play well back home.

He feels the world has got some things wrong about him, but even so he would rather not correct the record publicly. He was exasperated to be marked down as a conservative libertarian, for example (he is, he says, more moderate than has been reported), but declines to be more specific about his actual politics. It would simply alienate some people, he believes. He thinks journalists have speculated too much about his family (his father has visited him in Moscow), and misunderstood his relationship with Lindsay, the girlfriend he left behind in Hawaii; life is more complicated than the headlines. But, again, he won't go on the record to talk about them.

At the same time, the people closest to him have plainly told Snowden he has to raise his profile if he wants to win over US hearts and minds. And, from his periodic self-corrections and occasional stop-start answers, it is evident he is on a mission to make friends, not enemies. At the end of a diplomatic answer to a question about Germany, he breaks off in frustration. 'That's probably too political. I hate politics. Really, I mean, this is not me, you know. I hope you guys can tell the difference.'

The Snowden-as-traitor camp will take his reluctance to vouchsafe too many details as confirmation that he is, if not a double agent, then a 'useful idiot' for the Kremlin. He tackles some of these criticisms head-on. He didn't take a single document to Russia. He has no access to them there. He never initially sought to be in Russia – it happened 'entirely by accident'. It's a 'modern country ... and it's been good to me', but he would rather be free to travel. He repeats his criticisms of Russia's record on human rights and free speech, and tacitly concedes that his televised question to Vladimir Putin in April this year was an error.

What about the Russian spy thesis, advanced by the *Economist* writer Edward Lucas, among others? Lucas has said that, had Snowden come to him with the NSA documents, he would have marched him straight to a police station. 'Yeah, he's crazy,' Snowden sighs. 'He's not credible at all.'

One of the Lucas charges was a 'fishy' September 2010 trip to India, where he speculates Snowden may have met unspecified

Russians or intermediaries, and attended a hacking course. 'It's bullshit,' Snowden exclaims. 'I was on official visits, working at the US embassy. You know, it's not like they didn't know I was there. And the six-day course afterwards, it wasn't a security course, it was a programming course. But it doesn't matter. I mean, there are always going to be conspiracy theories. If my reputation is harmed by being here, there or any other place, that's OK, because it's not about me.

'I can give a blanket response to all the Russia questions,' he adds. 'If the government had the tiniest shred of evidence, not even that [I was an agent], but associating with the Russian government, it would be on the front page of the *New York Times* by lunchtime.'

What about the accusation that his leaks have caused untold damage to the intelligence capabilities of the West? 'The fact that people know communications can be monitored does not stop people from communicating [digitally]. Because the only choices are to accept the risk, or to not communicate at all,' he says, almost weary at having to spell out what he considers self-evident.

'And when we're talking about things like terrorist cells, nuclear proliferators – these are organised cells. These are things an individual cannot do on their own. So if they abstain from communicating, we've already won. If we've basically talked the terrorists out of using our modern communications networks, we have benefited in terms of security – we haven't lost.'

There still remains the charge that he has weakened the very democracy he professes he wants to protect. Al-Qaida, according to MI6 chief Sir John Sawers, have been 'rubbing their hands with glee'.

'I can tell you right now that in the wake of the last year, there are still terrorists getting hauled up, there are still communications being intercepted. There are still successes in intelligence operations that are being carried out all around the world.'

Why not let the agencies collect the haystacks of data so they can look for the needles within?

Snowden doesn't like the haystack metaphor, used exhaustively by politicians and intelligence chiefs in defence of mass data collections. 'I would argue that simply using the term "haystack" is misleading. This is a haystack of human lives. It's all the private records of the most intimate activities, that are aggregated and compiled again and again, and stored for increasing frequencies of time.

'It may be that by watching everywhere we go, by watching everything we do, by analysing every word we say, by waiting and passing judgment over every association we make and every person we love, that we could uncover a terrorist plot, or we could discover more criminals. But is that the kind of society we want to live in? That is the definition of a security state.'

When did he last read George Orwell's *Nineteen Eighty-Four*? 'Actually, quite some time ago. Contrary to popular belief, I don't think we are exactly in that universe. The danger is that we can see how [Orwell's] technologies now seem unimaginative and quaint. They talked about things like microphones implanted in bushes and cameras in TVs that look back at us. But now we've got webcams that go with us everywhere. We actually buy cell phones that are the equivalent of a network microphone that we carry around in our pockets voluntarily. Times have shown that the world is much more unpredictable and dangerous [than Orwell imagined].'

But the life he describes inside the closed walls of the NSA does have echoes of Big Brother omniscience. Snowden, sipping Pepsi from a bottle and speaking in perfectly composed sentences, recalls the period when he was working as an analyst, directing the work of others. There was a moment when he and, he says, other colleagues began to have severe doubts about the ethics of what they were doing.

Can he give an example of what made him feel uneasy? 'Many of the people searching through the haystacks were young, enlisted guys, 18 to 22 years old. They've suddenly been thrust into a position of extraordinary responsibility, where they now have access to all your private records. In the course of their daily work, they stumble across something that is completely unrelated in any sort of necessary sense – for example, an intimate nude photo of someone in a sexually compromising situation. But they're extremely attractive. So what do they do? They turn around in their chair and they show a co-worker. And their co-worker says, "Oh, hey, that's great. Send that to Bill down the way," and then Bill sends it to George, George sends it to Tom, and sooner or later this person's whole life has been seen by all of these other people.'

The analysts don't discuss such things in the NSA cafeterias, but back in the office 'anything goes, more or less. You're in a vaulted space. Everybody has sort of similar clearances, everybody knows everybody. It's a small world. It's never reported, because the auditing of these systems is incredibly weak. The fact that records of your intimate moments have been taken from your private communication stream, from the intended recipient, and given to the government, without any specific authorisation, without any specific need, is itself a violation of your rights. Why is that in the government database?'

How often do such things happen? 'I'd say probably every two months. It's routine enough. These are seen as sort of the fringe benefits of surveillance positions.'

And the auditing is really not good enough to pick up such abuses? 'A 29-year-old walked in and out of the NSA with all of their private records,' he shoots back. 'What does that say about their auditing? They didn't even know.'

He emphasises that his co-workers were not 'moustache-twirling villains' but 'people like you and me'. Still, most colleagues, even if they felt doubts, would not complain, having seen the fate of previous whistleblowers, who ended up vilified and 'pulled out of the shower at gunpoint, naked, in front of their families. We all have mortgages. We all have families.'

As the leaden skies darken beyond the net curtains, Snowden breaks to order a bowl of ice cream (chocolate, vanilla and strawberry sorbet). Afterwards, he warms to his theme, explaining how he and his colleagues relied heavily on 'metadata' – the information about our locations, searches and contacts that needed no warrants or court orders, but that betrays a huge amount about our lives. 'To an analyst, nine times out of 10, you don't care what was said in the phone call till very late in the investigative chain. What you care about is the metadata, because metadata does not lie. People lie in phone calls when they're involved in real criminal activity. They use code words, they talk around it. You can't trust what you're hearing, but you can trust the metadata. That's the reason metadata's often more intrusive.'

What about his own digital habits? He won't use Google or Skype for anything personal. Dropbox? He laughs. 'They just put Condoleezza Rice on their board, who is probably the most anti-privacy official you can imagine. She's one of the ones who oversaw [the warrantless wire-tapping program] Stellar Wind and thought it was a great idea. So they're very hostile to privacy.' Instead, he recommends SpiderOak, a fully encrypted end-to-end 'zero-knowledge' file-sharing system.

Why should we trust Google any more than we trust the state? 'One, you don't have to. Association with Google is voluntary. But it does raise an important question. And I would say, while there is a distinction – in that Google can't put you in jail, Google can't task a drone to drop a bomb on your house – we shouldn't trust them without verifying what their activities are, how they're using our data.'

He is extremely alarmed by the implications of the NSA and GCHQ documents, which showed their engineers hard at work undermining the basic security of the internet – something that has also concerned Sir Tim Berners-Lee, the man credited with inventing the World Wide Web. 'What people often overlook is the fact that, when you build a back door into a communication system, that back door can be discovered by anyone around the world. That can be a private individual or a security researcher at a university, but it can also be a criminal group or a foreign intelligence agency – say, the NSA's equivalent in a deeply irresponsible government. And now that foreign country can scrutinise not just your bank records, but your private communications all around the internet.'

The problem with the current system of political oversight is twofold, he says. First, the politicians and the security services are too close: no politician wants to defy intelligence chiefs who warn of the potential consequences of being seen to be 'weak'. And then there's the problem that, in most societies, the job of monitoring the security agencies goes to the most senior politicians or, in the UK, retired judges – most of whom, he believes, do not have the technical literacy to understand what it is they should be looking for, or regulating.

'What last year's revelations showed us was irrefutable evidence that unencrypted communications on the internet are no longer safe. Any communications should be encrypted by default.' This has big implications for anyone using email, text, cloud computing, or Skype, or phones, to communicate in circumstances where they have a professional duty of confidentiality. 'The work of journalism has become immeasurably harder. Journalists have to be particularly conscious about any sort of network signalling; any sort of connection; any sort of licence plate-reading device that they pass on their way to a meeting point; any place they use their credit card; any place they take their phone; any email contact they have with the source. Because that very first contact, before encrypted communications are established, is enough to give it all away.' To journalists, he would add 'lawyers, doctors, investigators, possibly even accountants. Anyone who has an obligation to protect the privacy of their clients is facing a new and challenging world.'

But ask Snowden if technology is compatible with privacy, and he answers with an unequivocal 'absolutely', mainly because he believes that technology itself will come up with the solutions.

'The question is, why are private details that are transmitted online any different from the details of our lives that are stored in our private journals? There shouldn't be this distinction between digital and printed information. But the US government, and many other countries, are increasingly seeking to make that distinction.'

Snowden is not against targeted surveillance. But he returns to the philosophical, ethical, legal and constitutional objections to security agencies routinely seizing digital material from innocent people, when they would not dream of entering their houses to plant spy cameras, or walk off with personal diaries and photographs. If these things are wrong in analogue life, why not in our digital lives? And where, he asks repeatedly, is the evidence that it is cost-effective? Or even effective?

Surely he would concede there are occasions when it is of benefit to police or intelligence agencies to be able to trawl collected records after a crime or terrorist event has taken place? He concedes there are 'hypotheticals' in which such a capability might have its uses, but he counters with questions of proportionality. America is not at war; terrorism should be treated as a criminal problem. He might personally draw the line in a different place in the event of a war, but, in any event, this is something that should be determined by democratic discussion.

'You have a tremendous population of young military enlisted individuals [in the NSA] who may not have had the number of life experiences to have felt the sense of being violated. And if we haven't been exposed to the dangers of having our liberties violated, how can we expect these individuals to reasonably represent our interests?'

He cites the German Stasi as an organisation staffed by people who thought they were 'protecting the stability of their political system, which they considered to be under threat. They were ordinary citizens like anyone else. They believed they were doing the right thing. But when we look at them in historic terms, what were they doing to their people? What were they doing to the countries around them? What was the net impact of their mass, indiscriminate spying campaigns?'

The skies over Moscow are darkening as Snowden prepares to go. We give him a fragment of a smashed-up hard drive, a memento of the *Guardian*'s tangles with GCHQ: a year ago this weekend, senior editors destroyed computers used to store Snowden's documents while GCHQ representatives watched. 'Wow, that is the real deal,' he mutters, as he examines the scarred circuit board. And then he speculates – maybe only half joking, for the tradecraft never quite goes – that it might have a tracking device in it. He says that he faces a logistical nightmare in getting home undetected tonight. A driver is waiting for him outside.

Will he be watching that night's World Cup semi-final between Holland and Argentina? 'You know, this is probably going to surprise a lot of people, but I'm not particularly athletic. I'm not a great sports fan.'

He wonders if we will want to shake his hand. We do. An adviser has warned him not to be offended if visitors are anxious about a photograph of a handshake that might come back to haunt them.

He means, if it turns out Snowden really is a Russian spy?

'Right, exactly. If you guys were running for office, then you'd be in trouble.'

And with that he picks up his rucksack and slips out of the room, back into the curious world of semi-anonymous exile that may be his fate for a long time to come.

'No one should die penniless and alone'

AMELIA GENTLEMAN

We know that David Clapson was actively searching for work when he died because a pile of CVs he had just printed out was found a few metres from his body. The last time he spoke to his sister, a few days before he died, he told her he was waiting to hear back about an application he had made to the supermarket chain Lidl.

But officials at the Jobcentre believed he was not taking his search for work seriously enough, and early last July, they sanctioned him – cutting off his benefit payments entirely, as a punishment for his failure to attend two appointments.

Clapson, 59, who had diabetes, died in his flat in Stevenage on 20 July 2013, from diabetic ketoacidosis (caused by an acute lack of insulin). When Gill Thompson, his younger sister, discovered his body, she found his electricity had been cut off (meaning that the fridge where he kept his insulin was no longer working). There was very little left to eat in the flat – six tea bags, an out-of-date tin of sardines and a can of tomato soup. His pay-as-you-go mobile phone had just 5p credit left on it and he had only £3.44 in his bank account. The autopsy notes reveal that his stomach was empty.

The circumstances of Clapson's death have been scrutinised by many of the groups campaigning for a reform of the government's increasingly punitive (or rigorous, depending on your perspective) sanctions system, by which the Department for Work and Pensions (DWP) stops benefits payments to claimants who have not met the agreed conditions every jobseeker signs up to when they start to claim support. While sanctions have long been a part of the benefits system, and have cross-party support, new regulations introduced in October 2012 have meant that they are being handed out with greater frequency and for longer stretches of time. In 2013, 871,000 people were sanctioned, losing some or all of their benefits payments for a minimum of four weeks, rising to three years in exceptional cases. There are hardship payments for those who are struggling, but only a minority are told about them, leaving many to survive on zero income.

Details of Clapson's death emerged just days after the publication of an independent review of sanctions, the Oakley report, commissioned by the DWP, which acknowledged that while the system as a whole was 'not fundamentally broken', it was 'clear that this is a system that can go wrong and, when that happens, individuals and families can suffer unfairly'. The report concluded that improvements were needed, 'particularly for more vulnerable individuals'. The government responded by agreeing to make all the proposed improvements. After a period of growing unease about the consequences of stricter sanctions, there appears now to be some official recognition that aspects of the system need to change.

Gill Thompson is uncomfortable about launching a public campaign, and talking about the way her brother died makes her cry, but she is forcing herself to speak about it because she wants the government to accept that improvements need to be made to the way sanctions are handed out. 'I don't want revenge or compensation; I just want lessons to be learned,' she says.

She is at pains to describe her brother as someone who had worked for 29 years, anxious to stress that he should not be seen as a 'scrounger'. He spent five years in the army, two of them serving in Belfast, 16 years working for BT and another eight at other companies, before he stopped working to care for their mother who had developed dementia. When she died three years ago, he began to look for a new job and was put on the government's new Work Programme, designed to help unemployed people find a job. He completed two periods of unpaid work experience, for B&Q and for a discount store. He told his sister he had enjoyed these sessions, and had hoped to be allowed to do more. He also completed a forklift truck training course. Although he struggled to use a computer, he had been trying to apply for jobs online. Thompson believes he was taking the process very seriously.

But at some point in May 2013, he missed two appointments with the Work Programme office, and was sent a letter informing him that his benefits would be stopped for a month; the last payment was made on 2 July, according to his sister. Six days later he was down to that last £3.44 (which he was unable to withdraw since it was less than £5). He died a fortnight later.

Thompson describes her brother as very quiet and private; he was not someone who liked to ask for help. 'I don't know what happened. He wasn't one for creating a fuss. He didn't tell me he had been sanctioned. He was very proud. If I'd known I would have gone over with food,' Thompson says. 'I could have sorted it out for him.'

A DWP spokesman says: 'Our sympathies are with the family of Mr Clapson. Decisions on sanctions aren't taken lightly – there is a chain of processes we follow before a sanction comes into effect, including taking every opportunity to contact the claimant several times. People can also appeal if they disagree. Mr Clapson did not appeal or ask for a reconsideration of the sanction or apply for a hardship payment.'

The DWP says Clapson was told during a phone call on 16 July that he could fill out a form to request hardship funds. He was sent a letter (dated 15 July) explaining how to apply for them, but his sister found it unopened in his flat. 'He was very bad at opening letters. People in his situation are frightened of these letters. They are never good news,' she says. Had he opened it, he might have found the language confusing. 'We cannot pay you your Jobseekers' Allowance from 28 June 2013,' the letter reads. 'This is because we recently told you that a decision would be made about a doubt: on whether you failed to comply with the requirements of the scheme to which you have been referred.'

Clapson's sister hopes now for a fuller investigation and wants to see reforms to the system so that people are treated with a greater degree of empathy. An online petition calling for an inquiry into his death has gathered 43,000 signatures.

'I don't think anyone should die like that in this country, alone, hungry and penniless,' she says. 'They must know that sanctioning people with diabetes is very dangerous. I am upset with the system; they are treating everyone as statistics and numbers.'

Several of the issues she raises chime with concerns highlighted in the Oakley report, which noted that many people found the letters they received 'complex and difficult to understand' and 'overly long and legalistic in their tone and content' and lacked 'personalised explanations of the reason for sanction referrals'. The correspondence was 'particularly difficult for the most vulnerable claimants to understand'. Another problem frequently highlighted was 'that letters could be left unopened or unread by claimants'.

For over a year, charities and welfare advice organisations have been warning the government over the increased use of sanctions. The food bank charity the Trussell Trust, which handed out over 900,000 three-day food parcels in 2013–14, said 83 per cent of its food banks reported that sanctioning is causing rising numbers to turn to them. Citizens Advice has seen a 60 per cent increase in the number of problems related to Jobseekers' Allowance sanctions since the minimum sanction period was increased from one week to four weeks in October 2012.

There was relief from some charities that the government-commissioned review recognised some of these issues. Leslie Morphy, chief executive of the homelessness charity Crisis, said: 'Sanctions are cruel and can leave people utterly destitute – without money even for food and at severe risk of homelessness.'

Charities question whether sanctions are achieving the stated aim, which is to encourage people back to work. The Oakley report also pointed out that so many people are having sanctions reviewed and overturned when they appeal against them that this 'results in a significant cost to the state'. Citizens Advice has noted the high success rate for those who appeal against sanctions, which chief executive Gillian Guy said 'reveals a culture of "sanction first and ask questions later"'. The charity warns that the longer minimum sanction period is counterproductive because 'claimants are distracted from job-hunting as they focus on putting food on the table and keeping a roof over their head'.

While Clapson's case has attracted front-page headlines, thousands of others have contacted advice centres, unhappy about the way their benefits have been stopped and overwhelmed by the challenge of looking for work at a time when they have no money for food, bus fares, phone calls and electricity.

Michael, 54, (who asked for his real name not to be published) was sanctioned for four months after failing to undertake a compulsory week's work experience at a local charity shop. He points out that it wasn't his fault he didn't do the work experience, because he was told by the charity shop that they didn't want him to work there.

'I was five minutes early, I was polite. I knew that if I didn't do the work, I would be sanctioned. I knew it was important. But they decided they didn't want me; I've no idea why that was. Two or three days later, when I tried to withdraw my Jobseekers' Allowance, there was no money in my account. I went to the cashpoint, put my card in and bingo! Nothing,' he says.

'I went to the Jobcentre and was told that my benefits had been sanctioned for four months. It was a huge shock.'

He didn't realise that he could appeal or that he was entitled to some hardship payments (and the Oakley report said only 23 per cent reported being told that they may qualify for emergency hardship payments if they had their out-of-work benefits stopped).

He was sanctioned early last September, and it was six weeks before (with the help of Citizens Advice) he began to get money again. In the meantime, he was left with no money to buy food, and no money to pay for his electricity. It was very difficult to rectify the problem because he had no money to pay for phone calls, and no money for the £4.50 return bus fare from his village to Witney, where the Jobcentre is based. Instead, he says he walked six miles there and six miles back (a journey that took two and a half hours each way) every week until his payments were reinstated.

He had no savings, no family to support him and few friends in the area. The little food he had in his cupboards was used up quickly and his electricity supply (on a card payment) ran out almost immediately. When, several weeks later, he found that there was a food bank he could get help from, about half of the food he was given was no good to him because it needed to be cooked. Occasionally he went into the corridor of his housing association home, at a time he was sure no one else would see him, and plugged his kettle into the communal socket to boil water for a cup of tea.

'It was bleak. You just give up,' he says. He denies that sanctions can prove a positive motivator, encouraging people to step up their search for work. On the contrary, it hampered his ability to find a job. 'It kills you. I haven't got a computer. I was limited to looking in shop windows for work.'

He makes light of feeling hungry. 'You deny it, I suppose. You go without. I went down to basics – a bag of crisps a day. You think it's only people abroad who live on scraps, but that's what you do.'

He has now found part-time work as a cook in a care home.

Terry Eaton, 58, worked most of his life as a builder, until he fell off a ladder and broke his ankles. He spent some time on sickness benefit, but more recently he was reassessed and found fit for work. Initially he was happy at the prospect of being sent on a programme to help him find work, but he struggled with the requirement to search for jobs on a computer ('I've never owned a computer; we didn't have computer lessons at school'), and to prove that he had applied for a fixed number of jobs a week. When he visits building sites, he has the impression he is rejected because of his age. He has been sanctioned several times this year.

'They don't tell you that you've been sanctioned. You go to the post office and find out that there is no money. Then you think there must have been some computer error, so you get on the phone, but you can't get through to talk to local people. You haven't got a clue who you're talking to. The calls aren't free, so after a while you can't afford to make any more.'

If you go to a payphone, you need to put 80p in just to get through to officials, he says; given that you are often left on hold, you usually need about £4 in your pocket to fund the call.

He was sanctioned a second time, when he was already sanctioned, because he didn't have the £5.50 return bus fare he needed to attend an appointment. He is the youngest of eight brothers and sisters, who have helped him. His four sisters have brought him meals and helped with electricity payments. 'I am very lucky. I don't know how other people manage.'

He appealed successfully, although he hasn't received back-dated payments and is no longer asking for them. 'I can't afford to keep chasing them. You call them and they just say: "That's not our department."'

Rita, 30, (also not her real name) was made redundant from her job at Wallis clothes shop two years ago. She has repeatedly been sanctioned, she believes in error, and most of these sanctions have subsequently been overturned, although not until after she has been left without money for long stretches of time. One time she was sanctioned because she was 10 minutes late for an appointment; another time she missed an appointment because she was doing work experience elsewhere (and had received permission from a Jobcentre official). 'It was difficult to tell my friends and family. It is embarrassing enough to be on benefits but to be on benefits and struggling is not something that you just blurt out. Coming out from university, I didn't think this would happen. I didn't know how to say to people that I couldn't afford to eat.

'There was no electricity, so I had to go to sit in the library. I couldn't make any calls, so I hoped my friends would call me. There were times when I just sat at the bus stop wondering: "What am I going to do?"' In the evenings, because there was no electricity, she would put on layers of clothes and lie on her bed in the dark and cold.

'I couldn't travel and I couldn't make any calls because I couldn't afford it. I couldn't even afford to get the bus to come and sign on, but I knew that if I didn't come in I would be suspended again.'

She got into debt, and is now fighting an eviction process because she owes over a thousand pounds in rent.

Some Jobcentre staff are uneasy at the new rules surrounding sanctioning. A Public and Commercial Services Union (PCS) survey published in May showed that 70 per cent of surveyed PCS members who worked for the DWP did not believe that sanctioning has a positive impact on helping a claimant find work, while 76 per cent had seen an increase in food bank referrals.

One group of former DWP employees has set up a free online advice service, jobseekersanctionadvice.com. The founder, a 54-year-old grandmother who left the DWP in 2011 and who asked to remain anonymous, says she became uncomfortable with having to implement policies that she believed were designed to punish people for making small errors. Last Monday morning the site had 200 emails, most of them requests for assistance, but six of them offers to help staff the site; two of them from former DWP employees.

The founder says she was an award-winning employee while she worked for the Jobcentre. 'I know sanctions don't work. There are other ways to motivate people.' She hopes that the system will be reformed. 'When people get sanctioned, they don't get told. They don't get a chance to put their side of events. It is the vulnerable who are hit. They are easy targets; they don't fight back and they usually don't understand the rules.'

Few question the need for sanctions, and the idea that the government needs some kind of stick to ensure that people take their responsibility to look for work seriously is broadly supported. The concerns rest on the sensitivity with which they are imposed.

The DWP spokesman says: 'The new JSA sanctions regime, which was introduced in October 2012, encourages people to engage with the support being offered by Jobcentres by making it clearer to claimants what they are expected to do in return for their benefits – and that they risk losing them if they don't stick to the rules.' But in response to the Oakley review, the government has promised to look at the way it communicates with claimants and to 'clarify guidance' about the hardship payment process.

Clapson's sister hopes that her brother's death may encourage greater sensitivity towards claimants who are struggling. 'There is no humanity and they are getting the little people. Why sanction vulnerable and needy people?'

4 AUGUST

Commonwealth Games 2014: not defined by the sport but by Glasgow itself

ANDY BULL

It began with a game of lawn bowls, at a quarter to nine on a sunny Thursday morning. Kelvingrove seats about 2,500, which is just a little more than the population of some of the countries the fans had come to see compete. Such as Norfolk Island, whose women's team beat South Africa, the reigning champions, that same day.

Now, no doubt lawn bowls has its constituency – there are 914 registered clubs in Scotland, with around 75,000 members – but even the most ardent devotee, and I asked a few of them, would struggle to argue that, say, Malaysia's match against Niue was must-see sport. Tickets started at £15 each, half that for concessions. Add in a couple of cups of coffee and Cokes, £2.50 a pop, four bacon rolls at £5 each, and travel into the city, and it's almost £100 for a family of four. And yet, by the end of the morning, the stands were pretty much full.

It was the same at each of the 13 venues, on all of the 11 days. They sold 187,000 tickets for the four sessions of rugby sevens at Ibrox, the best part of 50,000 for each of the morning sessions of athletics at Hampden, 10,000 for the last day of the boxing at the Hydro, 3,000 for the finals of the weightlifting, almost 2,000 for each day of the judo, netball and wrestling preliminaries. The organisers say they shifted well over one million tickets, more than 92 per cent of the total allocation. On Saturday I spoke to a Scottish colleague whose daughters had decided at the last minute that they wanted to go to the Games just because 'everyone else was'. The only tickets they could get were for the semi-finals of the squash doubles at Scotstoun stadium. Of course, they went anyway and had a ball.

The sport itself, despite all the BBC's insistence to the contrary, has not always been 'amazing', 'astonishing', 'astounding', or any of the other adjectives Gary Lineker and his fellow presenters have used to hype up what we've seen on screen. There have been moments of exquisite brilliance in amongst it all. The rugby sevens, for instance; the swimming, where the bright young talents of the four home nations went head-to-head with their Australian rivals; the netball, where the four best teams in the world tussled for the medals; and the squash, where the best male and female players in the world won gold in brutally competitive finals. And others too, of course, typically all in the few sports where the Commonwealth countries can muster a genuinely elite field.

As for some of the rest, well ... only four teams entered the men's 10m synchronised diving, which meant that the organisers did not feel able to award a bronze. But 2,000 people turned up at the Royal Commonwealth Pool to scream their support for Tom Daley anyway. In the women's pole vault, which admittedly took place in atrocious conditions, bronze was won with 3.80m. That would not even have qualified for the final at the World Junior Championships in Oregon last week. Which did not stop 50,000 fans from going potty when Wales's Sally Peake won silver with a vault of 4.25m. Just as they did for Usain Bolt the night before, when the great man turned up to run 44 strides in a relay heat against the likes of Montserrat's Alford Dyett (100m PB: 11.78sec).

Why have the Games been such a success? We could make like the BBC and pretend that they have been a festival of world-class sport. Or we could adopt one of the other common justifications given by those who feel the Games are in some way sacrosanct, which is that they give badly needed experience to good young athletes. It is true, but it still seems a desperately poor reason to spend £600m staging the event. We could point to the flush of patriotic satisfaction that the British must feel, since their nations have won 276 medals between them. They have come at a rate of more than one an hour, which makes it a little hard to keep track, and a little harder still to think: 'Yes! Another bronze!' England are top of the medal table. They have won 174. So, in your face, Fiji. Beat it, Belize. Even the table-top battle between England and Australia, which I've been guilty of whipping up myself, seems a little like a media construction, designed to flog a little life into stories we worry won't hold public attention on their own merit.

Or we could be honest, and admit that actually something far more interesting has been going on in Glasgow for the past fortnight. The people here didn't much care what they were watching. They didn't mind whether it was any good, because they were always going to cheer and sing. And plenty of them weren't fussed who won, because they just wanted to be able to say 'I was there'. These have been the first – horrible word – selfie Games. Everyone has been at it. Even the Queen and Prince Harry got up to a spot of photobombing.

As Bolt said: 'This new thing about selfies, they are really making the lap of honour long.' Almost every single event has ended with the winning, and losing, athletes taking a tour of the stands, stopping to pose for photos with the fans which can be shown to friends and shared on social media. It's all proof, you see, that they were part of something fun, something special. And so they were.

Mike Hooper, chief executive of the Commonwealth Games Federation, is fond of saying that the Games are 'unashamedly of and for the Commonwealth', as though this disparate group of 2.2 billion people are bound together by their shared interest in the triple jump and table tennis, rather than long-distant history and trade agreements. They're not. Very few tourists even travel to watch them. Fewer than 3 per cent of the tickets here were sold overseas.

Instead, the Games are unashamedly of and for the host city. If the locals aren't into it, don't enjoy it, then the Games look ridiculous and feel redundant, as they did in Delhi four years ago when 60 per cent of the tickets weren't sold. The enthusiasm of hundreds of thousands of Glaswegians has been the 'amazing', 'astonishing', 'astounding' thing about these Games, not the sport. This has been the city's success.

5 AUGUST–25 SEPTEMBER

Readers' letters:
The dog's politics

5 AUGUST

I cannot believe I am alone in feeling outraged and appalled by Nicholas Lezard's assertion (*Review*, 2 August) that dogs are inherently fascistic whereas cats are independently minded. Speaking as someone who has nearly always shared his life with both, it is unmistakable that dogs are community-minded, socialist, eager to make the world a better place. Now look at cats: smug, entitled and clearly interested only in themselves and their I'm-all-right-Jackery.

There will always be some dogs who are corrupted, misled and – like Stalin – born to the left but end up on the fascistic right. Just as there must be rare examples of cats who have abandoned their life of comfort – Che Guevara comes to mind – and given their lives to the betterment of others (though I am yet to meet one). Which brings us to the one undeniable truth shared by anyone, of any political persuasion, who has ever canvassed door to door: dogs vote Labour, cats vote Conservative.

Jonathan Myerson, London

7 AUGUST

Both correspondents (*Review*, 2 August; Letters, 5 August) are wrong. The dog votes slavishly for its master's preference, while the cat is the classic swing voter, offering itself to whoever offers most.

Brendan Martin, London

7 AUGUST

I am surprised to see that your correspondents have such politically minded cats. Ours just sits on the fence.

Ken Forman, Manchester

8 AUGUST

If Brendan Martin thinks a dog will do something slavishly for its owner, he has clearly never owned a West Highland terrier.

Kirsten Elliott, Bath

8 AUGUST

My old, sadly deceased, dog was definitely an anarchist. He loved peace camps, festivals and demonstrations and was keen on animal rights. Never voted, probably on principle. He did nip a Trotskyist's wagging finger at a Troops Out meeting once, the only one in the room brave enough to do what we all wanted to do.

Ross Bradshaw, Nottingham

11 AUGUST

My cat is a true socialist. He believes in claws four.

Veronica Porter, London

13 AUGUST

I have shared my life with several cats over the years and all of them knew the name of the founder of the Chinese Communist party.

Joe Corbett, London

14 AUGUST

In more than 50 years' canvassing, door-knocking and delivering literature on behalf of the Labour party, I have never been bitten

or attacked by a cat. Dogs are another thing, however, and I bear the scars as evidence. Dogs are definitely Tories.
John Sullivan, Oldbury, West Midlands

14 AUGUST
Did Joe Corbett's 'several cats ... all of [whom] knew the name of the founder of the Chinese Communist party' prefer Li Ta-chao or Ch'en Tu-hsiu?
Professor Alan Knight, St Antony's College, Oxford

16 AUGUST
It's obvious that dogs are the fascists ... have you ever seen a police cat? (Thanks to Dave Sheridan and Gilbert Shelton of *Fabulous Furry Freak Brothers* fame.)
Simon Hargreaves, Cromford, Derbyshire

18 AUGUST
Have you ever seen a cat guiding the blind, hearing for the deaf, tending the paralysed, warning of intruders, digging out people buried under avalanches and collapsed buildings, tracking the lost, stranded and injured or detecting explosives, harmful drugs and potential tumours merely by sniffing?
W Stephen Gilbert, Corsham, Wiltshire

25 SEPTEMBER
Some weeks ago I used these pages to advance my thesis that dogs vote Labour, cats vote Conservative. Bafflingly, there were some objections to this.

Yesterday we heard that the Queen purred down the line at Cameron [on hearing the result of the Scottish referendum]. I rest my case.
Jonathan Myerson, London

18 AUGUST

The perils of moving in with your parents at 40

PETE CASHMORE

Apparently, I'm not boiling my eggs correctly. My mistake, you see, is putting the eggs in water and then boiling for three minutes; I should be reducing the heat to a gentle, rolling boil, not leaving the eggs to their own devices in a wild, bubbling maelstrom. It doesn't matter that my method has served me perfectly well in all my years of egg-boiling. I'm doing it wrong. I know this because my mum tells me more or less every time I boil eggs, in the kitchen I share with her and my dad since I moved back in with them recently, at the age of 40.

That's not all I do wrong. Sometimes, I leave the saucepan boiling with the handle over another gas ring. This is also wrong – dangerous, in fact – because what if the other gas ring should accidentally ignite? The metal handle would become hazardously hot! Quite how the gas ring would do that of its own accord I don't know. It's just something my mum worries about when she's not monitoring my toast for potential burning. Because, oh yeah, my mum doesn't trust me to make toast properly, either. At 40.

I was made redundant just before my 40th birthday, and took the difficult decision to move home from London to Wolverhampton to freelance, stretch out my redundancy payment and regroup. I was planning to live in my parents' spare room for a month, maximum. Owing to the local estate agents' peculiar lack of alacrity, it has now been six weeks, with at least another five before I can move out. 'You're so lucky!' people tell me. 'Free bed and board, free meals, laundry done, no bills. What a result!'

A ha ha ha ha ha. NO.

Living with your parents at 40 is not good. There's just no way in which it's anything other than awful, no matter how clean and well-ironed your underpants are. It's like living in a hotel where the maids, concierges, serving staff and receptionists disapprove vocally of everything you do. The main issue is that, like all youngest children in their parents' eyes, I was effectively hermetically sealed, like a still-boxed *Star Wars* figure, at the age of 16, and am treated and spoken to as such. So it's open season on things like my tattoos, my beard and my hair, which make me look scruffy, which is of course *exactly the point.*

All the things you take for granted when you live alone – masturbating when and wherever you want; barrelling in drunk and ordering a pizza, leaving it out on the sofa overnight and then having the rest for breakfast; drinking wine at 10.30 a.m. on a Saturday – they're all out of the window.

Life as a grown man living with one's parents is a life of enforced abstinence and constant, agitated bafflement at the things they say (they suggested I phone a Spanish hotel ahead of a mini-break 'to check if they let you wear shorts'). Every morning over breakfast – which, inevitably, I prepare wrongly – I'm asked, 'What are you going to do today?', which means, of course, 'What are you going to do *to find work* today?' The honest answer – 'Probably have a pub lunch and then watch *Rise of the Planet of the Apes*' – just doesn't cut it. It should be the right of every recently redundant man or woman to waste the occasional weekday afternoon in the pub; after all, you can pitch ideas and hunt for jobs on a laptop in a beer garden much more pleasurably than you can in the spare bedroom where the laundry basket is kept. But, right now, the days of drinking a bottle and a half of red wine when I should be working seem like the stuff of a madman's most fevered imaginings.

The most obvious adjunct of all this is that my love life is hopelessly on hold, partly because I can't bring anyone home, but mainly because of the vastly diminished erotic appeal of a 40-year-old man who lives with his mum. You can probably imagine the conversation:

Me: Hi there, I'm Pete!

Her: Hi, I'm Generic Modern Professional Woman Name! What do you do?

Me: I'm a writer.

Her: Ooh, how interesting, I'm a Typical Exciting Noughties Media Professional. So, where do you live?

Me: A small village outside Wolverhampton. With my parents.

Her: ...

Until I move into my own place, I'm in limbo and purgatory, a transitory space stuffed with torment. When I use the bathroom, I can expect a review of the condition in which I've left it, whether I have been showering, shaving or ... other stuff. When I dine, I will be lambasted for the size and speed of my mouthfuls, although wolfing down my meal is the only thing preventing a double murder-suicide at the table. And when I put on jeans, I'll be told to put on a belt because my mum can see my pants, even though *that's how we wear jeans nowadays, Mum.* I spend every second wanting to scream, 'I'm 40 fucking years old!'

Having said all that, my mum's Sunday roasts are the absolute bomb and I'm not paying rent, so maybe I should shut my big, stupid, ungrateful face.

THE BEDSIDE GUARDIAN 2014

Pete's mum responds ...

JUNE CASHMORE

Dear Peter,

Before we start, your father and I would just like to thank you for allowing your piece to be published on his 74th birthday. We trust your fee will be paying for dinner. Your father is working in the greenhouse at the moment; I don't think he wants to talk to you. Your brother – a very successful veterinary surgeon – might be coming for dinner, by the way.

As for the rest of it, we're not sure where to start, as has been the case with you for a good 30 years now. I hope you have read the comments on the newspaper website and can now concede that a) a man of your age should not be wearing his jeans in such a way that we can see his underpants and a good inch of his bum cleft, and b) I was right all along about the eggs – when they're boiling, they're boiling; you don't need them to be bouncing and thrashing around like they're getting off with each other in a Jacuzzi.

The bottom line is, we know that you are beyond repair now, that those tattoos are not going to fall off overnight and that it's not within our rights to hold you down while you sleep and forcibly remove that ghastly beard. But the spare room, lest we forget, is *our spare room*; you just happen to be squatting in it, so when we go in there and find that it looks like someone has detonated a mini-bomb of spent underwear, empty Pepsi Max bottles and unsent CVs, we do feel we are within our rights to object. I see enough of your underpants looming up over the waistband of your jeans every day, I don't need to be picking them up off the floor as well. Likewise, we expect to go into the bathroom and not find the sink full of hair, not least because, if it's not coming from your face, then ... Well, we don't want to know.

I hope you read all of the comments. There is some very good advice in there ('You should move to Denmark' was quite a good one, although we also rather liked 'Are there no flats available in the area for this selfish git?'). Who knows? You may just listen to total strangers because you're certainly not listening to us. As it stands, though, at the time of writing, it is only 13 more days until you move into your new flat and I know that you are very excited about the move. Well, take that excitement, multiply it by two, throw in a vastly reduced grocery bill and one less slovenly ape-child, whose mess we have to clean up, moping around the house (in shorts and flip-flops) making it look untidy, and just imagine how thrilled we're going to be. And finally, stop swearing – you're supposed to be a writer.

With love,
Mum

19 AUGUST

Scottish writers on the referendum – independence day?

The late, great Michael Marra, the bard of Dundee, once wrote a heart-rending and witty song called 'Beefheart and Bones' about a couple divvying up their CD collection after a break-up. It sums up how I've come to feel about Scottish independence after a long time of swithering (a Scots word meaning 'swinging from one position to another'). For a long time, I couldn't make up my mind. In the 'Aye, naw, mibbe' discussion, I was a definite 'mibbe'. But neither side seems able definitively to answer my questions about what will happen after the referendum. Will we keep the pound? Will we get devo max? Will we drive Trident from our waters? Will we keep the Windsors?

Given that, the only basis I could find for making a choice is to look at the track record of what the Scottish parliament has done differently from Westminster since we've had some power restored to us. And, overwhelmingly, I prefer what we've done north of the border – free prescriptions, no student tuition fees, social care for elderly people. So, with a degree of trepidation, I'm going to nail my colours to the mast of aspiration and vote 'Yes'.

When you realise you're in a relationship in which the two of you want different things, where your hopes and dreams are taking you in different directions, you don't hesitate because you're not sure what you're going to get in the divorce settlement; you make the decision and then you sort things out afterwards. We shouldn't be held back because of the fear that seems to be the major plank of the Better Together campaign. And if we don't get the Beefheart CD, we can always go out and buy a new copy.

VAL MCDERMID

The 'Great' in 'Great Britain' is so often taken for a boastful adjective that we forget it's a comparator. It doesn't mean 'Excellent Britain'. It means 'great' as in 'great crested newt' or 'great auk' or 'Greater London'. We forget that 'Great Britain' is simply the geographical name for the largest island of the hundreds in the British archipelago. It's our Honshu; our Java. Perhaps 'Greater Britain' would be a clearer name, or 'Big Island'.

You can, and perhaps will, mark out a conceptual east–west line dividing the island in two, and decree that on either side of the line people will pay different taxes, deal with immigration in different ways, permit or not permit nuclear weapons. What you cannot do is physically make one island into two, or move the island elsewhere.

I can imagine a number of unhappy consequences of Scotland voting for independence in September. I can also imagine good ones. The assumption that political fragmentation means more nationalistic, inward-looking, self-aggrandising cultures in the separated nations, particularly England, might be wrong. What if the death of Britannia heightened awareness of the non-political culture that spans the entire archipelago – the islandic world?

It would be different were Scotland to be speaking a different language. But modern Scots hasn't been systemised in a way that makes it practical to learn to speak for everyday use, or to prepare Scots to accept hearing it spoken with a non-Scottish accent, and Ireland's experience suggests even universal Gaelic teaching doesn't make Gaelic a first language.

Adjacency, entwined histories, entwined families, a common language, vernaculars of everything from diet to architecture to sailing to hill walking to drinking – there is much in common in islandic culture, like Scandinavian, that will transcend islandic borders.

Last year I was invited to the book festival in Dún Laoghaire, near Dublin. I was on stage with AL Kennedy; two writers, brought up in Dundee, now living in London, speaking in Ireland. It was an islandic experience, and I found myself intoxicated by the pleasure of small differences. Dún Laoghaire was not quite like anywhere I had been before. But the way it seemed different from Brighton or Ayr was exactly the same as the way in which Brighton and Ayr seem different from each other. That's not something you change with a vote.

JAMES MEEK

I emailed a dozen yes-supporting friends and asked for a snap response to the question: 'Where are we at?' Their replies make up this 'poem'.

Aye!
We are rolling our tongues around a three-letter word.
We are finding our voice.
We're resisting the big-bank, multinational-dictated slip-
    page to the right ...
Only bruising, no blood.
It's about money.
It's not about money.
It isn't all about money.
It's about fear, faith, strength.
It can't come fast enough.
We're exploring a different way of organising a country.
This won't go back in the box.
We're questioning *everything*.
Peacefully, we're resisting all sorts of intimidation from
    the British establishment.
England has been a good neighbour, but ...
It's the choice between a maimed culture and a whole
    country.
Unionism has no new songs.
What a great time to be alive in Scotland!
We're one-thirds way round a big blind bend.

KATHLEEN JAMIE

23 AUGUST

The one that got away

JEANETTE WINTERSON

Nostalgia for lost love is cowardice disguised as poetry. It is easy to imagine that if life had moved a degree in a different direction, then the one that got away would be by our side, and we would both be living happily ever after. Memories of holiday romances or stray nights with strangers are part of the pleasure of the past. And I believe that anyone we have loved is someone we should be able to think about, talk about and recognise as a real piece of our emotional history.

To me, one of the best aspects of gay culture is that we work hard to stay friends with our exes – perhaps a survival mechanism from the bad old days of the ghetto, but a civilised arrangement, nonetheless. (It will be interesting to see if the normalising effect of marriage changes this.)

But recognising the past as our past, and being able to groan, giggle, blush, sigh and play with those memories, is not the same as a corrosive secret infatuation with the idea of that special someone we managed to mislay. Sighing over a fantasy drains energy from reality. What happens in our heads isn't private; it is unspoken, that's all. We all know what it's like to live in the stifling atmosphere of what is unsaid.

Love is hard work. We don't hear enough about that. Falling in love is the easy part – it's why affairs are so exciting and attractive – none of the toil, all of the fun. I used to have a lot of affairs until I realised it was like growing cress on a flannel – instant results, no roots. Adam Phillips has written eloquently, in *Missing Out*, on the strange discontent that prompts us to believe that the life we are not living would be better for us than the life that is ours. If only we had that job/house/girlfriend/husband/sex life, etc. In truth, the life that is ours is the one we make, and that includes our partners. If we really have been criminally careless with the love of our life, and driven him away, or let her go – well, then, we deserve to be unhappy, at least until that unhappiness prompts such a change in us that the miracle of a second chance (with someone else) is not thrown away.

I realised a few years ago that the script I was running through all my relationships was a narrative of loss. Either I chose, or let myself be chosen by, people who weren't free (those were the exciting ones), or I had bouts of duty where I tried to settle down in a way guaranteed to find me secret-sighing over someone else. Changing that story changed my relationship with myself – which is, after all, the relationship all other relationships must negotiate.

I have regrets about a couple of past partners, but no fleeting feelings of nostalgia for what might have been with 'someone'. 'Someone' is a fantasy. The person I love is real.

20 SEPTEMBER

This glorious failure could yet be Scotland's finest hour

IRVINE WELSH

They came out in their droves, in a last-ditch, stoic defence of the union, to staunch the seemingly irresistible tide towards independence. The no voters should take a bow: they delivered the

UK establishment a reprieve the enervated, confused and weak campaign of their masters certainly didn't deserve. They have bought time for the union, and many of them, people who will habitually support the status quo at almost any cost, will simply be relieved. Others in this disparate group, who want change, but decided to give the establishment one more chance, will be keenly looking south to see what is on offer. The Westminster parties now have to look closely at who the no voters are, especially the devo max ones they made the late pitch for. Many of them must now be at the limits of their patience, and they won't be remaining silently in that camp after any more fudges and broken promises.

At the start of the campaign, a narrow win for the political-class-led no would have been a nightmare result for the establishment. They originally expected a rout – the rationale behind Cameron leaving devo max off the ballot paper, before he had a humiliating rush north, in realisation that his abiding political legacy might be the end of the union.

The vibrant and euphoric yes movement, which, during the debate, evolved from a small base to come within a whisker of a sensational victory, will be massively disappointed that they didn't manage to get it done.

They will have to cool their ardour a while longer, although anybody believing they'll stop now is indulging in wishful thinking. Why would they? The process and the subsequent debate, which they won handsomely, took support for independence from around 30 per cent to 45 per cent and heading north. It's now established as the compelling narrative of the post-devolution generation, while no dominates only in a declining constituency of elderly voters. Yes may have lost this battle, but the war is being won.

There was much talk of how ineffective the no campaign was. In some ways this is unfair: you can only go with what you've got and they simply weren't packing much heat. The union they strove to protect was based on industry and empire and the esprit de corps from both world wars, and you can't maintain a political relationship on declining historical sentiment alone. With the big, inclusive postwar building blocks of the welfare state and the NHS being ripped apart by both major parties there's zero currency in campaigning on that, especially as they're only being preserved in Scotland by the devolved parliament. The boast of using oil revenues to fund privatisation projects and bail out bankers for their avarice and incompetence is never going to be a vote winner. Going negative was the only option.

The referendum was a disaster for Cameron personally, who almost lost the union. The Tories, with enough self-awareness to realise how detested they are in Scotland, stood aside to let Labour run the show on the basis they could deliver a convincing no vote. But for Labour, the outcome was at least as bad; when the dust settles they will be seen, probably on both sides of the border, to have used their power and influence against the aspiration towards democracy. Labour voters caught this ugly whiff, the number of them supporting independence doubling in a month from 17 per cent to 35 per cent. In the mid-term, the leadership may have simply acted as recruiting sergeants for the SNP.

As Cameron was at first absent and uninterested, then finally fearful, so Miliband looked just as ineffective and totally lost during this campaign. He became a figure of contempt in Scotland: Labour leaders have generally needed a period in office in order to achieve that distinction.

As social media came of age in a political campaign in these islands, the rest of the establishment will be for ever tarnished in the eyes of a generation of Scots. The senior officials of banks and supermarkets dancing to Whitehall's tune, their nonsense disseminated by the London press, was not unexpected, but the BBC extensively answered any questions about their role in a post-independent Scotland.

No sleep will be lost by the elites over that; the reason that this is such a bad result for the establishment is that it compels action; the narrow no decision, in tandem with the massive surge of momentum towards yes, leaves the issue unresolved. Though defeated in the poll, the independence movement emerged far stronger – from the narrow concern of a bourgeois civic nationalist party, to a righteous, vibrant, big-tent, pro-democracy movement. The referendum galvanised and excited Scots in a way that no UK-wide election has done. Like it or not, unless they come up with a winning devo max settlement, every general election in Scotland will now be dominated by the independence issue.

Scotland's post-devolution generation is a different breed to their predecessors; they've been building a new state in their imagination, from the basis of a limited but tangible parliament in Edinburgh. They see the possibilities in full statehood, and came from nowhere to deal a body blow to Britain's tired and out-of-touch elites. The smartest of them have always seen independence as a process, not an event, and having come so unexpectedly close, they won't be going into a depressive hungover funk. They'll be keen for a rematch, and they'll get it soon.

This vote ensures that Scotland will remain central on the UK agenda. The union was on death row and the no vote earned it a stay of execution; the establishment parties are now in the process of organising their appeal. That has to involve real decentralisation of power and an end to regional inequities. Do the political classes have the stomach and the spine for this? A devo max that gives Scotland the power to raise taxes to pay for welfare programmes, but not reduce them by opting out of Trident and other defence spending, while maintaining the oil flow south of the border, without even an investment or poverty alleviation fund, is a sham, especially as it was denied at the ballot box. It may be perceived as setting up the Scottish parliament to fail, and undermining devolution.

However, it's probably the case that anything more than that would be unlikely to be palatable to the major parties or the broader UK electorate. The biggest problem for the Westminster elites now is not just to decide what to do about Scotland but, crucially, to do it without antagonising English people – who might justly feel that the tail of 10 per cent is now starting to wag the dog of the rest of the UK.

The fact is that the majority of the 25 million who live in London and the south-east are perfectly fine with the bulk of tax pounds (to say nothing of the oil revenues) being spent on government, infrastructure and showcase projects in the capital – why wouldn't they be? The problem is that in a unitary, centralised state, the decision-making and civic wealth of the nation – and therefore practically all the large-scale private investment – lies in that region.

So how can you square the two? Scots are showing they won't go on committing their taxes or oil monies to building a London super-state on the global highway for the transnational rich, particularly when it's becoming unaffordable to their cockney comrades, driving them out of their own city to the M25 satellites.

English nationalism has always been the elephant in the room and it seems likely that demands made from north of the border will precipitate a reaction from the south, and encourage further political polarisation. Be careful of what you wish for was a taunt by Better Together, warning Scots of the potential hassles – real and fantasised – of extrication from the union. Now they have that headache, as they seek to work out how they can hold this mess together.

The major parties, particularly Labour, a poll- and press-conscious, focus group-driven concern, obsessed with the centrist support of middle England, may find that trying to reconcile the Scots' aspiration to autonomy with the maintenance of a unitary, centralised UK state is an impossible task. If Labour can't decentralise and provide autonomy to their own party in Scotland, it's hard to see how they can even start to do it for the UK. Scottish independence, with the party campaigning cheek by jowl alongside the Conservatives, provided more (and probably decisive) evidence for Labour voters of just how much their party has been co-opted by the establishment. Even more of them will be disinclined to pass on the now traditional 'put up and shut up' to 'keep the Tories out' offer. In the English Labour marginal constituencies, low turnouts could hurt them. The benefactors south of the border may be the latest xenophobic pack of establishment mules, Ukip, a BNP-with-standard-grades affair.

With Ukip's clear aim of removing the UK from Europe, Labour voters might reason that at least they know what they are voting for with this particular devil.

The Liberal Democrats and some on the left have been flirting with a federal solution to maintain the UK. But this back-of-a-cigarette-packet desperation only betrays the same top-down establishment thinking. There has to be some kind of demand from the people; imposing an unwanted parliament in Norwich on East Anglian folks would be as undemocratic as taking away the Scots one in Edinburgh. It seems more sensible and more painless just to accept that the UK is not politically homogenous and let its constituent parts find their own paths up the mountain. This is the quandary for the establishment to sort out and it's one that would tax bigger and more tolerant minds than their own.

Back in Scotland, many (including quite a few in the no camp) have become disenchanted by the negative, desperate campaign orchestrated from Westminster, and the establishment in general, particularly the way business and media interests have been nakedly shown to collude against democracy. If the yes campaign excited Scots to the possibilities of people power, the opposition one showed the political classes, their establishment masters and metropolitan groupies in the most cynical, opportunistic light. From the empty, manipulative celebrity 'love-bombing' to the crass threats and smears issued by the press, around half of Scotland might now feel as if it has been classified as the 'enemy within', that stock designation for all those who resist the dictates of the elites' centralised power.

The yes movement hit such heights because the UK state was seen as failed; antiquated, hierarchical, centralist, discriminatory, out of touch and acting against the people. This election will have done nothing to diminish that impression. Against this shabbiness the Scots struck a blow for democracy, with an unprecedented 97 per cent voter registration for an election the establishment wearily declared nobody wanted. It turns out that it was the only one people wanted. Whether this Scottish assertiveness kick-starts an unlikely UK-wide reform (unwanted in most of the English regions); or wearies southerners and precipitates a reaction to get rid of them; or the Scots, through the ballot box at general elections, decide to go the whole hog of their own accord; the old imperialist-based union is bust.

The Scots, so often regarded as a thrawn tribe with their best years behind them, have shown the western world that the corporate-led, neoliberal model for the development of this planet, through G7 'sphere of influence' states on bloated military budgets, has a limited appeal.

This country, when it was ever known on the global stage under the union, was associated with tragedy, in terrible events like Lockerbie and Dunblane; it's now synonymous with real people power. Forget Bannockburn or the Scottish Enlightenment, the Scots have just reinvented and re-established the idea of true democracy. This – one more – glorious failure might also, paradoxically, be their finest hour.

Index